FRESH
START

BY THE AUTHOR OF

Great Good Food

COAUTHOR OF

The New Basics Cookbook

*The Silver Palate
Good Times Cookbook*

The Silver Palate Cookbook

THE
GREAT
GOOD
FOOD
SERIES™

FRESH START

JULEE ROSSO

Illustrations by Annie Hoffman

Great low-fat recipes, day-by-day menus—
The savvy way to cook, eat and live

Crown Trade Paperbacks
New York

Published by Crown Trade Paperbacks, 201 East 50th Street,
New York, New York, 10022. Member of the Crown Publishing Group.

Random House, Inc. New York, Toronto, London, Sydney, Auckland

Crown Trade Paperbacks is a trademark of Crown Publishers, Inc.

Great Good Food is a trademark of Julee Rosso Associates Inc.

Printed in the United States of America

Library of Congress Cataloging in Publication Data is available upon request

ISBN 0-517-88523-9

10   9   8   7   6   5   4   3   2   1

First Edition

For my dad, "Shrank,"
who gave me a true love of the land,
a curiosity for its harvest, a funny bone and
the instinct for what is right.
And to Bert, who long ago opened my eyes to how what
we eat will affect our very well-being and
how we care for one another will nurture us all.
—Jul

A warm, sunbright "thanks"
to my husband, David; daughter, Bailey; and faithful dog,
Chester, for they helped me bring these sketches to life.
May the rest of my family and friends enjoy reading this
book as much as I enjoyed contributing to it.
—Annie

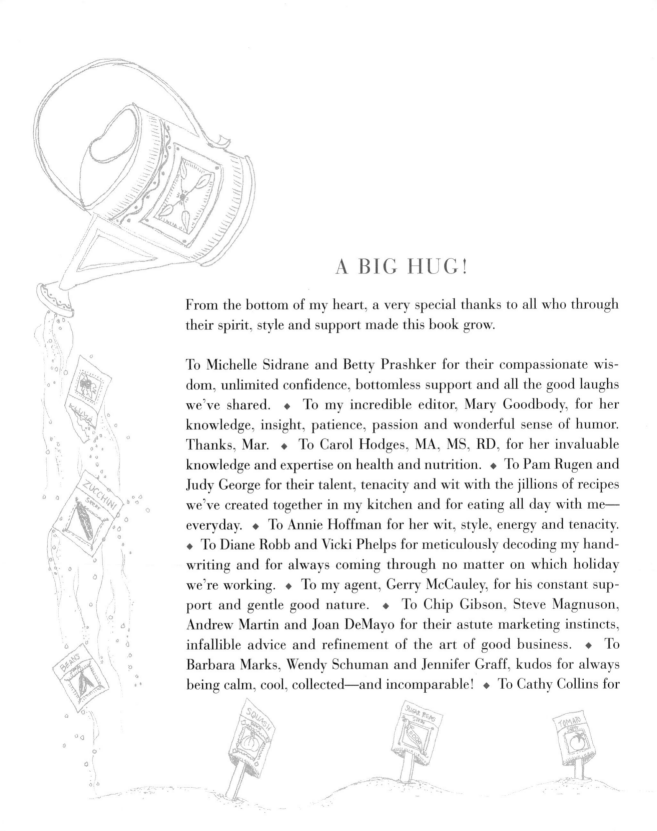

A BIG HUG!

From the bottom of my heart, a very special thanks to all who through their spirit, style and support made this book grow.

To Michelle Sidrane and Betty Prashker for their compassionate wisdom, unlimited confidence, bottomless support and all the good laughs we've shared. ◆ To my incredible editor, Mary Goodbody, for her knowledge, insight, patience, passion and wonderful sense of humor. Thanks, Mar. ◆ To Carol Hodges, MA, MS, RD, for her invaluable knowledge and expertise on health and nutrition. ◆ To Pam Rugen and Judy George for their talent, tenacity and wit with the jillions of recipes we've created together in my kitchen and for eating all day with me—everyday. ◆ To Annie Hoffman for her wit, style, energy and tenacity. ◆ To Diane Robb and Vicki Phelps for meticulously decoding my handwriting and for always coming through no matter on which holiday we're working. ◆ To my agent, Gerry McCauley, for his constant support and gentle good nature. ◆ To Chip Gibson, Steve Magnuson, Andrew Martin and Joan DeMayo for their astute marketing instincts, infallible advice and refinement of the art of good business. ◆ To Barbara Marks, Wendy Schuman and Jennifer Graff, kudos for always being calm, cool, collected—and incomparable! ◆ To Cathy Collins for

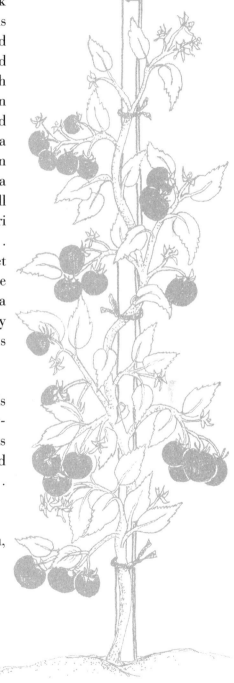

her many bright ideas and ability always to go the distance. ◆ To Jim Davis, Lauren Dong, Nancy Kenmore, Lynne Amft and Tom Lau for a perfectly beautiful fresh book design—inside and out. ◆ To Laurie Stark for her fabulous ability to set a schedule and keep us all to it with good humor. ◆ To Amy Boorstein, a deep bow of respect and admiration for how she does what she does with so much grace and compassion. ◆ To Jo Fagan, Sean Yule, Robin Strashun and Phyllis Fleiss for their marketing savvy and support. ◆ To Wendy Williams, Deborah Callan, Barbara Albright and Peter Goodbody for their precise passion on the computer and in the test kitchens. ◆ To Teresa Nicholas and Jane Searle for keeping one step ahead of all of us and making sure it all comes out right. ◆ To Merri Ann Morrell for her marvelous magic at the computer . . . she's created a new art form. ◆ To Libby Kessman, Janet McDonald and Carole Berglie for their broad experience and expertise in the art of fine tuning. ◆ To Dakila Divina for his charm and good-natured spirit. ◆ and ◆ to the very wonderful women of Wickwood who with their world-class graciousness support me endlessly.

And to my anchors: To Wills, who has been relentless in his love and support and has lived amid the pages while sharing some pretty lopsided meals with me. To Mom, who has seen it all and continues to make us laugh. To Bobbie and Banana, who have, too, been there every step of the way . . . always cheering!

And, finally, a fond "Skoal" to Ken Sansone. We all miss you, dear friend, and hope you are surrounded by fabulous art.

CONTENTS

My View ◆ 10

One Step at a Time ◆ 14

My View

*"How we spend our days is,
of course,
how we spend our lives."*
ANNIE DILLARD

My passion for cooking started almost thirty years ago and continues to this day as strong as ever. I marvel at how far we've evolved in this country regarding food and how my own life in the kitchen has unfolded. I began cooking with Julia Child's *The French Chef*, and over the years discovered how to create the big, vibrant, intense, magnified flavors that would become my cooking signature.

Concerns about healthful eating began in the early '70s, for me, when my father had one of the first heart bypass operations. Having always taken after my dad and being a "working woman"—then still a fairly unique commodity—I remember wondering if heart disease would be my fate, too, even though in those days it was never considered a major health problem for women. And so, over the next several decades, I read every new report on the effects of diet on health, trying to understand how they might affect me. At the same time, my interest in new ingredients, dishes and exotic cooking methods expanded. Flavors I tasted on my travels to France, Italy, Spain, Greece, the Caribbean, Japan, the South Pacific, Scandinavia, Mexico and Morocco influenced me. Wherever I went I visited markets, restaurants, food shops, and homes, tasting simple and elaborate traditional dishes and studying the region's history, always noting how differently Americans eat from the rest of the world and always wondering what impact this had on our health. Yet I was busy searching for ways to make the richest crème brûlée, the chunkiest, chocolate chip cookies and the tangiest, most buttery lemon tart. I loved discovering the "latest" or newest ingredient available at the farmers' market and making it intensely explosive and exciting to the palate.

Ten years ago, after coauthoring my first two cookbooks, tasting food nearly all day long at The Silver Palate (the Manhattan gourmet take-out store I cofounded and later sold) and indulging in big lunches and late-night dinners at the latest and greatest restaurants in New York, around the country and the world, my weight was at an all-time high. I felt sluggish and logy. The emerging health research continued to unfold, confirming that we were all eating far too much fat and it was linked with an increased risk of life-threatening diseases and degenerative conditions. I knew something had to be done, yet restrictive diets weren't the answer. (Believe me, I tried them all, from cottage cheese and pineapple to grapefruit, rice and Optifast—long before Oprah!)

In the end, it finally dawned on me that my commonsense instincts about fresh natural food and my growing interest in health had come together in a sensible fusion. It was simply time to start cooking at home again! It was clear that only by getting back into my own kitchen could I control what I was eating.

Once there, I was willing to give up fat, but I refused to give up the intensely flavored dishes that had become my passion. It was then that I made another wonderful discovery in my own kitchen: Most of the flavors I loved had little to do with fat! True, fat is often a great transmitter of flavors, but it does not have to be present in large amounts to do that job. Nor does it have to be the predominant flavor. Over and over again I found that by simply cooking differently, I could enjoy the same foods made with far less fat but with the same vibrant flavors.

"Things which matter most must never be at the mercy of things which matter least."
GOETHE

Best of all, I barely missed the butter because the flavors had become so fresh and magnified.

When the flavor of a dish was truly terrific, I forgot the fat was gone!

Thank goodness there were so many intense flavors that had no fat connection at all: the fresh taste of herbs, the spark of ginger, the tang of hot and sweet peppers, the bite of horseradish and wasabi, the saltiness of soy. There was the spunk of vinegar, the warmth of freshly ground spices, the smokiness of grilled foods and the intrigue of vanilla. They all made it simple. And surprisingly, everything suddenly tasted fresher and even more exciting—all with very little fat! Every day, I continued to learn something new or discovered a better way to reduce fat while intensifying flavor.

And then, in 1993, one of life's mysterious coincidences happened. I was on a book tour for *Great Good Food: Luscious Lower-Fat Cooking* and was scheduled to be on a Sacramento, California, radio talk show with Dr. Ted Diethrich—the same Arizona doctor who had operated on my father more than twenty years earlier! Dr. Diethrich had just written *Women and Heart Disease*, which I read, mesmerized, on my way to San Francisco that afternoon. In it he confirmed my own health concerns. According to Dr. Diethrich, women are indeed at risk for heart disease and are succumbing from it in numbers equal to men—almost 500,000 women a year, compared to the 44,000 lost to breast cancer. But the symptoms are somewhat elusive and very different from those of men, complicated by hormones, which bring difficulties in detection. Dr. Diethrich strongly emphasized that there is a great deal of research yet to be done for us to understand heart disease in women.

"You must do the thing you think you cannot do."
ELEANOR ROOSEVELT

From that moment on, when women at my cooking workshops asked me for advice on cooking for their *husbands'* health, it became my mission to urge them to make changes for their *own* health's sake as well. Lowering the fat in our diets has to be a priority for us all, sparking a new way of eating for the rest of our lives! After testing well over 4,000 reduced-fat recipes in the past decade, I am now totally convinced that good food and good health are utterly and deliciously compatible! As long as we're conscious of what and how much we're eating and how it's prepared, we do not have to give up the foods from around the world that we've come to love. And the only way to accomplish this is to start cooking again.

The menus and recipes in this book are intended to get you started on the right path to a lifetime of good eating habits. There's no magic to lower-fat cooking except your own cooking flair. You won't find any synthetic miracle ingredients or long, time-consuming, complicated recipes in *Fresh Start*. All you need are the best, freshest ingredients of the season, some simple cooking techniques and, most of all, the desire and intention to change the way you and your family eat every day—forever.

Don't panic. Change need not be radical. Start by taking it slowly—recipe by recipe, meal by meal, day by day. Use the information here as a guideline to incorporate wherever and whenever you can in your busy life. Before you know it, you'll view food differently. The foods you choose will taste fresher, cleaner, more satisfying. You'll honestly crave pasta, rice, breads, fruits and vegetables, and find that your sweet tooth beckons less often for the taste of pecan pie than for a perfectly ripened peach. Meat, dairy, fats and even fish will become an accent, not the main event. When you do indulge, you'll find rich isn't nearly as appealing as you remember it being, and a little goes a long way. Just keep in mind that when the flavor is there, you forget the fat is gone!

Best of all, you'll start feeling differently.

You'll have more energy. You'll feel lighter and even think more clearly. Being outdoors and exercising will become a happy addiction, not a chore to be scratched off your list. Each day it will become easier—a way of life for the rest of your life.

And my hunch is you'll laugh a lot more, too. Just ask anyone out on the bicycle path, jogging around the reservoir or powerwalking in the park who's already made the switch! You can do it, too!!

JULEE ROSSO MILLER
Saugatuck, Michigan

"Shoot for the moon. Even if you miss it, you will land among the stars."
LES BROWN

13

One Step at a Time

"Pasta Is Fattening," "Exercise Moderately—No, Exercise More!" "Eggs Are Bad/Not So Bad," "Drink Wine!" If it's Tuesday, this must be another health proclamation. And somehow, the latest one seems to conflict with the health news we read just last week. No wonder we've become a nation of food skeptics. Admittedly, we're overweight skeptics—with convenience and junk food habits, an eye for quantity and alarming rates of heart disease, cancer and other ailments linked to lifestyle. But we're skeptics nonetheless. Wearied by the roller-coaster ride of medical and nutritional information, lots of people are throwing up their hands and just eating what they want. Longevity be damned! Let's eat cheese! Beef is back! Live for today!

While it would be easier to agree, we must remember that individual studies are only steppingstones to scientific consensus. We can't overreact to each and every one. We have to rely on established facts and recommendations regarding the relationship between diet and health, such as the Framingham Study, the oldest ongoing research project on cardiovascular disease, which has well-documented results of the positive effect of lower-fat diets on heart disease over the years.

I find America's disease statistics far too disturbing to ignore. For too many of us, our lifestyles and family histories are frightening. I am particularly concerned about women and heart disease, which is now recognized as the leading cause of death for women, just as it is for men. And the American culture of abundance has made us the fattest nation on earth. In this century alone, our average fat intake has risen to 37 percent of total daily calories, a figure that can quickly spike higher on any given day.

Research repeatedly shows that in cultures around the world where people eat less fat and more carbohydrate-based foods—combined with other lifestyle differences such as exercise and lowered stress—heart disease rates and those for cancer, stroke and other "modern" diseases are dramatically lower.

Is there a "miracle" diet that we in America

14

*"If you have made mistakes . . . .
there is always another chance for you.
You may have a fresh start
any moment you choose,
for this thing we call 'failure' is not
the falling down,
but the staying down."*
MARY PICKFORD

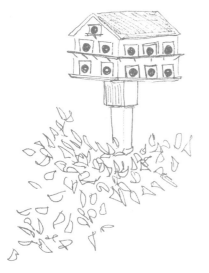

don't know about? No, it's simply a diet similar to what our ancestors ate and the one many of the world's populations consume today. It is a diet based on grains, legumes, fruits and vegetables, with only occasional meat, dairy products and fat. It is a diet that because we have so very much abundance in America today, we have forgotten. It is the diet represented in the USDA Food Pyramid.

But all this news doesn't have to be overwhelming or depressing. It just makes it very clear that it's possible to help our health simply by changing how we eat and live today. And once you begin to make these changes, you'll feel better, have more energy and truly believe that for the first time ever *you're* in charge of your own healthful destiny!

It's Your Fresh Start

My goal in writing this cookbook is to make healthful cooking simple and delicious enough to become a daily habit. *Fresh Start* isn't about tricks or gimmicks, synthetic ingredients, magic potions or food combinations. This is not a weight loss plan, although that may well be a benefit. This book is meant to be a primer for helping you to change your cooking habits and learn to truly enjoy lower-fat foods. It's about fresh, wholesome ingredients and common sense. It's about glorious flavors achieved without the burden of fat. It's about the big, intense tastes I've come to know and love in perfect harmony with today's goal of a healthy, balanced, always-on-the-go lifestyle. And there's only one secret to cooking with less fat —replace it with flavor!

In *Fresh Start*, I don't suggest—even for a minute—that you'll have to sacrifice the pleasure of eating or swap "real foods" for synthetic substitutes. Nor will you have to give up the foods you've come to love. In the recipes that follow I have either adjusted the ingredients or modified the cooking method to lower the fat. Where it is not to my taste to give up the intrinsic flavor of one of my favorite ingredients—such as Parmesan (I use less) or in the case of whipped cream and coconut—it becomes an indulgence to be enjoyed less frequently. Yet all of the recipes are simple and quick. After cooking them for a while, you will easily know how to adapt most of your own favorite. So let's begin . . . .

Eating Habits Around the World:
The Secrets of the Pyramids

Most of the world eats more healthfully than we do. This is why we're hearing so much about Asian, Mediterranean and other *traditional* diets.

Traditionally, the Chinese and Japanese, with their rice-based diets, eat a third less fat, double the carbohydrates and one-tenth the animal protein we do. They eat minuscule amounts of meat and virtually no dairy products. Consequently, they have long been known for their large long-living elderly population. Recently, since Japan's urban working population has converted to Western eating habits, they've begun suffering from "Western" rates of certain diseases,

such as cancer and heart disease.

Throughout the Mediterranean, people have classically eaten a light breakfast, a large lunch at midday (followed by a break from daily toil) and a modest supper, often made up of lunch leftovers with a little soup or salad. It is a diet plentiful in fruits, vegetables, legumes and grains, with meat eaten only on very special occasions. Wine is consumed in moderation with meals, and olive oil (high in monounsaturated fat) is the main source of fat. Once again, unless they have adopted American habits, the people in this region suffer only a fraction of our rates of coronary artery disease.

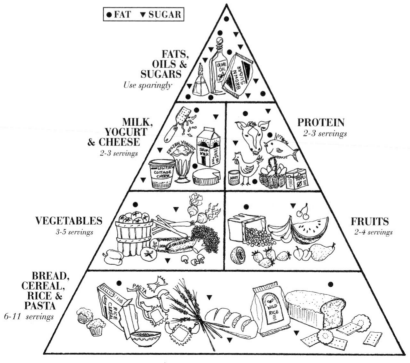

THE USDA FOOD PYRAMID

The French Paradox, attributed in part to drinking two glasses of red wine daily for health, was also about centuries of the rural French diet. Based on vegetables and grains, it regarded meat as a once-a-week event and wine as an everyday ritual. Even today, there are significant differences in the food ways of the French. They eat more vegetables and fruits, bread, grains and beans but never eat between meals. And they still drink wine. Again, in the cities where American eating habits—particularly meat consumption and stress—are present, the health ramifications are becoming apparent.

The fact is, the diet Americans have forsaken in the name of lush abundance looks a lot like the USDA/H.H.S. Food Pyramid—the nation's prescription for healthy eating since 1992. It makes the bread, cereal, pasta and rice group the foundation of a healthy diet, with protein playing a far less central role and fats, oils and sweets used only sparingly. The pyramid's emphasis on breads, pastas, rices, grains, legumes, potatoes, fruits and vegetables (with meat and dairy used as condiments and fat kept to a minimum) is in fact modeled after the diets found in parts of the world where obesity and heart disease are rarities. We need to remember that rice is the staple food for more than half the earth's population, supplying 55 percent of the daily food requirement. Compare the Mediterranean pyramid with the USDA pyramid and you'll see they're very similar, with meat given a smaller role and olive oil a larger one in the Mediterranean model. Most important, this pyramid reminds us to exercise!

In essence, the USDA pyramid/the Mediter-

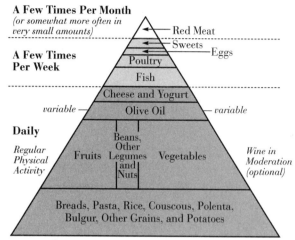

THE TRADITIONAL HEALTHY MEDITERRANEAN DIET PYRAMID

Copyright © 1994 Oldways Preservation & Exchange Trust

ranean pyramid, our ancestors' diets and eating habits around the world are all telling us the same thing: The healthiest diet is based on complex carbohydrates. We need to eat more fruits and vegetables. Fat consumption is linked to risks of our most serious diseases. Cutting fat and increasing carbohydrates and fiber can lower them. This is the foundation of *Fresh Start*. It's a sensible approach to lower-fat eating based on the information we already know and the magnificent, intense flavors we already love. New studies and theories can be "food for thought," but the groundwork is already there.

A balanced diet, exercise, stress management and other healthy habits are all part of the equation for a healthy life that will allow us to age well with vibrant health. Today we understand the results of centuries of healthy eating patterns around the world. Now, it's time for all of us to make a *Fresh Start*!

17

How to Eat Right

The USDA Food Pyramid presents a good, sensible blueprint for eating right—but putting it to work for you everyday can be confusing. On pages 24 to 39, I detail the food categories recommended by the pyramid, explaining what constitutes a serving size, describing the various foods that fall into a specific category, why you need to include them in your diet and how to establish some new habits regarding them. Then, there is a chart on page 49 that you can photocopy and keep handy for recording your new daily meals and habits until they become second nature.

Your everyday goals will be to:

◆ Strive to eat a balanced diet that includes the following: 6 to 11 servings of complex carbohydrates such as grains and cereals that supply good amounts of fiber; 3 to 5 servings of vegetables and 2 to 4 servings of fruits (also complex carbohydrates and sources of fiber); 2 to 3 servings of dairy products; and 2 to 3 servings of protein (poultry, fish, meat, dry beans, eggs).

◆ Simultaneously reduce fats to your own daily goal

◆ Watch your intake of sugar and sodium

◆ Drink at *least* eight glasses of water a day

◆ Exercise for a minimum of 30 minutes every day!

Sound hard? It's not—it's easy! Start gradually by following the daily menu plans in the book. If you don't use them every day, try to do so several times a week. As you cut the fat and increase the flavor, you'll feel better, more energized. I promise!

So that you will know what's in store in this book, and to help you better understand my philosophy, I have codified the most important points:

◆ Set your own personal goals. Once you understand what you want to achieve, don't stop there. You need to take action. Don't talk about it to your friends and family—this is your own personal endeavor. Don't intellectualize. This is the time to break old habits and develop new ones. Stop using confusion over dietary information as an excuse to do nothing. It's time to "just do it"—for a lifetime!

◆ Make a commitment to cook and eat at home more often. This way, you will know exactly what you are eating.

Daily Calorie Requirements
Recommended Energy Intake For You

TYPE OF PERSON AND ACTIVITY LEVEL	CALORIES PER DAY	TYPE OF PERSON AND ACTIVITY LEVEL	CALORIES PER DAY
Minimum calories for adequate nutrition	1000–1200	Very active women Average men 50+ Boys 11 to 14	2200–2600
Sedentary women	1600		
Moderately active women Children 4 to 6 Women 51+	1800	Active men Teen boys	2600–2800
		Men 25 to 50 light to heavy activity, Athletes in training	3000–4000
Active women Sedentary men, teen girls Children 7 to 10	2000–2200		

CONSULT WITH YOUR DOCTOR AND NUTRITIONIST TO CONFIRM YOUR GOAL

SOURCE: U.S. Department of Health, Human Services, Food and Drug Administration, FDA Special Report, May 1993, p. 44, Washington, D.C.

◆ Strive to increase your level of exercise. Without this, your new healthful diet alone can't improve well-being for long.

◆ Talk to your doctor about your health and a registered dietician (R.D.) to set your own personal dietary goals. To find an accredited nutritionist in your area, call the American Dietetic Association Hotline (800-366-1655).

◆ Know the goals that are best for your own lifestyle. Refer to the chart above and on page 37 to find your own daily calorie requirements and daily fat-gram allowances.

◆ Routinely keep track of what you're eating. It's the only way you'll know if you're eating the way you think you are.

◆ Average your fat intake over three to four days instead of measuring it at every meal. Think of fat as a daily "allowance" that allows for flexibility if you're traveling or indulging and helps you get back on the healthy track quickly. Take it day by day, meal by meal, recipe by recipe until new habits develop.

◆ Become familiar with the fat grams and percentages of fat to calories for various foods. Feel comfortable with them and use them to help you order in restaurants and buy take-out food.

"Life itself is the proper binge."
JULIA CHILD

Please continue to read the introduction (I will try to make it as clear and interesting as possible). You really need to understand the reasoning behind your new goals.

Then, read through the entire book to get an overview of what's ahead—the menus, the recipes, the nutritional analyses and the boxes of information to get the lay of the land. I've included lots of charts and helpful nuggets of advice to make your metamorphosis easier and more fun!

Later in the book, you'll find four weeks of menus designed to get those of you who strive to understand low fat off to a fresh start and give those of you who already have begun the healthy eating habit a new idea or two. Each day's menu includes breakfast, lunch, dinner and one or two snacks. They are meant as a guide to cooking at home, ordering in a restaurant or mixing and matching recipes to the menus. The recipes can be easily increased or decreased as you need. Or, if you prefer, eat six minimeals a day. The menus are based on:

◆ 2,000 daily calories. If your age, weight and activity level are enough to consume

more calories or if you need to eat fewer, increase or decrease the portions accordingly.

◆ A limit of between 15 and 20 percent of total calories from fat to be averaged over three to four days.

◆ Increased carbohydrates, fiber, fruits and vegetables (based on guidelines developed by the USDA).

◆ Decreased emphasis on meats, dairy, fats, sodium and sugars.

Try to follow the menus as closely as possible until eating at your fat goal level becomes second nature. Most other goals will fall into place naturally.

While I don't expect anybody to make every single recipe for every meal during the month, I hope you will want to try many of them. Most are very simple. You can also use them to guide you when you're ordering in a restaurant or dining with friends.

Don't get discouraged if you slip or don't notice rapid, dramatic change. You are changing a lifetime of cooking and eating habits, many of which feel as comfortable as an old shoe. You don't have to do it at once. Take small steps and make little changes. Don't announce to the world—or even your family—that you're cooking "low fat." This is your own personal agreement with yourself. Just do it. If you slip, start again! *It's important because this concerns the rest of your life.*

*"Nothing great was
ever achieved without enthusiasm."*
RALPH WALDO EMERSON

When the Flavor Is There, You Forget the Fat Is Gone!

The biggest secret to cooking with less fat is to replace it with flavor! It's easy for me because my cooking style has always included big, intense, magnified flavors that taste fresh, clear and clean—and are immediately and easily identifiable.

The wonderful thing of all is that most of these big, bold flavors come from foods with little, if any, fat. And those that do have a lot (*), such as nuts and olives, have flavors so bold that a little bit goes a long way.

- Anchovies*
  fillets
  paste
  rolled with capers
- Broths
  chicken
  beef
  fish
  vegetable
- Capers
- Chilies, fresh, dried,
    roasted
  habañero
  jalapeño
  poblano
  Scotch bonnet
  serrano
- Chili paste
- Chutney
- Citrus juice
  grapefruit
  lemons
  limes
  oranges
- Citrus zest
  lemon
  lime
  orange
- Cocoa powder*
  alkalized
  nonalkalized
- Coconut milk*

- Coffee and tea
- Dried fruits
  apples
  apricots
  bananas
  currants
  peaches
  prunes
  raisins
- Fruit and vegetable
    juices extracted
    in a juicer
  hand-squeezed
  store-bought
- Fruit-only jams and
    preserves
- Garlic
  fresh
  pureed
  roasted
- Ginger
  crystallized
  fresh
  powdered
- Herbs
  fresh
  dried
- Honey
- Horseradish
  fresh
  prepared
  wasabi
- Lemongrass

- Mushrooms, fresh and
    dried
  cepes
  Chinese black
  morels
  porcini
  shiitake
- Mustards
  Dijon
  powdered
  prepared yellow
  spicy brown
- Nuts*
  roasted
  salted
  toasted
- Olives*
- Peppercorns
  black
  green
  red
  white
- Pestos*
- Prepared sauces
  hoisin
  hot pepper (such as
    Tabasco)
  Pickapeppa
  soy
  tamari
  Worcestershire
- Red bell peppers
  fresh

  roasted
  grilled
- Salsas
  homemade
  store-bought
- Shredded coconut*
- Spices
  freshly ground in a
    mortar and pestle
  freshly ground in a
    mini food
    processor
  dry rubs
  spice blends
- Sun-dried tomatoes
  dry-packed
  oil-packed*
- Tomato paste
- Vanilla extract and
    bean
- Vinegars
  balsamic
  cider
  herb-infused
  red wine
  rice wine
  white distilled
  white wine
- Wines
  fortified wine
  table wine

What to Eat—and How Much of It to Eat

Restructuring how you eat every day is easy when you visualize the Food Pyramid: start at the bottom of the pyramid—think of it as starting or building a foundation. Eat more grains and legumes then anything else and don't skimp on fruits and vegetables, either. Go easy on dairy products and meat, poultry and fish. Work your way up to the point to use fat only to enhance flavors! No more thickly spreading on the butter or pouring on the olive oil! Trust me, after a few weeks of eating this way, you will hardly miss the fat. And when you do eat a high-fat dish, you will find that a little bit goes a long, long way. After several months you will wonder how you ever managed to eat that tremendous slice of cheesecake or plateful of bacon, eggs and hash browns.

Great! You are ready to begin eating sensibly and healthfully. But what *exactly* is a serving of fruit? How large is a serving of meat or poultry? Is a glass of milk bad for you? When do you know if you've overdone the butter or oil?

The following pages explain it all: from serving sizes to helpful hints on incorporating all these good foods into habits. You will find that most of the foods you will be eating are the same foods you have always eaten and loved—but you may find you are eating more rice and fresh fruit, for example, and less red meat and cheese. This is healthy eating for a lifetime.

As you consider how to include more grains, legumes, fruits and vegetables into your diet, remember that the big, bold flavors I have long loved and cooked with shine through in these recipes. They replace the fat, so that you won't miss it for a minute! A squeeze of tangy lemon juice, a sprinkle of sweet balsamic vinegar, a spoonful of aromatic chopped fresh herbs or a pinch of pungent ground spices enliven nearly everything. The flavors of the food come alive, dancing on your palate in a pleasingly delicious medley of taste sensations.

"The secret of success is consistency of purpose."
Benjamin Disraeli

Fabulous Flavors

Over the years, I've discovered flavors for foods from all around the world. Some of the flavors have a lot of fat, but many of our favorites have very little fat. Once you know which are which, you'll know how to use them and in what quantities.

	CAL.	FAT (G)		CAL.	FAT (G)
Almonds, 1 T.	38	3	Lemon juice, 1 T.	4	0.02
Anchovies, 1	8	0.4	Lemon zest, 1 T.	6	0.02
Balsamic vinegar,			Mustard, 1 T.	11	0.7
1 T.	2	0	Nutmeg, 1 T.	37	2
Basil, fresh, 1 T.	0.5	0	Red pepper flakes,		
Black olives, 1	12	1	1 tsp.	11	0.3
Black pepper, 1 T.	16	0.3	Red pepper, sweet,		
Capers, 1 oz.	1	0.1	1 T.	2.2	0.02
Caraway seed, 1 T.	7	0.1	Red wine, 1 T.	11	0
Catsup, 1 T.	16	0.1	Salsa, 1 T.	3	0
Cinnamon, 1 T.	18	0.2	Spinach pesto, 1 T.	24	1.5
Coconut, 1 T.	18	1.8	Sun-dried tomatoes,		
Currants, 1 T.	26	0.02	1 T.	9	0.1
Dried mushrooms,			Sun-dried tomatoes,		
1 T.	11	0.04	oil packed, 1 T.	30	2
Fresh mushrooms,			Tabasco, 1 T.	2	0.09
¼ cup	2	0.03	Tamari, 1 T.	9	0.01
Garlic, 1 T.	13	0.04	Tomato paste, 1 T.	14	0.1
Ginger root, 1 T.	4	0.04	Vanilla, 1 T.	28	0
Green olives, 1	7	0.7	White wine, 1 T.	10	0
Hoisin sauce, 1 T.	30	0.8	Worcestershire sauce,		
Horseradish, 1 T.	6	0	1 T.	11	0

Bread, Cereal, Rice, and Pasta

6 to 11 servings daily
One serving = 1 slice of bread,
1 ounce ready-to-eat cereal,
½ cup cooked cereal, rice or pasta,
1 pancake,
½ sandwich bun,
3 to 4 small crackers

Carbohydrates are the body's number-one source of energy. Current guidelines recommend they make up 55 to 75 percent of your total calories, mostly in the form of complex carbohydrates found in bread, pasta, rice and other grains, potatoes and cereal, fruit, vegetables and legumes.

Foods high in carbohydrates contain essential micronutrients and other components, some of which may actually protect you from cancer and heart disease. They're vital in regulating fat metabolism, sparing protein from being used to provide energy when it is needed for ongoing body maintenance and repair. And here's a big bonus: A diet high in complex carbohydrates is more likely to leave you feeling satisfied—for lots longer—than a low-carbohydrate diet with the same number of calories.

Carbohydrates supply 4 calories per gram.

Foods high in complex carbohydrates include vegetables; many fruits; legumes; grain-based foods such as polenta, corn bread, tortillas, bread, pasta, cereal, low-fat muffins; whole grains such as kasha, quinoa, rice, couscous, barley, oats, bulgur, millet, wheat berries, cracked wheat and wheat flakes and foods in which they predominate. Sugars are simple carbohydrates.

Fiber (roughage) is another benefit of a diet high in complex carbohydrates. Found in plant foods, fiber aids digestion. Eat a fiber-rich diet and you'll feel more satisfied after a meal—with fewer calories. Grains, legumes, nuts, fruits and vegetables are good sources. Aim for 25 to 35 grams of fiber every day.

Remember, it's what you put on top of bread, rice, potatoes, or pasta that makes them high in fat.

Fiber Facts

Fiber is the indigestible part of plants. You need it for optimum health.

Insoluble fiber, which doesn't dissolve in water, aids digestion and may protect against certain types of cancer. Whole-grain foods are the best sources.

Soluble fiber dissolves and forms gels that help delay the absorption of certain substances. It appears to be beneficial in controlling cholesterol. Legumes have the most soluble fiber; it's also in oat bran, barley, bananas, berries, pears, apples, grapefruit, apricots, potatoes, yams, corn, carrots, cabbage and many more fruits and vegetables.

◆ In grains, the closer to "whole," the greater the fiber, vitamins and minerals.

◆ In bread, look for whole-grain clues such as "100% whole wheat flour," "stone-ground whole-wheat flour," "wheat berries," "sprouted wheat," "oatmeal," "rye," "millet," and the like. These should appear at the beginning of the ingredients list, since ingredients are listed in order of predominance by weight in the product.

◆ Try whole-wheat versions of pasta.

◆ Start the day with a high-fiber cereal (10 to 40 grams per serving). It'll be easier to meet your fiber quota.

◆ Serve bread at most meals. Look in the bakery and farmers' market for country-style multi-grain breads. Eat bread plain or with a nonfat topping (see page 130).

FOOD SOURCES OF FIBER IN GRAMS/DAILY GOAL 25 TO 35 GRAMS

Food	Grams	Food	Grams
Apple, large (1)	4*	Lentils (¾ c. cooked)	6*
Baked potato w/skin, medium (1)	4*	Navy beans (¾ c. cooked)	9
Banana, medium (1)	2	Peas or winter squash (½ c. cooked)	3
Black-eyed peas (¾ c. cooked)	12*	Pear	4
Broccoli or spinach (½ c. cooked)	2	Pinto beans (¾ c. cooked)	8*
Brown rice (1 c. prepared)	3	Prunes, dried (5)	4
Brussels sprouts (½ c. cooked)	3*	Raisins (¼ c.)	2
Bulgur (cracked wheat) (1 c. prepared)	8	Split peas (¾ c. cooked)	4*
Carrot, raw (1)	2	Sweet potato, w/o skin, medium (1)	3*
Chickpeas (garbanzos) (¾ c. cooked)	7*	Wheat bran (½ c.)	13
Corn (½ c. cooked)	3	Whole-wheat spaghetti (1 c. prepared)	6
Figs, dried (3)	5		
Kidney beans (¾ c. cooked)	14		

*Soluble and insoluble fiber have not been measured in most foods. Foods that have been analyzed and contain at least 1 gram per serving of soluble fiber are marked by an *.

Fruits

2 to 4 servings daily
One serving = 1 medium piece of fruit, ¹/₂ cup chopped, canned or cooked fruit,
³/₄ cup fruit juice, ¹/₄ cup dried fruit

Fruit is naturally sweet, juicy (it's 80 to 95 percent water) and low in calories. It has little sodium, virtually no fat and certainly no cholesterol. As a complex carbohydrate, it's Mother Nature's gift to your sweet tooth.

Fruits are loaded with fiber, both insoluble and soluble. Their chief contributions are vitamins A, C and beta-carotene, which is particularly high in melons, citrus fruit and berries. They also supply potassium, iron, calcium and magnesium. Like vegetables, they contain anti-carcinogenic compounds. The ellagic acid in grapes and strawberries and a natural flavoring agent in oranges and citrus may protect you against cancer, for example.

Fruit is a great replacement for high-sugar, high-fat sweets. It satisfies your sweet tooth naturally. More than a snack or dessert, it can add subtle sweetness to other dishes.

Ripeness is the key; the fruit softens, changes color, its vitamin content increases and it sweetens, developing a heavenly aroma.

Dried fruits offer concentrated energy and fiber. Whole fruits are higher in fiber than are fruit juices; choose natural juices over sugary drinks diluted with water.

Just remember: The low-fat, high-fiber benefits of fruits and vegetables won't be as great if you add fats and sweets.

◆ Aim for the National Cancer Institute and the Produce for Better Health Foundation's "Five a Day for Better Health" goal, and eat at least five fruits (and vegetables) a day.

◆ Keep a bowl of fruit as a "movable snack." Put it on the counter or table, by the back door, by the telephone or the TV. Just get it out of the fridge. If your family sees it, they'll eat it.

◆ Don't throw away the peel if it's edible. Peels are full of nutrients. Just wash it well.

◆ Start with two pieces of fruit for breakfast.

◆ At breakfast, top your pancakes with fruit instead of syrup. Add sliced bananas or strawberries to your cereal.

◆ Serve wedges of fruit with chicken or shrimp salad, roasted chicken, pork or fish.

◆ Add fruit to rice and green salads, muffins, cakes or cookies.

◆ Always have a big bowl of lemons, limes and oranges within easy reach to use in cooking and for serving. Both the juice and the

Fruit Is Nature's Sweetener

FRUIT (1 whole medium size or 1 cup)	CAL.	FAT (G)
Apple	81	0.5
Apricot	37	0.1
Banana	105	0.6
Blackberries,	24	0.6
Blueberries	82	0.6
Cantaloupe	57	0.5
Green Grapes	90	0.9
Kiwi	47	0.3
Mango	68	0.6
Orange	62	0.1
Papaya	118	0.4
Peach	37	0.1
Pear	98	0.7
Pineapple	73	0.7
Plum	36	0.4
Pomegranate	104	0.5
Raspberries,	61	0.7
Strawberries	45	0.5
Tangerine	37	0.2
Watermelon	50	0.7

zest (colorful peel) magnify the flavors of other foods.

◆ Pack dried fruit as a portable snack.

◆ Use fresh, frozen fruit or fruit purees for frozen yogurt, sorbets or smoothies.

◆ Let fruits take over for your sweet tooth. You'll be surprised how cloying sugary desserts seem after a while.

◆ Finish your meal with a piece of perfectly ripened fruit, presented in a special way (sliced and put in a pretty bowl, for instance). Add a small piece of great cheese, a cookie or a good glass of wine, and you have dessert!

Vegetables

3 to 5 servings daily
One serving = 1 cup raw leafy vegetables, ½ cup cooked or raw vegetables
¾ cup vegetable juice

It's time to take vegetables out of the side-dish category. They're the cornerstones of a healthy diet. Full of fiber, vegetables are rich in a variety of vitamins, minerals and phytochemicals linked to disease prevention, particularly cancer and heart disease. Virtually fat- and cholesterol-free, they're nutrient dense, giving you a lot of nutrition "punch" for just a few calories.

Vegetables can be divided into three groups: dark green, "starchy" and red-yellow-orange vegetables. Dark green vegetables contain fiber, vitamins A, beta-carotene, C, E, folacin, riboflavin, iron and magnesium. They include broccoli, salad and field greens and some members of the cabbage family.

"Starchy" vegetables include beans, peas, corn, dried beans and peas and all root vegetables, including potatoes, parsnips, rutabagas, carrots and radishes. They're complex carbohydrates, offering starch and fiber as well as protein. And they'll give you a whole range of important vitamins, minerals and phytochemicals. The red-yellow-orange group, including carrots, red peppers, squash and tomatoes, contains fiber, vitamins A, beta-carotene, C, E and folacin.

Try to eat vegetables both raw and cooked. Raw and undercooked, they generally retain more nutrients. Yet carrots yield more beta-carotene after cooking, even more after pureeing. Vitamin C–rich vegetables can lose up to half their nutrients when boiled. Always serve promptly after cooking to minimize nutrient loss.

Exposure to light, air and long soakings in water will also deplete nutrients. And watch what you peel—many nutrients are just under the skin. Leaves and stems are good for you, too.

◆ Freshly harvested vegetables have more vitamins than those that have been stored. Grow your own or frequent the farmers' market.

◆ Try to have two servings of vegetables at lunch and two at dinner.

◆ Eat vegetables as crunchy snacks all day long. They travel well in a resealable plastic bag.

◆ For beta-carotene, choose deep yellow, dark green and cruciferous vegetables such as carrots, sweet potatoes, winter squash, pumpkin, spinach, kale, brussels sprouts, cauliflower, broccoli, broccoflower (or broccoli rabe), kale, mustard greens, cabbage (green, red, savoy, bok choy), turnips, rutabaga and kohlrabi.

◆ Choose dark greens for salads: arugula, chicory, dandelion greens, mustard greens, spinach and watercress.

◆ Don't spoil a good thing by drowning vegetables or salads in oil.

28

- Get to know peppers, both sweet and hot, and how they vary in taste.

- Understand the nuances of beans, rices and grains—explore their nutty, herby or smoky flavors. Cook them in broth with herbs, citrus juice or onions and garlic to infuse them with flavor.

- Steam or microwave vegetables with flavored steaming liquids (see page 306), and lightly seasoned and spiced waters which infuse flavor into steamed vegetables, making them taste more exciting.

- Sprinkle lemon juice or balsamic vinegar and freshly ground pepper on steamed or roasted vegetables.

- Learn to enjoy cooked vegetables naturally, with nothing more on top than perhaps freshly ground pepper and a sprinkle of salt.

- Be creative in getting your 3 to 5 servings per day. Mix vegetables into main dishes, tuck them into sandwiches and add as "extras" to salads. Be sure to eat a variety of vegetables for a variety of nutrients.

Versatile Vegetables

VEGETABLES (1 whole or 1 cup)	CAL.	FAT (G)	VEGETABLES (1 whole or 1 cup)	CAL.	FAT (G)
Acorn squash (baked)	115	0.3	Fennel (raw)	27	0.2
Artichoke	60	0.2	Green beans (boiled)	44	0.4
Arugula	12	0.2	Mushrooms (raw)	57	0.9
Asparagus (steamed)	44	0.6	Onion (raw)	42	0.2
Beets (boiled)	52	0.3	Peas (raw)	117	0.6
Broccoli (raw)	24	0.3	Potato (baked)	227	0.3
Brussels sprouts (boiled)	60	0.8	Romaine lettuce	8	0.1/10
Cabbage (raw)	18	0.2	Spaghetti squash (baked)	45	0.4
Carrots	31	0.1	Spinach (raw)	12	0.2
Cauliflower	25	0.2	Sweet Potato (baked)	206	0.2
Celery	6	0.2	Tomato	26	0.5
Corn (boiled)	133	0.1	Watercress	4	0.1
Eggplant (raw)	21	0.1	Zucchini (raw)	18	0.2

Protein

2 to 3 servings daily
One serving = 2 to 3 ounces cooked lean meat, poultry or fish,
½ cup cooked dry beans,
1 egg, 2 tablespoons peanut butter, 1 to 2 ounces low-fat cheese

Somewhere along the line, a lot of us bought into the notion that protein was the most important nutrient. When healthy eating became a concern, we worried about getting enough.

Protein can provide fuel for energy. But that is not its role. Protein is essential for transporting nutrients, regulating body processes and building, maintaining and repairing body tissues. If you eat enough complex carbohydrates, the protein you eat can be reserved for its construction and regulatory roles. But we need far less protein than we ever imagined—only about 10 to 15 percent of total calories, or a Recommended Daily Allowance of 40 to 60 grams a day, depending on age and gender. The average American consumes 160 grams. That's three to four times the protein we need. Excess protein doesn't build more muscles (only strength training can do that), it just forces the kidneys to excrete the extra by-products of metabolism.

Doubly significant is the fact that 70 percent of our protein is from animal foods, natural carriers of fat and cholesterol. That's the best reason of all to limit consumption or to choose alternative sources of protein. Meat is the protein of choice and habit for most Americans. The Chinese consume only 7 percent of their protein as meat. The Western diseases of affluence—heart disease, diabetes and cancer—are found in areas of China where people eat the most animal protein. Fish and poultry, particularly white meat, are the leanest animal foods. Breeders have responded to consumer demand for leaner cuts of meat by bringing leaner animals to market.

You don't need to get protein from meat. Vegetarians obtain adequate protein by combining grains, legumes and nuts or seeds, or adding dairy products or eggs to a meatless diet. A "complete" protein contains all nine essential amino acids, found in virtually all meat. But legumes, grains and nuts or seeds all contain some essential amino acids. If you eat them with another plant food that supplies the missing amino acids at the same meal or later in the day, the protein will still be "complete." Tacos with beans; risotto with peas; rice with beans; minestrone with noodles; and beans and pea soup with whole-wheat bread are all examples of complementary protein combinations.

Beans, especially soybeans, contain protein in amounts almost comparable to complete protein foods, with minimal fat and a fiber bonus.

Eggs, long considered "nature's perfect food," are an inexpensive source of high-quality protein, and not as prohibitive in terms of fat and cholesterol as recently thought. Because only 2 grams of an egg's 5 grams of fat are saturated fat, which has a greater impact on blood cholesterol than dietary cholesterol, the American Heart Association has raised its weekly acceptable egg intake for healthy people from three to four eggs. If you have an elevated cholesterol level, you should discuss your diet with a doctor. But egg whites can be used freely. They're almost perfect, pure protein, with no fat or cholesterol.

◆ Limit animal protein (poultry, fish, cheese, eggs) to 6 ounces a day. When thinking of poultry or fish, this amount represents a serving about the size of a deck of cards. Limit red meat to 12 ounces a week.

◆ Always trim all visible fat from meats and remove the skin from poultry before serving.

◆ Use condiments, such as mustard, preserves and chutneys, as tasty glazes on broiled and grilled meat and poultry.

◆ Emphasize fish, poultry and nonanimal sources of protein.

◆ Eating fish twice a week is a good way to get the benefits of essential fatty acids, which are most evident in oily fish such as salmon and mackerel.

◆ Sprinkle fish before and during broiling or grilling with lemon juice and fresh herbs.

◆ Substitute ground turkey or chicken for ground beef, pork, lamb or veal.

◆ Farm-raised game is surprisingly lean, better tasting and more readily available today than it used to be. This is also called "free-range" or "natural" poultry or game.

◆ Whenever possible, substitute two egg whites for one egg yolk.

◆ Nuts and seeds are good sources of protein, minerals and vitamins, but they are loaded with fat and calories (130 to 200 calories per ounce), so go easy on them.

◆ Combine foods to make complete proteins: pasta with beans; lentils with whole-wheat bread; hummus with tortilla chips; black beans or sugar snap peas with rice. Whole grains combined with beans, peas, nuts or seeds result in the same high-quality protein as meat, fish or poultry.

◆ Don't be shy about using herbs and spices to enhance the flavor of protein.

Alternative Sources of Protein

	PORTION	CAL.	PROT. (G)	FAT (G)/%
Almonds	3 oz.	501	17	44/79
Apple w/peel	1 med.	81	0.3	0.5/6
Baked potato w/skin	1 med.	227	4	0.3/1
Banana	1 med.	105	1	0.6/5
Beef tenderloin	3 oz.	179	20	9/43
Black beans	½ cup	113	8	0.5/4
Broccoli	1 cup	50	7	0.6/10
Brown rice	1 cup	315	7	3/7
Chicken, skinless	3 oz.	148	17	4/23
Corn	½ cup	86	3	1/10
Cottage cheese, nonfat	¼ cup	38	7	0/0
Egg noodles	1 cup	210	7	2/10
Egg, white	1	16	4	0/0
Egg, whole	1	75	6	5/60
Green beans	½ cup	17	1	0/0
Green peas	½ cup	59	4	0.3/5
Lemon sole	3 oz.	100	16	1/9
Lentils	½ cup	325	27	1/3
Linguine	3 oz.	120	4	0.6/5
Nonfat yogurt	3 oz.	45	5	0/0
Oatmeal	1 cup	145	6	2/14
Peanut butter	1 T.	94	4	8/77
Raisins	1 cup	495	5	0.8/1
Salad greens	1 cup	9.5	1	0.1/11
Sweet potato	1 med.	117	2	0.1/1
Tofu	⅓ cup	75	7	4/48
Tuna, in water	3 oz.	99	22	1/9
Turkey breast	3 oz.	134	21	3/20
Whole-wheat bagel	2 oz.	149	6	0.8/5
Whole-wheat bread	1 slice	86	3	1.5/16

Milk, Yogurt and Cheese

2 to 3 servings daily
One serving = 1 cup milk, 8 ounces yogurt,
1½ ounces natural cheese, 2 ounces processed cheese

The dairy group is a rich source of high-quality protein, calcium and important nutrients needed by people of all ages. But because dairy products naturally contain saturated fat and cholesterol, you need to choose them carefully. One glass of whole milk has the same amount of fat as three strips of bacon.

Luckily, there are now lots of great low-fat or nonfat dairy alternatives. All have the nutrients intact (and then some, if they're fortified), without the fat. Low-fat and skim milk are required by the FDA to be fortified with vitamin A. All commercially available milk is vitamin D–fortified.

Milk and milk products are the leading source of calcium in the American diet. Calcium and vitamin D–rich foods are important to building and maintaining bone health and preventing osteoporosis, a degenerative condition characterized by loss of bone density and increased risk of debilitating fractures. With 300 mg per cup, two to three servings of milk go a long way toward fulfilling the recommended intake of 800 to 2000 mg of calcium a day, which varies depending on age and gender. But because one cup of whole milk has 8 grams of fat and 2% milk has 5 grams, 1% or skim milk are wiser choices for anyone over the age of two. Butter is a dairy product, too, but it is all fat (much of it saturated) and contains cholesterol, so it is best grouped with Fats and Oils.

Cheese labels that say "lite" must now have a third fewer calories or half the fat of the reference food. "Low-fat" must have no more than 3 grams of fat per serving. Only a few cheeses are truly lower in fat—part-skim mozzarella, fat-free cream cheese, low-fat goat cheese (chèvre) and nonfat cottage cheese. You can use a little of a stronger-flavored "real" cheese and make it stretch a long way with nonfat cottage cheese or yogurt.

Watch out for ice cream and other frozen treats. "Real" ice cream may get 80 to 90 percent of its calories from fat, much of it saturated. Frozen yogurt may or may not be low in fat. Check the label—there are good low-fat and nonfat versions, too.

◆ Choose nonfat or low-fat varieties of dairy to your taste. There is one for almost every dairy product.

◆ If you are trying to switch to skim milk and find it unappealing, start gradually, beginning with whole milk and moving to 2%, 1% and then skim. You might also try adding

Dairy

PRODUCT (per 1-cup serving)	CAL.	CHOL. (MG)	FAT (G)/%
Buttermilk	99	9	2/8
Cream cheese	792	176	80/91
Evaporated skim milk	198	10	0.5/2
Fat-free cream cheese	200	40	0/0
Heavy cream	821	326	80/88
Light sour cream	400	0	32/72
Low-fat cottage cheese	164	10	2/11
Low-fat cream cheese	640	40	56/79
Low-fat ricotta cheese	160	60	8/45
Low-fat yogurt	128	12	3/22
Mayonnaise	1600	80	176/99
Mayonnaise, light	800	80	80/91
Neufchâtel cheese	560	160	48/77
Nonfat Blend	130	0	0.7/5
Nonfat cottage cheese	140	10	0/0
Nonfat yogurt	120	0	0/0
Nonfat yogurt cheese	219	0	0/0
1% milk	102	10	2.6/23
2% milk	121	18	4.7/35
Parmesan cheese	888	152	56/57
Part-skim mozzarella cheese	576	128	40/63
Ricotta cheese	400	120	32/72
Skim milk	86	4	0.6/4
Sour cream	512	trace	48/84
Whole milk	150	33	8/48
Yogurt	150	30	8/48

flavorings such as vanilla and other extracts, spices, instant coffee, frozen fruit juice concentrates or fresh juice. Or add nonfat dry milk to 1% or skim to make it taste richer.

◆ Substitute canned evaporated skim milk for heavy cream. Use low-fat milk in recipes calling for milk and cream.

◆ When appropriate, use nonfat yogurt, nonfat cottage cheese or Nonfat Blend (see page 298) instead of cream in baking.

◆ Substitute Neufchâtel cheese (also called low-fat cream cheese) for regular cream cheese.

◆ Use Nonfat Blend (see page 298) flavored with a little mayonnaise to dress chicken or tuna salad.

◆ Make a white sauce using potato flakes and add flavor from herbs, pesto, mustard, nutmeg, tomato paste, pureed vegetables, salt and pepper or one tablespoon of butter added at the very end of cooking.

◆ The best sources of calcium are milk and yogurt, cheese, calcium-fortified orange juice, some cereals, broccoli, tofu with calcium and canned fish with bones.

Fats, Oils and Sweets

Use sparingly

By now, the effects of too much fat in the diet have been fairly well established. In study after study, a high-fat diet has been linked to cardiovascular disease, cancer, stroke, diabetes, chronic liver disease, osteoporosis and other diseases. Fat literally makes fat, as evidenced by the 40 percent of Americans who are overweight.

You really *do* need *some* fat. It regulates hormones, cushions your organs and protects them in extreme weather conditions, keeps your skin soft, helps transport the fat-soluble vitamins A, D, E and K and helps maintain protective HDL cholesterol levels. Fat is also

an important body fuel. But it's hard not to get enough fat! A tablespoon a day will do the trick.

The average American consumes the equivalent of six to eight tablespoons a day, 37 to 41 percent of their total diet. The USDA recommends limiting fat intake to 30% of daily calories, but many health and medical experts consider 15 to 20 percent healthier. And some cardiologists set a limit of 10% for patients with existing heart disease. In *Fresh Start*, I aim for the 15 to 20 percent level. Of course, not everything you eat will be 15 to 20 percent fat. Much will be less. Some will be more, to be

Cholesterol

Cholesterol is a waxy, fatlike substance that along with other plaquelike substances in the blood can clog veins and arteries, narrowing them and sometimes triggering a heart attack or stroke. Like fat, your body requires some cholesterol, but your liver manufactures all you need. Cholesterol is found in all animal foods such as meat and cheese. If something you ate once had a liver (or is the product of an animal), it has cholesterol, too. Limit cholesterol to 300 mg per day.

Americans are watching their cholesterol, and many of us have succeeded in lowering our intake. But there is a dangerous lack of awareness that saturated fat is thought to have a greater impact on heart disease than the consumption of cholesterol-containing foods. A food product can still have 2 grams per portion of saturated fat and still carry the label "no cholesterol," misleading many to think it's a healthy food. Avocados, olives, coconuts, nuts, seeds, cocoa butter and palm oil are all high in saturated fat, but as non-animal sources, they have no cholesterol. That doesn't make them any less harmful because saturated fat raises blood cholesterol in the body.

The average American under the age of thirty has a cholesterol count of 180 mg/dl; above thirty, 200 mg/dl, down from 210 just a few years ago. But according to Dr. Castelli, a level of 150 or below is even better, offering as much protection as possible from heart disease. *If your cholesterol level is above 200, you need to find out your HDL/LDL ratio and triglcycerides, then, seek out a cardiac specialist and begin taking his or her advice.*

averaged over three to four days. Cutting back on fat means using common sense, being aware, keeping track, learning, understanding and making the right choices.

Dietary fat has three forms: saturated fat, polyunsaturated fat and monounsaturated fat. Most foods are a combination of all three forms.

Saturated Fat is an artery-damaging fat found mostly in animal products such as lard, meat fat, butter and whole milk products.

According to Dr. William Castelli, medical director of the Framingham Study, the country's oldest ongoing study of heart disease, "For most Americans, the reason their cholesterol is too high is more because they eat too much saturated fat than because they eat too much cholesterol." Saturated fat is solid at room temperature and gives foods a pleasant velvety texture. There's less in poultry and fish than in red meat, but many animal foods and even some vegetable oils are high in saturated fat. No more than 7 percent of your total daily fat intake should be consumed in the form of saturated fat.

Polyunsaturated Fats are liquid at room temperature. They're found in cooking oils of vegetable origin, such as corn, safflower and sesame oils. These fats lower both LDL (bad cholesterol) and, to a lesser extent, HDL (good cholesterol). Polyunsaturated Omega-3 fatty acids (found in seafood—especially oily fish) have an anticlotting action, helping prevent heart attacks and strokes.

Monounsaturated Fat is liquid at room temperature, viscous or hard when refrigerated. It's found in high amounts in olive, canola and peanut oils. This fat reduces LDL

Daily Fat Gram and Fat Calorie Allowances

(select your total daily fat percentage goal)

AVERAGE CALORIES PER DAY	15%		20%		25%	
	FAT (G)	FAT CAL.	FAT (G)	FAT CAL.	FAT (G)	FAT CAL.
1000	17	150	22	200	28	250
1200	20	180	27	240	33	300
1400	23	210	31	280	39	350
1600	27	240	36	320	44	400
1800	30	270	40	360	50	450
2000	33	300	44	400	56	500
2200	37	330	49	440	61	550
2400	40	360	53	480	67	600
2600	43	390	58	520	72	650
2800	47	420	62	560	75	700

but not HDL cholesterol. Canola and olive oil are thought to lower cholesterol when they replace saturated fat. But limit these fats too.

Remember, all oils are 100 percent fat and all have some saturated fat, an average of about 14 percent. But oils that are liquid at room temperature are best. A manufacturing process called *hydrogenation* adds hydrogen atoms to unsaturated fatty acids, making them more saturated and solid at room temperature. Hydrogenation increases shelf life and enhances texture in processed foods. It also creates elements called "trans-fatty acids." They're in more foods than you can

Sugar

The Food Pyramid recommends that sugar be consumed as sparingly as fat. Sugar contributes to dental cavities and obesity, particularly as it often goes hand in hand with high-fat foods such as cakes and cookies. Watch for its many forms in prepared foods: brown sugar, corn sweetener, Demerara sugar, dextrose, fructose, fruit juice concentrate, glucose, high-fructose corn syrup, honey, invert sugar, malt, maltose, molasses, raw sugar, sucrose, syrup and treacle.

Sugars are simple carbohydrates. Honey, molasses, table sugar and its many other forms don't give you much more than an energy boost.

imagine—practically everything that comes in a box or package in the grocery store. Trans-fatty acids can be unhealthy if you're eating more than a small amount. They appear to raise cholesterol just as much as saturated fat. You can avoid them by checking labels for the terms "hydrogenated" and partially hydrogenated.

The butter/margarine controversy confuses more people than any other. Butter is a saturated fat and contains cholesterol. Margarine contains varying amounts of hydrogenated oils, which act like saturated fats in raising blood cholesterol. Unprocessed liquid vegetable oils are preferable to either.

The bottom line: Reduce fat intake in general and cut back gradually, so you don't feel deprived. The habit really sticks.

FOR LOWER-FAT COOKING EVERY DAY, ALWAYS KEEP THESE TASTY FLAVORS IN STOCK

- Chicken broth—low-fat, low-sodium
- Beef broth
- Nonfat yogurt
- Nonfat cottage cheese
- Nonfat buttermilk
- Spices in small quantities to ensure freshness
- Fresh herbs—a variety, always
- A variety of mustards
- Tamari, hoisin and soy sauce
- Pestos, bean pastes
- Crushed red pepper flakes
- Capers, curry pastes
- Anchovies, sardines, smoked fish
- Tomato paste, tomato sauce
- Salsa
- Honey, molasses, brown sugar
- Smoked meats and sausage
- Olives
- Citrus fruit—for juice and zest
- Concentrated frozen fruit juices
- Vinegars—red and white wine, balsamic, cider, herb- and spice-infused
- Onions, garlic, shallots, scallions
- Low-fat ricotta, part-skim mozzarella and Parmesan cheeses
- Big-flavored real cheeses
- Kosher salt and sea salt
- Black, white and dried green peppercorns
- Mushrooms—fresh and dried
- Hot and sweet peppers
- Vanilla extract and beans
- Barbecue sauce, and the makings for yours
- Fortified wines, alcohol and liquers
- Coffee, espresso
- Tea—herbal and caffeinated
- Frozen berries

Types of Oils & Fats

All fats and oils have approximately 14 grams of fat or 120 calories per tablespoon. Saturated fats turn to cholesterol in the body.

OILS	% POLY-UNSATURATED	% MONO-UNSATURATED	% SATURATED	% UNDEFINED FATTY ACIDS	CHOL. (MG)
Almond	18	73	8	1	0
Avocado	13	71	4	12	0
Canola/rapeseed	30	59	7	4	0
Coconut	2	6	86	7	0
Corn	59	24	13	4	0
Cottonseed	52	18	26	4	0
Grapeseed	69	0	10	21	0
Hazelnut	10	78	7	5	0
Palm	9	37	49	5	0
Peanut	32	46	17	5	0
Olive	8	74	13	5	0
Safflower	13	9	0	78	0
Sesame	42	40	14	4	0
Soy	16	25	15	40	0
Sunflower	68	21	11	5	0
Vegetable	74	12	9	5	0
Walnut	67	24	9	5	0
FATS					
Butter	5	31	64	9	33
Chicken fat	21	45	30	4	24
Duck fat	14	51	35	0	13
Lard	11	48	41	0	12
Turkey fat	24	45	31	0	13

Remember, all fats are 100% fat.

Plan Three Meals and Three Snacks

A regular schedule is important for controlling your eating. Choose three meals and three low-fat, high-fiber snacks, or divide the day's intake more evenly into five or six mini-meals. Just make sure you don't eat more *and* more often.

Planning is essential. A week's worth of menus will make marketing easier and help you meet your nutritional goals. Yet be flexible enough so that you can switch Monday night with Sunday lunch, if you please.

Breakfast is a vital jump start after eight to ten hours of fasting. It affects how you feel and what you eat for the rest of the day. Skip it, and you might binge later. You'll feel most satisfied and have the most energy when breakfast offers complex carbohydrates for energy and fiber, a good source of protein and an abundance of vitamins and minerals. Start with hearty breads, cereals and fruit. Vary the menu so you don't give up in boredom. Save eggs, bacon and croissants for *very* special occasions.

Lunch refuels in the middle of the day. Lunch at home alone can be lonely and filled with temptation; lunch out can be social and filled with temptation. Planning helps. Are you having protein for dinner? Should this be your big meal of the day? Some people relish routine and eat the same thing every day. Do whatever works.

Choose salads, soups, lean meat or fish and whole-grain pasta or sandwiches. Pass on processed meats and the deli sandwich in favor of fish or turkey. Don't automatically slather butter or mayo on your sandwiches, or mayo or sour cream in your salads. Be selective at the salad bar. If you must, carry your own dressing.

Dinner is usually the most social meal of the day. Flaunt tradition and make it lighter and leaner, with an emphasis on carbohydrates (potatoes, pasta, grains) and vegetables. Begin with an appetizer salad served with a crusty bread, the best and most interesting you can find. Make soup, salad or a stir-fry the main event, with meat as an accent or side dish. Serve two vegetables, one unadorned, one more special. Finish with a flourish—a simple fruit dessert or frozen yogurt and coffee or biscotti and a glass of Vin Santo. Try to eat three to four hours before bedtime.

Snacks can help keep blood sugar levels steady and keep you from mindless munching. Choose fresh foods over commercial snacks and have a variety on hand. Choose fruits, raw vegetables, fruit and vegetable juices, smoothies, air-popped popcorn, soups, bagels, low-fat crackers, nonfat frozen yogurt, low-fat cookies, cereal, fruit yogurt, dried fruit or sorbets. Be creative!

Cook at Home as Often as You Can

It's daunting once you realize you've got to throw out the dietary rules you were brought up with and reinvent the repertoire of dishes your family loves. But I promise that if you make changes recipe by recipe, meal by meal, the big picture won't seem half as large. After a few weeks, it'll all start to click. You'll look at food differently. You'll feel better. And cooking will become second nature once again.

So take it one step at a time. Your pantry will change, your cooking methods will evolve, but the food will taste as good as ever. I've talked with literally thousands of cooks and those who have made the change and say they're not going back to their old cooking methods ever again. They feel too good!

AT THE MARKET

◆ Plan ahead and market for a week or minimally three to four days at a time. You won't have to market every time you cook and you'll have the flexibility to plan the vegetable, fruit and carbohydrate first with the protein last, and to reduce the emphasis on meat and dairy. Try to plan two to three pasta, two bean and two rice dishes per week, and potatoes three to four times a week, with a variety of breads. Work in meat primarily as a side dish, and when you do choose it, figure only three to six ounces per person.

◆ Shop with the seasons. Choose what's in season. Select produce at its prime and your dishes will naturally taste better. Nature's combinations of food flavors complement each other naturally. And you'll get the best buys.

*"Watch a French housewife
as she makes her way slowly
along the loaded stalls...
searching for the peak of ripeness
and flavor...
What you are seeing is a true artist
at work, patiently assembling
all the materials of her craft,
just as the painter squeezes the oil colors
onto his palette ready to create
a masterpiece."*
KEITH FLOYD

◆ Buy the best ingredients available, even if you have to spend a little more. Find the best local sources for fresh fish, walking-around (free-range) chicken, game and meat. Buy the best herbs, the finest, most pungent spices and the best oils and vinegars, anchovies, capers, and so on. If you're eating less, you want it to taste the very best. Flavor is paramount—get the most that you can from your flavor ingredients.

◆ Know your sources. At the farmers' market, get to know the people who grow your fruit and produce. Find out how they grow it. Talk to the butcher, the baker and the fishmonger and let them know you're interested in the freshest and the best. Fresh, natural foods are better for you and less expensive in the long run.

42

◆ Find a great local bakery, one with a variety of hearty, country-style, multi-grain breads. Then store the bread in a breadbox, a bread drawer or a brisker to keep it fresh and readily available at all times.

◆ Grow your own herbs. Start with pots of herbs on the patio, a small terrace or windowsill—then let it stretch into an herb garden, a few tomato plants, a patch of lettuces and *one* zucchini plant. You'll get in touch with the soil and the weather and learn how to garden without chemicals.

◆ Read labels. The new nutrition labels help, once you understand them. Pay close attention to serving size and learn to recognize the number of fat calories compared to the number of calories or grams per portion. Learn to read labels (see page 52).

IN THE PANTRY

◆ Variety is the spice of life. Make sure you have choices in your pantry. All grains, beans and rices don't taste alike.

◆ Stock a variety of fats and oils for various uses. Have a fruity extra-virgin olive oil for salads and drizzling on potatoes, bread or pizza; a lighter and less expensive one for everyday cooking. Then, if you choose, use a neutral vegetable oil for cooking and baking. (Throughout the book, I urge you to use oil sprays to cut back on fat. You can buy these or make your own using a spritzer.) Add to these selections a variety of oils for varying flavors—hazelnut oil, walnut oil, sesame oil, hot chili oil or oils infused with herbs or spices. Complement these with a variety of vinegars—balsamic, red and white wine, cider and those infused with fruits, herbs and spices. They give you flexibility in cooking.

◆ Think small. Stock your pantry and refrigerator with small amounts of the best and keep the inventory turning. With age, coffee loses its aroma, spices their punch, oil its freshness and we all know about fish and greens.

◆ Reevaluate your kitchen storage. How, when, where and at what temperature you store your ingredients can make a difference. Keep lots of space for a wide variety of ingredients.

◆ Substitute. Find foods similar in texture and taste as replacements for the foods you're cutting back on—always with less fat, sugar or salt than the original. Your own taste will be the key.

◆ Clear away kitchen clutter. "Decorate" with the texture of beans, grains and pastas in clear storage jars. Keep spices in view so you don't have to search. Keep onions, garlic, potatoes, citrus fruit and squash in baskets where you'll remember them.

A Word on Dining Out

We're all dining out more—sometimes for up to half of the week's meals. We need to learn to control eating habits away from home, too. Use the recipes in this book and study the ingredients as a guide to ordering when out.

Restaurants aim to please, and most are aware of the new dietary goals. They may even have special healthy menu sections.

Many restaurants may even help you out with portion sizes and cooking methods. Let your server know what you're looking for and then let the chef do his thing. He can usually lighten a dish so you don't have to have the sauce on the side, or toss a salad with less oil or with vinegar or lemon juice alone a lot more easily in the kitchen than you can at the table. No one will be offended if you ask for help. But they will if you don't come back because you didn't.

43
◆

Healthy Cooking Techniques

Using nonstick pans and spray oils goes a long way toward making the food you cook more healthful and lower in fat. There are numerous cooking methods that contribute equally to a good-for-you diet.

Bake/Roast: Oven is preheated well to seal in the juices; spray pan with olive oil.

Blanch: Vegetables are partially cooked rapidly in a large amount of lightly salted boiling water.

Braise: Food is cooked in liquid, in a covered pan, to the desired tenderness. Near the end of cooking, the cover is often removed and the liquid reduced to create a sauce. Braise foods that take a long time to cook, such as leeks and garlic cloves. Add to them a little broth, cover and cook until tender. Remove cover, increase heat and cook the food, turning as necessary, to a golden color. The point is to cook food with moisture.

Dry Sear: Meat is cooked in a pan without any oil. A few drops of stock may be added with the vegetables, if any. As the liquid hits the pan, it steams the vegetables.

Grill/Broil: Food is cooked near direct or indirect dry heat without salt, which extracts moisture.

Microwave: Vegetables, fish and grains are covered (usually) and cooked quickly, with or without added liquid.

Oven-Fry: Spray food with vegetable oil or coat with egg whites and breading, then bake until crisp.

Sauté: To cook quickly over high heat. Instead of using fat, sauté food in hot broth.

Steam: Vegetables or fish are quickly steamed, tightly covered, in a basket set over one to two inches of rapidly boiling liquid.

Stew: Slow cooking merges flavors.

Stir-Fry: Quick cooking over a stovetop in a wok or large shallow frying or sauté pan with a little oil and broth.

Cooking With Less Fat

♦ Measure all of the fat you add to foods—even one teaspoon goes a long way to aid the flavor, sheen and texture of foods.

♦ Use vegetable oil and olive oil sprays for lighter cooking.

♦ Trim the fat on all meats and remove the skin from poultry before eating.

♦ Reduce and replace the oils in salad dressings with homemade chicken broth, canned beef consommé, broth (less viscous than the first two), fruit and vegetable juices and buttermilk. Use egg white–based salad dressings or vinegar, broth and fruit juices to bind a vinaigrette. Take the bite out with just a spoonful of sugar. Use a spray bottle for salad dressing—lightly spritz and toss.

♦ Be consciously aware of where fat is in all foods. Educate yourself.

♦ Consume only liquid fats. Choose a "healthier" fat—canola, olive, safflower, corn and others—rather than highly saturated butter, lard or tropical oils.

♦ Learn how to count fat grams and figure fat percentages in recipes and labeled foods.

♦ Read ingredient labels for fat, saturated fat, hydrogenated fat and cholesterol.

♦ Know the "better" oils from the "just good" oils.

♦ Learn how to cook with less fat. You might not really know how much fat you're putting in a dish. Measure. Learn what a tablespoon of oil looks like, the size of a 3- to 4-ounce portion of meat, and how to recognize a tablespoon of salad dressing on 2 cups of salad greens.

♦ If you want the taste of butter, just add a little bit at the end.

♦ Know your maximum daily fat intake, but average it over several days so you can have some of the foods you really want.

♦ It's what you put on top of bread, rice, potatoes or pasta that makes them high in fat. Go easy on the butter, sour cream and rich sauces.

♦ Don't be shy when adding herbs. Get to know their flavors so you will feel confident about adding them liberally.

♦ Know spices and learn how to combine them for deep, slow-cooked flavors that can then be refreshed with fresh herbs.

♦ Feel comfortable adding wines, fortified wines and liqueurs to foods—experiment with them to best know how to use them to flavor foods.

LEARN TO USE LIQUIDS TO MOISTEN AND BASTE WITHOUT FAT

◆ Cook rices, grains and beans in defatted chicken, beef or vegetable broth—add herbs, garlic or shallots for even bigger taste.

◆ Every chance you get, make broth and freeze it—chicken, vegetable, beef, fish. Save broth from cooking vegetables, reduce and freeze. Freeze deeply flavored defatted and reduced pan juices from roasting meats, poultry and vegetables to add flavor to rices, beans, soups and stews.

◆ Poach fish in tomato or vegetable broth.

◆ Marinate in wines, soy sauce or concentrated or fresh fruit and vegetable juices.

◆ Sauté vegetables and scaloppine meats with 1 to 2 tablespoons defatted broth, water, juice or wine instead of oil in a nonstick pan. Keep the heat high and add more liquid if it evaporates before the food is browned.

◆ Use wines or other alcoholic ingredients for richness and flavor without fat or cholesterol. Add them early in the cooking so that their flavors will penetrate and concentrate.

◆ Use fruit juices to transmit flavor and moisten food.

◆ Reduce defatted pan juices and thicken with potato starch, cornstarch or arrowroot to create intensely flavored thickened sauces.

◆ Puree vegetables, alone or in creative combinations. Smooth with broth, blended nonfat cottage cheese or Neufchâtel cheese.

REMOVE AS MUCH FAT AS POSSIBLE

◆ Trim all extra fat from meat and poultry. You can leave the skin on poultry until after it's cooked—almost no fat will penetrate the flesh—but take it off before it goes to the table to avoid temptation.

◆ Build in time to chill soups and stews so the fats rise to the top, harden and can be spooned off.

◆ Skim off as much fat as you can, then blot up the rest with a paper towel.

◆ Use a defatting cup or ladle, or a special brush that attracts fat (it looks like a large pastry brush). Rinse under warm water after each collection.

◆ Tip the pan or skillet so you can spoon off most of the fat.

◆ Cut the fat where you won't miss it. But rather than give up the flavor of nuts, coconut, chocolate chips, olives and bacon, experiment and reduce the quantity by 25 to 75 percent.

COOK WITH FLAVOR INSTEAD OF FAT AND USE HEALTHIER COOKING METHODS

◆ Find the perfect cookware: it should conduct and hold heat well, clean easily and be nonreactive. Most important, look for a surface that is nonstick or requires the smallest amount of oil for cooking.

BAKE SMARTER

◆ Cut back sugar by 25 percent. A pinch of cinnamon, nutmeg or allspice will enhance the perception of sweetness. (Beware: Cutting back sugar in cakes, cookies and some other baked goods can affect texture or volume.)

◆ Rely on the natural sweetness of fruit for desserts.

DON'T SKIMP ON PRESENTATION

◆ Remember: Cooking is a visual art, too. But keep it simple.

◆ Subscribe to the "lush and abundant" school of presentation by serving in smaller but overflowing bowls.

◆ Serve on oversized dinner plates for drama.

"Some people like to
paint pictures,
or do gardening, or build a boat
in the basement.
Other people get a tremendous
pleasure out of the kitchen,
because cooking is just as creative
and imaginative an activity
as drawing,
or wood carving or music."
JULIA CHILD

47

The Healthy Basics for a Lifetime

Here are the seven basic strategies to achieve success and a fresh start:

1. EAT A VARIETY OF FOODS. The best way to get adequate vitamins, minerals and other important health-protective substances from natural sources is to eat a variety of foods. There are no "bad" foods. It's a matter of moderation and balancing your fat intake. See the Fresh Start Game Plan Everyday Food Goals (opposite).

2. EAT MORE FIBER. We should consume 25 to 35 grams of fiber a day (about 2 grams for every 100 calories). Fiber satisfies, allowing you to eat a lot less fat (and more fiber-containing foods) without feeling deprived. Choose the fiber that occurs naturally in foods, not supplements.

3. REDUCE OVERALL FAT AND SELECT FATS CAREFULLY. It's your choice to set your own goals: 10, 15, 20 or 30 percent of fat calories of total calories per day.

4. DRINK WATER. Water replenishes, cleanses and makes you "work" better. When you feel the urge to snack, you may actually be thirsty. Get in the habit of drinking eight to twelve glasses a day, sipping all day long and at meals to help you feel full. Water quenches your thirst the best of any liquid—coffee and tea are dehydrating, as is anything with caffeine. Sodas and diet sodas are "engineered" foods (just read the label) and the jury's still out on them as far as their long-range effects on health.

5. EXERCISE. When you exercise regularly, your basal metabolism rate changes, making you a more efficient calorie burner, an effect that can last for hours. You feel more energetic, too. Experts say moderate daily exercise is a must for weight control. Exercise is for a lifetime—for a longer, healthier, more agile life and stronger bones.

◆ Increase your physical activity—a minimum of 30 minutes every day. For maximum health benefits, exercise vigorously at least 45 minutes three times a week. (*Be sure to check with your doctor before beginning an exercise program.*)

◆ Step up your lifestyle activity—take the stairs, walk to the store, take up gardening.

◆ Find the time—Get up a half-hour earlier, skip a TV program, make exercise a part of each day, get a partner, join a club.

6. LIMIT SUGAR. It's easy to reach for sugar when you're trying to reduce fat. But sugar crowds out room for the nutritious foods you need and contributes to dental cavities. Try to use a minimum of sugar. It'll help you break the cycle of overindulgence and cravings (it's just as bad with sugar substitutes—and some may be carcinogenic).

7. REDUCE SALT INTAKE. Guidelines call for less than 2400 mg a day (your body needs less than 500 mg). Too much can lead to hypertension and strokes, and increase the risk of kidney and cardiovascular disease in people who are sodium sensitive. Salt is readily available in most processed foods and easy to obtain naturally in many foods.

FRESH START GAME PLAN
Everyday Goals

Today_____   Weather_____

CARBOHYDRATES:
6–11 servings*; 60–75% of Total Calories
1 slice of bread, 1 oz. ready-to-eat cereal,
½ c. cooked cereal, ½ c. pasta, ½ c. rice, 1
pancake, 3–4 small crackers or ½ sandwich bun:

___ ___ ___ ___ ___ ___ ___

___ ___ ___ ___

FIBER 25–35 grams
___5 g ___5 g ___5 g ___5 g ___5 g

VEGETABLES 3–5 servings*
1 c. raw leafy vegetables, ½ c. cooked
vegetables, ½ c. raw vegetables or ¾ c.
vegetable juice:

___ ___ ___ ___ ___

FRUITS 2–4 servings*
1 medium piece of fruit, ½ c. chopped
fruit, ½ c. cooked fruit, ½ c. canned fruit,
¾ c. fruit juice or ¼ c. dried fruit:

___ ___ ___ ___

MILK, YOGURT and CHEESE
2–3 servings*
1 c. milk, 8 oz. yogurt, 1½ oz. natural
cheese or 2 oz. processed cheese:

___ ___ ___

PROTEIN
2–3 servings*; 10–15% of Total Calories
2–3 oz. cooked lean meat, 2–3 oz. poultry,
2–3 oz. fish, ½ c. cooked dry beans, 1 egg,
2 tablespoons peanut butter or 1–2 oz.
low-fat cheese: ___ ___ ___

FATS and OILS Use sparingly.
No more than 15 to 20 percent of total
calories, including fats found in foods,
such as meats and dairy products.
Total 1 tablespoon. Record per gram.
Total calories_____ Total g_____
Total %____

CHOLESTEROL 200–300 mg.

SATURATED FAT No more than 10
percent (see Fats and Oils)

SUGARS Use sparingly. Aim for 5
percent of total calories, including sugars
found in foods.

WATER 8–12 glasses

SODIUM No more than 2400 mg

EXERCISE Thirty minutes every day;
45 minutes more vigorously 3 times a
week. ___30 minutes ___45 minutes
Type of exercise_____

_____

_____

*Servings are intended to span a wide range of body sizes
and activity levels. If you're a small, relatively sedentary
woman, choose the lower amounts; if you're an athletic sev-
enteen-year-old male, go for the maximum. (Adapted from
the USDA Food Pyramid)

49
◆

(Please photocopy this chart and keep one with you every day to count your food in every category.)

How to Get the Most from
Fresh Start

This book is intended as a primer—a step-by-step introduction to low-fat cooking. It is designed for people who have had a hard time getting started with a healthful diet either because the whole routine seemed overwhelming or because of a fear that low-fat food just wouldn't taste good. For those people already well on their way to eating healthfully, *Fresh Start* offers easy new recipes while acting as a useful reference guide. Regardless of the category you fall into, it's all here: the information you need to switch to a health-conscious lifestyle that includes great food.

My goal is to eliminate the confusion. In doing so, I explain various eating plans, including the Food Pyramids (page 16), and help you figure out how to make carbohydrates the foundation of your diet. Plus, you will learn how to eat all those fruits and vegetables every day, while cutting back on protein, sweets and fats—most of all fats!

My suggestions:

◆ Use the menus and recipes as guides that fit with your busy life. By reading the ingredients and studying the breakdowns of fats and calories, you will see how to incorporate very little fat into your daily diet. Note the example of Day 2 on page 53.

◆ Feel free to mix and match similar recipes among menus and, if you're ordering from a restaurant menu, to use the ingredients as a guide. Just tuck the book into your purse or briefcase and carry it with you.

◆ If you slip and overindulge, begin again. The order of the recipes is not important here;

You may be disappointed if you fail . . . but you're doomed if you don't try."
BEVERLY SILLS

50
◆

the menus do not constitute a lesson plan in food combining. They are meant only to be helpful and inspiring.

◆ Most of the recipes serve two or four people, although some serve six and eight. All are very easy to cook and can easily be doubled or halved. Exceptions include baked goods and desserts where the ratio of time to energy is too precious to reduce the amounts—so you may have a cake that serves far more than four included in a menu otherwise designed for four. Share it with a neighbor.

◆ For each day, the menu is listed in the front of the assigned section. However, for the specific foods and nutritional breakdowns for each meal, you will need to consult the charts called Breakfast, Morning Snack, Lunch, Afternoon Snack, Dinner and Evening Snack. Of course, you can eat any meal at any time during the day, as it fits into your life.

◆ The menus are based on approximately 2,000 calories a day, with between 15 to 20 percent of those calories coming from fat. You will need to adjust the portion amounts upwards or downwards depending on your Daily Calorie Requirements (see page 17) and your own goals concerning daily fat intake (see page 37). Also keep in mind that while I have figured the nutritional values for each recipe to the nearest tenth, when I list the day's totals, *I have rounded off the number.* I hope this makes life easier for you!

◆ Recipes included in the book are indicated by an asterisk (*) beside the title listed in the daily meal menus. If a recipe does not actually appear on that day's pages, it will have a reference page number to help you locate it elsewhere in the book.

◆ Consult a doctor, registered nutritionist or dietitian before you begin to set your goals for low-fat eating.

◆ Remember, take it day by day, recipe by recipe and meal by meal. You're bound to succeed!

Fat Grams/Fat Percentage

Learn to count fat grams, which you'll find easily on fat tables, food labels and in the recipes in this book. Be able to convert grams to percentage of fat by multiplying the number of fat grams by 9 (calories per gram), dividing that figure by the total number of calories in the food and then multiplying by 100. For example, a food portion has 142 calories with 2 grams of fat:

2 fat grams per serving × 9 calories per fat gram = 18 calories of fat

18 (fat calories per serving) ÷ 142 (number of calories per serving) = .1276

.1276 × 100 = 12.76% of total calories are fat calories

Rounded off, this means approximately 13% of the calories of that particular food come from fat.

Label Lingo

◆ To understand this box and learn to read the new product labels, find one of your favorite products and prop it up in front of you while you continue to read.

◆ Note that today's new product labels are based on total recommended daily calories of 2,000 calories. For women especially, 2,000 calories per day may be too high.

◆ Beware of the "total fat" percentage of daily value. This tells you the percentage of fat a serving of this food represents of the *whole* day's fat allowance, based on a 2,000-calorie diet. It *doesn't* tell you what percentage of the food is fat. This is very misleading to most people. To figure the percentage of fat in this particular food, divide the "calories from fat per serving" by the "calories per serving" then multiply by 100. If it's over 20 percent—watch out!

◆ Pay close attention to serving size. It may be larger than a pyramid portion or so small it's ridiculous.

◆ Fats may be listed in grams, which means you may need to convert it to calories or percentage of fat, depending on your daily accounting system.

◆ Scan the ingredients list. Look for hydrogenated and partially hydrogenated oils. And avoid them whenever possible. Watch for saturated fat (the most damaging kind).

◆ Some labels shout "97% Fat Free" on the front of the package, but when you learn the calories per portion and the total grams or fat calories per portion, it may prove to be another matter.

Fresh Start Nutritional Analysis of Recipes

The recipes·in this book have been analyzed by Nutrinfo or on "The Food Processor" by Esha Research. Please note the following:

♦ "Salt and freshly ground black pepper, to taste" in a recipe are always at the cook's discretion and are not included in the nutritional analysis.

♦ "Optional" ingredients are not included in the analysis.

♦ Chicken cooked with the skin is analyzed with it taken off—assuming that either the cook or the diner will remove it after cooking and before consuming. Fat absorbed by the meat during cooking from the skin is minimal.

♦ Meats have been trimmed of all possible fats.

♦ All recipes with "collected pan juices" assume that the cook will defat them.

♦ When noting the percentages of fat calories to total calories in each recipe analysis, remember that some dishes are so low in calories that the percentage of fat becomes disproportionately high. For instance, a whole pound of green beans—140 calories—has less than 1 gram of fat. Add 2 teaspoons of walnut oil and it jumps to 10 grams or 64 percent of the calories of the dish. That appears very high, but of course when this is divided by four people, it's ½ teaspoon per serving—not much fat at all.

♦ Unless otherwise indicated, the analysis is based on one serving.

Fat Adds Up Fast

To illustrate how quickly fat adds up, we took the menu for Day 2, which has 2007 calories, 40 grams of fat and 18 percent fat, and added:

Breakfast: 1 tablespoon butter on toast
Lunch: 1 ounce tortilla chips
Dinner: 2 tablespoons ranch dressing
Snack: ½ cup *real* ice cream

The calories increased to 2,813, fat increased to 120 grams or 38 percent of total calories. As you can see, it doesn't take much!

First Impressions

◆

This day is the first of a lifetime filled with food that tastes so great, you'll never notice that it's good for you. And if you don't announce this new beginning, everyone else will just simply love it. Some of your favorite snack flavors are here, too, and along with them some of the day's fat.

Monday
DAY 1

Fresh Orange Juice

Banana-Mint Slush*

Cinnamon Toast*

Turkey Ham Slices

◆

Salad Greens with Pesto Dressing*

Pure and Simple Onion Soup*

Country French Bread

Tropical Fruit Salad*

◆

Salad Greens with Roquefort Dressing*

Roasted Chicken with Fresh Figs and
Kalamata Olives*

Brown Rice

Ginger Carrots*

Green Beans

Whole-wheat Rolls

Blackberry Frozen Yogurt*

Breakfast Menu

Foods (per serving)	Cal.	Carb. (g)	Prot. (g)	Chol. (mg)	Fat (g)/%	Sod. (mg)
Orange juice, 6 oz.	83.5	19.4	1.4	0	0.3/3	1.2
Banana-Mint Slush*	98	20	5	2	1/9	63.8
Cinnamon Toast*	65	2	14	0	0/0	91
Turkey ham slices, 4 oz.	120	2	18	70	5/38	1320
Morning Snack						
Apple, 3½ oz.	59	15	0.2	0	0.4/6	0
Peanut butter, 1 T.	94	3.5	3.9	0	8/77	28

Smoothie Strategy

Sometimes you're half asleep and sometimes you're a bundle of energy as you whip together an early morning smoothie.

Either way, little thinking is required to make a smoothie. Once you're in the swing of the strategy, you can't go wrong.

Clear a space to make smoothies and keep the blender handy.

Add the sweetener last; fruits vary in their sweetness. Bananas with black speckles are sweetest.

BASE: Skim milk, frozen fruit juice concentrate, fresh fruit juice, nonfat yogurt, nonfat frozen yogurt, banana

FRUIT: Any fresh, frozen or canned, banana, cantaloupe, peaches or the like

FLAVORINGS: Coffee, vanilla extract, nutmeg, cinnamon, chocolate

PROTEIN: Powdered milk, nonfat cottage cheese, peanut butter, wheat germ

SWEETENERS: Honey, brown sugar, maple syrup, all-fruit spread

56

BREAKFAST

Good Morning!

No matter what you ate yesterday, you still have to fuel your body today, making the "breaking of the fast" critically important after nine or ten hours without eating.

But don't rely on simple carbohydrates (a muffin or a Danish) sloshed down with coffee to jump-start your engine. And don't skip breakfast. You'll push yourself to the point of hunger pangs, encouraging a grab for sweets or high-calorie, high-fat foods.

A good, balanced, energizing meal helps you feel and perform much better. A healthy breakfast should emphasize energy foods such as:

- ◆ fresh fruits
- ◆ whole-grain cereals
- ◆ breadstuffs
- ◆ yogurt or skim milk

Banana-Mint Slush

SERVES 2

1 ripe banana   *1 cup skim milk*
6 mint leaves   *4 or 5 ice cubes*
Grated zest of 1 lime

Place the banana in a blender and puree until smooth. Add the remaining ingredients and blend until slushy. Serve immediately.

CAL. 98   CARB. 20G   PROT. 5G   CHOL. 2MG   FAT 1G/9%   SOD. 63.8MG

57
◆

<blockquote>
"A thousand-mile journey begins with the first step."

<small>HENRY DAVID THOREAU</small>
</blockquote>

Cinnamon Toast

It's possible to enjoy this childhood favorite without guilt. Of course, some fat is added, depending on how long you spray the butter-flavored spray (see page 73), but its amount is small compared to the old-fashioned method of buttering the toast.

SERVES 2

1 tablespoon sugar
1/4 teaspoon cinnamon
2 slices nonfat whole-wheat bread
Butter-flavored oil spray

In a small bowl, mix the sugar and cinnamon. Spray each slice of bread lightly with butter-flavored oil. Sprinkle half the cinnamon sugar on 1 slice and the remaining on the other. Spray each slice again briefly and toast for 3 to 4 minutes in a toaster oven until the sugar is melted and the bread is golden.

CAL. 65   CARB. 2G   PROT. 14G   CHOL. 0MG   FAT 0G/0%   SOD. 91MG

Lunch Menu

Foods (per serving)	Cal.	Carb. (g)	Prot. (g)	Chol. (mg)	Fat (g)/%	Sod. (mg)
Salad greens, 1 cup	9.5	1.6	0.9	0	0.1/11	14
Pesto Dressing* (p. 118), 1 T.	17	0.5	0.4	0.4	1.5/80	0.2
Pure and Simple Onion Soup*	310	44	11	6	3/9	291
French bread, 1 slice	96	18	3	0	1/9	213
Tropical Fruit Salad*	110	25	2	0	1.9/14	12
AFTERNOON SNACK						
Sun-Dried Tomato Dip* (p. 163), 2 T.	24	1.8	3	2.4	0.8/30	108
Tortilla Chips* (p. 158), 6	108	24	3	0	0/0	336

"No one can persuade another to change. Each of us guards a gate of change that can only be opened from the inside."

MARVYN FERGUSES

Tropical Fruit Salad

You'll think you've taken a little trip to the Caribbean!

SERVES 2

2 cups cubed fresh pineapple
1½ cups cubed fresh cantaloupe
¼ star fruit, sliced (optional)
1 kiwi, peeled and sliced
4 teaspoons shredded sweetened coconut
2½ tablespoons passion fruit juice or orange juice
Pinch of cinnamon
2 teaspoons sugar, or to taste

Place the ingredients in a large mixing bowl and toss gently to coat with the juices. Serve slightly chilled.

CAL. 110   CARB. 25G   PROT. 2G   CHOL. 0MG   FAT 1.9G/14%   SOD. 12MG

58

Pure and Simple Onion Soup

"The best kind of onion soup is the simplest kind."

Ambrose Bierce

This is the most simplistic of onion soups, but it has become my favorite! The long simmering brings out the sweetness of the onion, making the soup's flavor surprisingly delicate.

SERVES 2

4 large onions, halved and thinly sliced (about 3½ cups)
1 quart beef broth
½ cup red wine
¼ teaspoon crushed red pepper flakes
1½ teaspoons finely minced fresh sage
2 slices French bread
2 tablespoons grated Parmesan cheese

1. In a medium-sized stockpot, combine the onions, broth, wine, red pepper flakes and sage. Bring to a boil over medium-high heat. Reduce the heat and simmer, covered, for about 2 hours, or until the onions are almost dissolved.

2. Preheat the broiler.

3. Sprinkle the slices of French bread evenly with cheese and broil until the cheese is melted and golden brown and the croutons are toasted. Ladle the soup into the bowls and top each with a cheese-topped crouton. Serve immediately.

CAL. 310   CARB. 44G   PROT. 11G   CHOL. 6MG   FAT 3G/9%   SOD. 291MG

59

ONION SOUP

Great onion soup variations extend around the globe. Italian-inspired versions, such as the one on this page, are clear, simple and very delicious.

In the French countryside, wild mushrooms and sherry are added. In Normandy, Calvados, of course. A tomato puree is added in Bordeaux; garlic, herbs and Madeira in Lyon. In Burgundy, it's topped with a poached egg.

Spain enhances onion soup with almonds. In Portugal, it's sweet wine and raisins. Middle Eastern countries serve it sparked with lentils, yogurt or meat. The English add Stilton; the Moroccans, minced chicken. Germans put their dark beer to good use. And in Latin America, it's transformed with coconut milk, peppers and local cheeses.

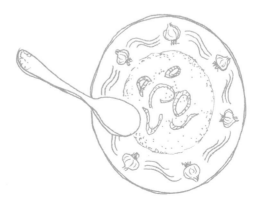

Roasted Chicken with Fresh Figs and Kalamata Olives

A favorite chicken dish with the distinctive flavors of fresh figs, capers and black olives, this is great hot or at room temperature. Fresh figs are unbelievable here, but if they are out of season, use dried figs, dried apricots or prunes. With the fat dramatically reduced, you'll want to serve it often.

"Before supper walk a little, after supper do the same."
ERASMUS

SERVES 2

3 chicken breast halves, halved, on the bone, skin removed
¼ cup finely minced garlic
¼ cup low-fat, low-sodium chicken broth
1 tablespoon dried oregano
¼ teaspoon freshly ground black pepper
2 tablespoons red wine vinegar
2 tablespoons pitted Kalamata olives (6 or 7 olives)
2 tablespoons capers with a little juice
3 bay leaves
3 tablespoons light brown sugar
½ cup dry white wine
¾ cup fresh figs, cut into halves, or ½ cup dried figs, dried apricots or prunes

60

1. In a large bowl, combine the chicken, garlic, broth, oregano, pepper, vinegar, olives, capers with juice and bay leaves. (If using dried figs, dried apricots or prunes, add them now.) Cover, refrigerate and marinate overnight or for at least 8 hours.

2. Preheat the oven to 350°F.

3. Arrange the chicken in a shallow baking dish and cover with the marinade. Sprinkle with brown sugar and pour wine around the pieces. Bake for about 1 hour, basting every 10 minutes, or until the chicken is cooked through. After 15 minutes of cooking, add the fresh figs. Remove and discard the bay leaves. Garnish each serving with sauce, olives and figs and serve immediately.

CAL. 300   CARB. 36G   PROT. 23G   CHOL. 55MG   FAT 4.5G/13%   SOD. 632MG

Three squares were once the rule. But for many, munching five or six minimeals and low-fat, high-fiber snacks makes adopting new health habits easier.

Minimeals help break the no-breakfast, fast-food lunch, famished-before-dinner routine. You're never hungry. Your body won't suffer the stress of a big meal. You stay energized. And you'll likely consume less fat.

◆ Divide, don't double. Cut your meals in two and space them two to three hours apart.

◆ Fill up on high-fiber foods low in fat and sugar: fruit, veggies or whole-grain bread.

◆ Learn the portion sizes recommended in the food pyramid (see page 16).

◆ Travel with healthy snacks: boxes of cereal, fruit, flavored rice cakes, pretzels, nonfat yogurt, veggies.

◆ In restaurants, order appetizer portions, eat just half or take it home.

Ginger Carrots

Although similar recipes rely on butter, I've substituted water to melt the brown sugar and coat the carrots.

SERVES 2

½ pound baby carrots, peeled and cleaned
½ teaspoon ground ginger
2 tablespoons light brown sugar
½ teaspoon caraway seeds

1. In a medium-sized saucepan, cover the carrots with water. Cook, covered, over medium-high heat for 10 to 12 minutes, or until tender.

2. Meanwhile, in a small bowl, combine the ginger, sugar and 1 tablespoon water.

3. Drain the carrots and return to the pan. Add the sugar water and toss well. Cook over medium heat for 2 to 3 minutes, until the carrots are well coated. Add the caraway seeds, toss and serve immediately.

CAL. 88   CARB. 21G   PROT. 1G   CHOL. 0MG   FAT 0.3G/3%   SOD. 78MG

61

Dinner Menu

FOODS (PER SERVING)	CAL.	CARB. (G)	PROT. (G)	CHOL. (MG)	FAT (G)/%	SOD. (MG)
Salad greens, 1 cup	9.5	1.6	0.9	0	0.1/11	14
Roquefort Dressing* (p. 120), 1 T.	9	7	7	1	0.4/36	29
Roasted Chicken with Fresh Figs and Kalamata Olives*	300	36	23	55	4.5/13	632
Brown rice, ½ cup	108	23	2.5	0	0.9/7	4.9
Ginger Carrots*	88	21	1	0	0.3/3	78
Steamed green beans, 1 cup	35	8.1	2	0	0.2/5	6.4
Whole-wheat roll, 1	93	18	3	0	1.6/15	167
Blackberry Frozen Yogurt* (p. 108), ½ cup	140	29	6.3	0.6	0.4/3	134
EVENING SNACK						
Popcorn (air-popped), 2 cups	61	13	2	0	0.7/10	0.6
Today's Totals	**2038**	**334**	**114**	**137**	**32/14**	**3544**

In Short Order

◆

Cooking with a new mind set will quickly become second nature once you realize that the foods can be prepared quickly, you can mix and match menus and everything will always taste delicious.

Tuesday
DAY 2

Great Granola* with Skim Milk

Fresh Strawberries

Whole-wheat Toast

◆

Rosy Shrimp Salad*

Breadsticks

Fresh Green Grapes

◆

Fresh Spinach Salad with
Orange-Basil Dressing*

My Favorite Pasta Carbonara*

Sourdough Roll

Honeydew Melon with Lime

Breakfast Menu

Foods (per serving)	Cal.	Carb. (g)	Prot. (g)	Chol. (mg)	Fat (g)/%	Sod. (mg)
Great Granola*, ½ cup	282	56	7	0	5/16	57
Skim milk, ½ cup	43	6	4	2	0.2/4	62
Strawberries, ½ cup	25	6	0.5	0	0.3/11	0.8
Whole-wheat toast, 1 slice	107	23	4	0	0.4/3	136
Morning Snack						
Fruit yogurt, 6 oz.	180	33	8	10	1.5/7.5	105

Great Granola

Here are all the golden crunch, sweetness and clumps you love in the higher-fat varieties of granola. A half-cup serving really gets your engine started! I've made a lot because it stores so well.

MAKES 6 CUPS

3 cups uncooked rolled oats (not instant)

3 cups crisp rice cereal (such as Rice Krispies)

1 cup multi-grain cereal

1 very ripe banana (about 4 ounces)

¼ cup honey

½ cup unsweetened applesauce

⅓ cup frozen apple juice concentrate, thawed

1 tablespoon cinnamon

1 tablespoon vanilla extract

½ cup blanched almonds, toasted

1 cup golden raisins or dried cherries

1. Preheat the oven to 300°F. Place the oats and both cereals in a large bowl and toss well.

2. In a small bowl, mash the banana. Add the honey, applesauce, apple juice concentrate, cinnamon and vanilla and mix well. Pour over the oat mixture and toss with your hands. Do not break the clumps apart.

3. Pour onto a baking sheet, spread evenly and bake for 45 to 50 minutes, tossing gently occasionally. Add the almonds and raisins, mix well and set the baking sheet on a wire rack to cool completely. Store in an airtight container.

Cal. 282   Carb. 56g   Prot. 7g   Chol. 0mg   Fat 5g/16%   Sod. 57mg
(Analyzed per ½-cup serving)

CEREALS

Roman goddess of grain Ceres honored women who scattered and harvested the seed—hence the name "cereal." Cereals are a part of every culture; no food in history has been more vital in providing nourishment.

Cereals are high in carbohydrates and are good, filling, satisfying food. Most grains are milled to remove the outer bran covering, making them more digestible. The germ is also removed to increase shelf life. "Whole grain" means the bran plus germ are intact.

Enriched and whole-grain cereals are the source of a variety of vitamins and minerals; whole grains provide fiber and important vegetable oils. Eaten with other grains and legumes, nuts and seeds, they make a complete protein.

The Very Best Hot and Cold Cereals

A high-fiber, low-fat breakfast helps the body perform more efficiently. It improves mental ability throughout the day and keeps your energy level high. Those who skip a nutritious and satisfying breakfast tend to eat more during the day or late at night. So start the day right with a bowl of the good stuff and add skim milk and fruit for sweetness.

COLD (1 CUP)	CAL.	CARB. (G)	PROT. (G)	FIBER (G)	FAT (G)
All-Bran	160	44	8	31	2
Bran Buds	210	42	9	32	3
Corn Chex	88	21	2	0.5	0
Corn Flakes	110	26	2	0.2	0
Fiber One	120	48	4	28	2
Granola, low-fat	315	65	8	2	13
Grape-Nuts	400	94	12	11	2
Great Granola*	282	56	7	5	5
Mueslix	194	44	4	7	1
Puffed rice	60	14	1	0.2	0
Puffed wheat	50	10	2	0.6	0
Raisin Bran	170	43	4	6	1
Rice Krispies	120	28	3	0.3	0
Rice Chex	120	27	2	0.5	0
Shredded Wheat	170	41	5	4	1
Special K	110	21	6	0.7	0
Wheat Chex	253	55	7	4	1
HOT (¾ CUP), COOKED					
Cream of Wheat	90	19	2	1	0
Oatmeal, rolled	156	27	5	5	3
Oatmeal, steel cut	230	41	8	5	5

L u n c h   M e n u

Foods (per serving)	Cal.	Carb. (g)	Prot. (g)	Chol. (mg)	Fat (g)/%	Sod. (mg)
Rosy Shrimp Salad*	243	22	24	176	8/28	310
Breadsticks, 2	160	26	12	0	4/22	420
Grapes, 1 cup	114	29	1	0	0.9/7	3
Afternoon Snack						
Brie, 1 oz.	95	0.1	6	28	7.9/75	178
Crackers, nonfat, 3	60	13	2	0	0/0	150

Rosy Shrimp Salad

Shrimp, tomato and cucumber are tossed into a salad and dressed with a lovely creamy tarragon dressing.

SERVES 2

12 sprigs fresh thyme
6 cloves garlic, peeled
12 large raw shrimp, peeled,
 deveined and halved
 lengthwise (about 8 ounces)
1 small tomato, finely chopped
 (about ½ cup)
1 rib celery, finely chopped
 (about ⅓ cup)
Sixteen ¼-inch slices
 English cucumber,
 minced

1 tablespoon finely minced
 fresh tarragon
½ teaspoon tomato paste
3 tablespoons Nonfat Blend
 (see page 298)
1 tablespoon mayonnaise
Pinch of cayenne
Salt and freshly ground black
 pepper to taste
Lettuce leaves, for garnish
Honeydew melon and straw-
 berries, for garnish (optional)

1. In enough water to cover the shrimp, combine the thyme and garlic cloves. Bring to a boil. Add the shrimp and cook for 3 to 4 minutes, until tender and pink. Drain and rinse with cold water.

2. In a large bowl, combine the tomato, celery, cucumber and tarragon. Add the shrimp and toss.

3. In a small bowl, blend the tomato paste, Nonfat Blend, mayonnaise, cayenne and salt and pepper. Taste to adjust the seasonings and then toss with the shrimp to coat well. Chill.

4. To serve, place 2 lettuce leaves on 2 plates and divide the salad between them. If desired, arrange 2 slices of honeydew on each plate, with 3 strawberries next to them.

Cal. 243　Carb. 22g　Prot. 24g　Chol. 176mg　Fat 8g/28%　Sod. 310mg

Bet you thought skipping lunch was a nifty way to lose weight, right?

Wrong. When you starve yourself, all you do is depress your body's ability to burn food calories. Metabolism slows. You lose weight more slowly, if at all. How's your body to know you're starving just to lose weight?

It's a long way till dinner. And there's that 4:00 P.M. slump. So go ahead, eat lunch. And try to find the time to take a brisk walk afterward.

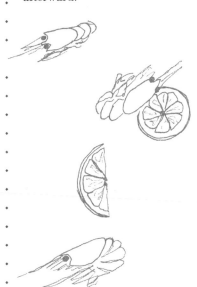

"There is no such
thing as
a little garlic."
Arthur Baer

My Favorite Pasta Carbonara

The story goes that this dish was created in the last days of World War II. American soldiers brought bacon and eggs to Italian cooks, requesting that they be prepared. They were, of course, made into a pasta sauce. My version doesn't even use eggs!

SERVES 2

⅔ cup dry white wine
¼ pound linguine, dried
3 tablespoons low-fat, low-sodium chicken broth
1 tablespoon finely minced garlic
½ cup diced onion

¼ cup sliced turkey ham (or torn into strips)
½ cup Parmesan shards
¼ cup chopped fresh parsley
1 teaspoon dried sage (optional)
Freshly ground black pepper to taste

1. In a medium-sized saucepan, reduce the wine to ½ cup over medium heat. Remove from the heat.

2. Bring 4 quarts of water to a rolling boil and cook the linguine for 8 to 10 minutes, or until al dente.

3. While the pasta is cooking, heat 2 tablespoons of broth in a large skillet. Add the garlic and onion and sauté for 2 to 3 minutes, until lightly browned. Add the reduced wine and simmer over low heat for 1 minute.

4. Drain the pasta and add to the skillet with sauce. Add the ham, cheese, parsley, sage if desired, pepper and remaining tablespoon of broth. Toss well, making sure the cheese melts, and serve.

CAL. 431   CARB. 52G   PROT. 22G   CHOL. 27MG   FAT 9.3G/20%   SOD. 722MG

PARMESAN SHARDS

For long, broad curls or shards of Parmesan, peel with a vegetable peeler as you would a potato. Always invest in the *real* aged Parmigiano-Reggiano. Its sweet nutty flavor is well worth it. Sixteen 3-inch Parmesan shards equal about ¼ cup.

67

Dinner Menu

FOODS (PER SERVING)	CAL.	CARB. (G)	PROT. (G)	CHOL. (MG)	FAT (G)/%	SOD. (MG)
Spinach, 1 cup, ½ cup mushrooms, ¼ cup red onion	90.6	15.4	8	0	0.8/8	183
Orange-Basil Dressing* (p. 121), 1 T.	3.4	0.7	0.05	0	0.01/3	0.09
My Favorite Pasta Carbonara*	431	52	22	27	9.3/20	722
Sourdough roll, 1	93	18	3	0	1.6/15	167
Honeydew melon, ¼, with lime, 1 t.	80	19	1	0	0.2/2	22
Today's Totals	**2007**	**308**	**102**	**244**	**40/18**	**2507**

Mediterranean Treasures

◆

For centuries, cooks who live in the countries surrounding the Mediterranean have known that if you respect raw ingredients, select them carefully and use them at their prime, their magical, intense flavors will allow great-tasting dishes to be attained with little effort.

Wednesday
DAY 3

Fresh Orange Juice

Grapes-Grapes*

English Muffin with
Honey and Peanut Butter

◆

Salad Greens with Lemon Dressing*

Ratatouille Sandwich*

Fresh Fruit Salad

◆

Tomato and Cucumber Salad

Italian Meatloaf* with
Fluffy Mashed Potatoes*

Individual Eggplant Towers*

Country Bread

Cantaloupe with Honey

Chocolate Chip Bites*

Breakfast Menu

Foods (per serving)	Cal.	Carb. (g)	Prot. (g)	Chol. (mg)	Fat (g)/%	Sod. (mg)
Orange juice, 6 oz.	83.5	19.4	1.4	0	0.3/3	1.2
Grapes–Grapes*	101	25	1.4	0	0.6/5	12
English muffin with honey, 1 T., and peanut butter, ½ T. (p. 124)	231	44	7	0	5/19	240
Morning Snack						
Apple, 3½ oz.	59	15	0.2	0	0.4/6	0

Grapes-Grapes

Here's a classic, refreshing sauce that's great with peaches, berries, apples, pears or plums—in fact, just about any fruit imaginable.

SERVES 4

2 tablespoons plus 1 teaspoons light brown sugar
2 tablespoons plus 1½ teaspoons lemon juice
4½ tablespoons nonfat sour cream
3 cups whole green grapes

In a medium mixing bowl, combine the sugar, lemon juice and sour cream and whisk well. Add the grapes and toss to coat. Chill for at least 2 hours to blend the flavors before serving.

Cal. 101   Carb. 25g   Prot. 1.4g   Chol. 0mg   Fat 0.6g/5%   Sod. 12mg

70

Lunch Menu

Foods (per serving)	Cal.	Carb. (g)	Prot. (g)	Chol. (mg)	Fat (g)/%	Sod. (mg)
Salad greens, 1 cup	9.5	1.6	0.9	0	0.1/11	14
Lemon Dressing* (p. 118), 1 T.	17	0.4	0.1	0	1.8/92	0.3
Ratatouille Sandwich*	270	57	9	0	6/20	239
Fresh fruit (honeydew, strawberries), 1 cup	79	20	1	0	0.4/5	8
Afternoon Snack						
Crackers, nonfat, 3	60	13	2	0	0/0	150
Neufchâtel cream cheese, 1 oz.	70	0.2	3	20	6/77	120

"Do you go for a walk every morning? —Every morning. And what if the weather is bad? —Then I walk in bad weather."

Colette

GET UP AND MOVE!

Research shows only 22 percent of adults are active enough, 54 percent are somewhat active and 24 percent are sedentary.

Thirty minutes a day are all you need to help decrease the risks of osteoporosis and coronary artery disease.

No time? Find it!

◆ Dance the night away.
◆ Pedal a stationary bike while watching the news.
◆ Weed the garden.
◆ Do housework.
◆ Walk three miles briskly, indoors or out.
◆ Play golf.
◆ Mow and rake the grass.
◆ Canoe.
◆ Row, row, row a boat.
◆ Play tennis.
◆ Stretch with simple bands of rubber.
◆ Stair-step.
◆ Play volleyball.
◆ Ice-skate.
◆ Play Ping-Pong.
◆ Roller-blade.
◆ Mountain-climb.
◆ Ride a horse.
◆ Snow- or water-ski.
◆ Rock-climb.
◆ Exercise with weights.
◆ Use the stairs.
◆ Walk your pet in the fresh air.

Ratatouille Sandwich

The flavors of roasted ratatouille are intensified by herbes de Provence. If you have none on hand, use equal amounts of dried thyme, sage, marjoram and rosemary.

SERVES 4

2 small zucchinis, cut into 8 slices lengthwise (about 1 pound)
2 red onions, thinly sliced
2 small red bell peppers, seeded and cut into 8 strips
Eight ¼-inch slices eggplant, cut lengthwise (about 1 pound)
2 tablespoons herbes de Provence
½ cup balsamic vinegar
Freshly ground black pepper to taste
4 teaspoons olive oil
2 tablespoons finely minced
*   Italian parsley*
¼ cup hot water
4 teaspoons finely minced garlic
4 teaspoons sugar
8 slices multi-grain bread, lightly toasted
1½ cups arugula, spinach or watercress

1. Preheat the oven to 400° F. Spray a baking sheet with olive oil spray.

2. In a mixing bowl, toss the zucchini, onion, red bell pepper, eggplant, herbes de Provence, 6 tablespoons balsamic vinegar and pepper. Toss to coat and spread on the baking sheet. Bake for about 30 minutes, tossing and spraying lightly again with oil spray after 15 minutes.

3. In a small bowl, whisk together the oil, parsley, water, garlic, sugar and remaining vinegar. Spoon about a tablespoon of the dressing over each slice of toast, allowing it to soak in. Use all of the dressing.

4. Divide the mixed vegetables equally onto 4 slices of toast. Top each with arugula. Place the other slices on top, dressing side down, and serve immediately.

CAL. 270   CARB. 57G   PROT. 9G   CHOL. 0MG   FAT 6G/20%   SOD. 239MG

71
◆

Italian Meatloaf

If you want a beefy-tasting meatloaf, this will still do the trick—but, if you prefer, increase the turkey and decrease the beef to fit your own taste and health goals. To see how the fat ratio is affected in a hamburger, turn to page 266.

SERVES 4

1¼ pounds lean ground sirloin

⅓ pound ground turkey breast

⅓ cup coarsely chopped onion

4 teaspoons finely minced garlic

1 teaspoon dried basil

1 teaspoon dried oregano

⅓ cup crushed tomatoes, drained

1 whole roasted red pepper, peeled, seeded and coarsely chopped (see page 107)

¼ cup grated aged Parmesan cheese

1⅓ cups coarsely chopped arugula

Freshly ground black pepper to taste

1 large egg white, lightly beaten with a fork

⅔ cup bread cubes

1. Preheat the oven to 400°F. Spray a 9 × 5 × 3-inch loaf pan with olive oil spray.

2. In a large mixing bowl, combine all ingredients except the egg whites and bread cubes. Using your hands, mix well. Add the egg whites and bread cubes. Combine thoroughly until all of the egg has been absorbed.

3. Transfer to the loaf pan and press into place. Bake for 50 minutes to 1 hour, or until cooked through. Cool for 10 to 15 minutes, pour off any excess fat and serve.

CAL. 237   CARB. 6.5G   PROT. 34G   CHOL. 84MG   FAT 8G/31%   SOD. 199MG

FLUFFY MASHED POTATOES

To this basic recipe you could add several garlic cloves minced, basil, low-fat pesto, nonfat sour cream, nonfat cream cheese, fresh dill, Italian parsley or chives—just about anything to suit your own taste!

SERVES 4 GENEROUSLY

4 medium-sized russet (baking) potatoes, peeled and quartered

⅔ cup skim milk (or more, depending on the stiffness you prefer), warmed

Salt and freshly ground black pepper to taste

1. Place the potatoes in a saucepan and cover with water. Boil over medium-high heat for 25 to 30 minutes, until the potatoes begin to fall apart. Drain.

2. Mash the potatoes with a hand mixer until smooth. Add the milk, ⅓ cup at a time, beating well after each addition, until the potatoes are fluffy. Season with salt and pepper, mix, taste and adjust the seasonings. Serve immediately.

CAL. 102   CARB. 22G   PROT. 4G   CHOL. 0.7MG   FAT 0.2G/2%   SOD. 26MG

Individual Eggplant Towers

Here's a lighter version of the Italian classic Eggplant Parmigiana.

SERVES 4

2 small eggplants, each cut horizontally into six ½-inch slices
¾ cup Quick Tomato Sauce (see page 304)
¾ cup grated part-skim mozzarella
2 tablespoons finely minced garlic
4 tablespoons finely minced fresh Italian parsley
4 tablespoons grated Parmesan cheese
4 tablespoons finely minced fresh basil

1. Preheat the oven to 400° F. Spray 2 baking sheets with olive oil spray. Lay the eggplant slices on the sheets in a single layer and bake for about 10 minutes on each side, spraying the eggplant when you flip it, until fork-tender. Cool for about 10 minutes.

2. Spray a baking sheet with olive oil spray and place 4 slices of eggplant on it. Begin layering—each individual tower has 3 identical layers: 1 tablespoon sauce, 1 tablespoon mozzarella, ½ teaspoon garlic, 1 teaspoon parsley, 1 teaspoon Parmesan, 1 teaspoon basil. Repeat twice. Bake, uncovered, for 25 to 30 minutes, until the cheese is golden brown.

CAL. 144   CARB. 11G   PROT. 10G   CHOL. 16.4MG   FAT 5.7G/36%   SOD. 395MG

Dinner Menu

FOODS (PER SERVING)	CAL.	CARB. (G)	PROT. (G)	CHOL. (MG)	FAT (G)/%	SOD. (MG)
Tomato and cucumber salad w/dash of vinegar	23	5.7	0.6	0	0.2/7	6
Italian Meatloaf*	237	6.5	34	84	8/31	199
Fluffy Mashed Potatoes*	102	22	4	0.7	0.2/2	26
Individual Eggplant Towers*	144	11	10	16.4	5.7/36	395
Country bread, 1 slice	93	18	3	0	1.7/15	167
Cantaloupe, ¼, with honey, 1 t.	78	20	0.8	0	0.1/1	1
Chocolate Chip Bites* (p. 141), 6	156	24	1.9	7.2	6.6/37	126
EVENING SNACK						
Strawberry Frozen Yogurt* (p. 108), ½ cup	159	36	4	1	0.4/2	48
Today's Totals	**1972**	**301**	**82**	**129**	**44/20**	**1751**

"The only joy in the world is to begin."
CESARE PAVESE

SPRAY OILS

Olive and vegetable oil sprays are now widely available in supermarkets and groceries. And, of course, you can always make your own. They're particularly popular because they provide a natural, even, light coating of oil on a baking sheet, roasting pan, skillet or on a salad or ingredients to be broiled or roasted.

Best of all, a little sprayed oil goes a long way. It takes eight one-second sprays to equal ½ teaspoon oil. Next time you spray, count "1001, 1002 … " and you'll see why the fat content of foods sprayed with oil becomes negligible.

73

FRUIT SMOOTHIES

Smoothies are a fabulous way to begin your regimen of five fruits a day and start adding up your intake of fiber, vitamins A, B, C and D, calcium, boron, thiamin, potassium, but very little fat. Fresh fruit starts the day on a naturally sweet note, whether you're at home or on the go. Any time of day, fruits whipped in the blender until smooth are deliciously sippable. The combinations are endless—limited only by your imagination.

STRAWBERRY-ORANGE SMOOTHIE

SERVES 1

$1/2$ cup strawberries, cleaned and halved
$1/2$ cup fresh pineapple chunks
$1/4$ cup orange juice

Process all of the ingredients in a blender until smooth. Serve immediately.

CAL. 88 CARB. 21G PROT. 1G
CHOL. 0MG FAT 0.7G/7% SOD. 2MG

CANTALOUPE SMOOTHIE

SERVES 1

$1/4$ cantaloupe, cubed (about 1 cup)
1 banana
1 tablespoon passion fruit juice (optional)
Ice cubes
Pinch of cinnamon

Process all of the ingredients in a blender until smooth. Serve immediately.

CAL. 161 CARB. 40G PROT. 3G
CHOL. 0MG FAT 1G/5% SOD. 15MG

COFFEE SIP

SERVES 1

1 cup strong brewed coffee, cooled to room temperature
$1/4$ cup nonfat plain yogurt
$1/2$ cup skim milk
Sugar to taste
Ice cubes

Process the coffee and yogurt in a blender until smooth. Add the milk and sugar. Add the ice cubes and blend to the desired consistency; strain if you like. Serve immediately over more ice.

CAL. 81 CARB. 12G PROT. 7G
CHOL. 2MG FAT 0.6G/6% SOD. 0MG

BANANA-ORANGE SMOOTHIE

SERVES 1

1 banana
1 orange, sectioned
$1 1/2$ teaspoons honey
$1/2$ cup skim milk
$1 1/2$ teaspoons lemon juice
$1/2$ teaspoon vanilla extract

Process all of the ingredients in a blender until smooth. Serve immediately.

CAL. 273 CARB. 64G PROT. 7G
CHOL. 2MG FAT 1G/3%
SOD. 65MG

STRAWBERRY SMOOTHIE

SERVES 1

1 cup fresh strawberries, cleaned and halved
1 banana
$1/2$ cup orange juice

Process all of the ingredients in a blender until smooth. Serve immediately.

CAL. 204 CARB. 49G PROT. 3G
CHOL. 0MG FAT 0.24G/5%
SOD. 4MG

GINGER-MELON SHAKE

SERVES 1

1/4 honeydew melon, peeled, seeded and cut into chunks (about 1 cup)
1 tablespoon crystallized ginger
1 cup skim milk
Ice cubes

Process the melon and ginger in a blender until smooth. Add the milk and ice cubes and blend to the desired consistency. Serve immediately.

CAL. 87 CARB. 16G PROT. 5G
CHOL. 2MG FAT 0.5G/5% SOD. 0MG

RED BERRY SHAKE

SERVES 1

1/2 cup hulled and halved fresh strawberries
1/2 cup fresh pineapple chunks
1/4 cup fresh raspberries
1 tablespoon frozen limeade concentrate

Process all of the ingredients in a blender until smooth. Serve immediately.

CAL. 66 CARB. 17G PROT. 2.5G
CHOL. 0MG FAT 0.5G/7% SOD. 4MG

STRAWBERRY SLUSH

SERVES 1

1 cup hulled and halved fresh strawberries
1 tablespoon fresh mint leaves
Sugar to taste
1/2 cup orange juice
1 tablespoon fresh lemon or lime juice

In a blender, puree the strawberries and mint until smooth. Add the sugar and strain if you like. Add the juices, blend and serve immediately over ice.

CAL. 107 CARB. 25G PROT. 2G
CHOL. 0MG FAT 0.8G/6% SOD. 0MG

RASPBERRY SMOOTHIE

SERVES 1

1/2 cup raspberries
1/2 cup skim milk
1/2 banana
1 tablespoon honey

Process all of the ingredients in a blender until smooth. Serve immediately.

CAL. 190 CARB. 44G PROT. 5G
CHOL. 2MG FAT 0.8G/4%
SOD. 64MG

HONEYDEW SMOOTHIE

SERVES 1

1/4 honeydew melon, cut into chunks (about 1 cup)
2 tablespoons nonfat plain yogurt
1 tablespoon honey
Juice of 1/2 lime
Sprig of mint

Process all of the ingredients, except the mint, in a blender until smooth. Garnish with the mint sprig and serve immediately.

CAL. 157 CARB. 41G PROT. 3G
CHOL. 0.5MG FAT 0.3G/2%
SOD. 42MG

PINEAPPLE SMOOTHIE

SERVES 1

1 cup chopped fresh pineapple
1 banana
1/2 cup skim milk

Process all of the ingredients in a blender until smooth. Serve immediately.

CAL. 224 CARB. 52G PROT. 6G
CHOL. 2MG FAT 1.4G/5%
SOD. 66MG

Food for All Seasons

◆

Every season brings us new taste treasures, and if you flow with their natural bounty, craving each in succession, your menus will have naturally complementary flavors. Best of all, the foods will fit the weather, and you'll be cooking with each ingredient at its best. Visit your local farmers' market first when you shop for groceries.

Thursday
DAY 4

Fresh Raspberries
Your Favorite Cereal with Yogurt
Toasted Cinnamon-Raisin Bagel

◆

Rosy Tomato Soup*
Caesar Salad with Pepper Croutons*
Country Bread
Fresh Fruit Salad

◆

Turkey Paillard Piccata*
Brown Rice with Asparagus
and Almonds*
Fresh Broccoli Florets
Angel Food Cake
with Fresh Strawberries

Breakfast Menu

Foods (per serving)	Cal.	Carb. (g)	Prot. (g)	Chol. (mg)	Fat (g)/%	Sod. (mg)
Raspberries, 1 cup	60	14	1	0	0.7/9	0
Favorite cereal, 2 T.	70.5	14	1.8	0	1.25/14	14
Nonfat yogurt, ¼ cup	30	4	4	1	0/0	47
Skim milk, ½ cup	43	6	4	2	0.2/4	62
Cinnamon-raisin bagel, 1	200	41	7	0	1.5/6	295
Morning Snack						
Orange, 1	62	16	1	0	0.2/3	0
Graham crackers, 2 whole	120	25	2	0	1.5/11	210

Lunch

Rosy Tomato Soup

This tomato soup truly warms the cockles of your heart. The flavor really shines in a full-bodied soup without a drop of cream.

SERVES 4

1¼ cups low-fat, low-sodium chicken broth
1 onion, coarsely chopped (about ¾ cup)
2 tablespoons finely minced garlic
One 28-ounce can tomatoes, crushed with a fork, juice reserved
5 tablespoons orange juice
1 tablespoon finely minced orange zest
¼ teaspoon cinnamon
½ teaspoon grated nutmeg
¼ teaspoon ground ginger
Salt and freshly ground black pepper to taste
¼ cup finely minced fresh mint

1. In a medium stockpot, heat the broth over medium heat and sauté the onion and garlic for 10 minutes, until tender. Add the tomatoes and their juice, orange juice, orange zest, cinnamon, nutmeg, ginger, and salt and pepper. Bring to a boil over high heat, reduce the heat to medium-high and simmer, partially covered, for about 30 minutes, until the flavors are well blended.

2. Cool slightly. Puree, using an immersion blender or food processor fitted with a metal blade. Reheat, garnish with the mint and serve immediately.

CAL. 82   CARB. 17G   PROT. 3.4G   CHOL. 0MG   FAT 0.7G/0.8%   SOD. 327MG

78

"Raspberries are best not washed. After all, one must have faith in something."

ANN BATCHELDER

FOR THE LONG HAUL

Vibrant health is based on natural principles. It develops over time with regular exercise, proper nutrition, adequate rest, a healthy mind and avoidance of what is harmful to the body.

If longevity is your goal, there's a 1995 Harvard School of Public Health study that shows only "vigorous exercise that raises the metabolic rate to six or more times the rate at rest" will likely lengthen your life. In other words, you might conclude that the more active you are, the longer you're likely to live. Such vigorous pursuits include:

◆ Walking at 4 to 5 mph for 45 minutes 5 times a week
◆ Playing one hour of singles tennis 3 days a week
◆ Swimming laps for 3 hours a week
◆ Jogging at 6 to 7 mph 3 hours a week
◆ Roller-blading 2½ hours a week

In the study, men who burned at least 1,500 calories per week through vigorous activity had a 25 percent lower death rate. Men who expended 2,500 calories a week in any activity lived significantly longer than those who burned fewer calories through exercise. It may take vigorous activity to live longer, but moderate exercise will lead to a healthier life.

The message is clear: Get up! Get out! Get moving!

Caesar Salad with Pepper Croutons

Over the years, I've lightened this classic many times. I like it to have a creamy, lemon-cheese flavor, and I *never* even miss the anchovies, egg or oil!

SERVES 4

*8 firmly packed cups romaine lettuce, torn into bite-sized
    pieces
1 cup Pepper Croutons (see page 300)
¼ cup nonfat cottage cheese
½ cup nonfat plain yogurt
2 tablespoons lemon juice, or to taste
4 teaspoons finely minced garlic
¼ cup grated Parmesan cheese
Salt and freshly ground black pepper to taste
Twelve 3-inch Parmesan shards
    (see page 67)*

1. Place the lettuce and Pepper Croutons in a salad bowl.

2. In a blender, process the cottage cheese until smooth.

3. In a small mixing bowl, combine the cottage cheese, yogurt, lemon juice, garlic and Parmesan cheese. Mix until blended, taste and adjust seasonings.

4. Toss the lettuce and croutons with ¼ cup of the dressing until well coated. (Refrigerate the remaining dressing in a tightly lidded jar.) Season with salt and pepper. Divide the salad onto 4 large plates, top each with 3 Parmesan shards and serve immediately.

NOTE: Use the leftover dressing within the next week.

CAL. 218   CARB. 29G   PROT. 16G   CHOL. 14MG   FAT 6.5G/25%   SOD. 546MG

79
◆

Lunch Menu

FOODS (PER SERVING)	CAL.	CARB. (G)	PROT. (G)	CHOL. (MG)	FAT (G)/%	SOD. (MG)
Rosy Tomato Soup*	82	17	3.4	0	0.7/0.8	327
Caesar Salad with Pepper Croutons*	218	29	16	14	6.5/25	546
Country bread, 2 slices	186	36	6	0	3.4/15	334
Fresh fruit salad, 1 cup	79	20	1	0	0.4/5	9
AFTERNOON SNACK						
Popcorn (air-popped), 2 cups	61	13	2	0	0.7/10	0.6
Cheddar cheese, 1 oz.	114	0.4	7	30	10/75	176

Turkey Paillard Piccata

This has the flavors of a lemony veal piccata with far less fat!

SERVES 4

1½ pounds turkey breast, presliced or thinly sliced on the
   bias into 8 slices (paillards)
6 tablespoons low-fat, low-sodium chicken broth
1 cup dry white wine
¼ cup finely minced lemon zest
¼ cup lemon juice
Salt and freshly ground black pepper to taste
2 tablespoons unsalted butter
¼ cup chopped Italian parsley

1. Preheat the oven to 200°F. Using a meat mallet or heavy pan, pound the turkey until thin.

2. In a large nonstick skillet, heat the broth over medium heat, add the turkey and cook for 2 to 3 minutes on each side, until white. Remove to a plate and keep warm in the oven.

3. Add the wine, lemon zest, lemon juice, salt and pepper to the skillet. Simmer for about 5 minutes over medium heat, until reduced by half. Increase the heat slightly if necessary. Add the butter and cook, stirring, for 1 minute longer.

4. Pour the sauce over the turkey, sprinkle with parsley and serve immediately.

CAL. 279   CARB. 3G   PROT. 41G   CHOL. 96MG   FAT 7.8G/25%   SOD. 188MG

80

IS BUTTER BETTER?

If you switched to margarine thinking you were doing your heart a favor, think again. Margarine contains trans-fatty acids, formed during the hydrogenation of vegetable oils to make them solid or semisolid.

Trans-fatty acids appear to increase risk factors for coronary artery disease by raising blood cholesterol levels. They're in the kind of fat that's used in commercially made foods, such as french fries, doughnuts, cakes, pies and cookies. But you won't find "trans-fatty acids" on the label. Instead they are called *partially hydrogenated oils and fats* Remember to use all fats sparingly, but choose unprocessed vegetable oils over the solid or semisolid partially hydrogenated variety whenever possible. And don't be fooled by the "no fat" labels. Look again.

If it's butter's flavor you want, a teaspoon or a tablespoon stirred into a sauce, stew or soup at the end of cooking will do the trick.

Brown Rice with Asparagus and Almonds

Rice is the staple food for more than half of the earth's population. It's a great source of fiber, a good source of protein, has almost no fat, is cholesterol-free and offers unlimited possibilities for flavor combinations. No longer for health nuts, but for all of us!

"A bear,
however hard
he tries,
grows tubby without
exercise. . . ."

POOH'S WORKOUT BOOK

SERVES 4

1 cup brown rice
¼ cup coarsely chopped onion
1 tablespoon finely minced
  garlic
2 cups low-fat, low-sodium
  chicken broth
¼ pound asparagus,
  cut into 1-inch pieces
  (about 1 cup)

¼ pound green beans, trimmed
  and cut into 2-inch pieces
  (about 1 cup)
1 tablespoon lemon juice
2 tablespoons sliced almonds,
  toasted and coarsely
  chopped
Salt and freshly ground black
  pepper to taste

1. In a medium-sized saucepan, combine the rice, onion, garlic and broth and bring to a boil over medium-high heat. Cover, reduce the heat to medium and simmer for 30 to 40 minutes, or until the rice is tender. Let stand for about 5 minutes.

2. Meanwhile, in a steaming basket set over about 1 inch of boiling water, steam the asparagus and green beans for 3 to 4 minutes, until tender. Set aside.

3. Fluff the rice with a fork and transfer to a serving bowl. Add the asparagus, green beans, lemon juice and almonds and stir. Season with salt and pepper and serve immediately.

CAL. 222   CARB. 42G   PROT. 7G   CHOL. 0MG   FAT 3G/12%   SOD. 287MG

81
◆

Dinner Menu

FOODS (PER SERVING)	CAL.	CARB. (G)	PROT. (G)	CHOL. (MG)	FAT (G)/%	SOD. (MG)
Turkey Paillard Piccata*	279	3	41	96	7.8/25	188
Brown Rice with Asparagus and Almonds*	222	42	7	0	3/12	287
Broccoli, steamed, 1 cup	44	8	5	0	0.5/10	42
Angel food cake	103	22	4	0	0.1/1	126
with Strawberries, 1 cup	50	12	1	0	0.6/11	1.6
Today's Totals	**2023**	**322**	**114**	**143**	**41/18**	**2666**

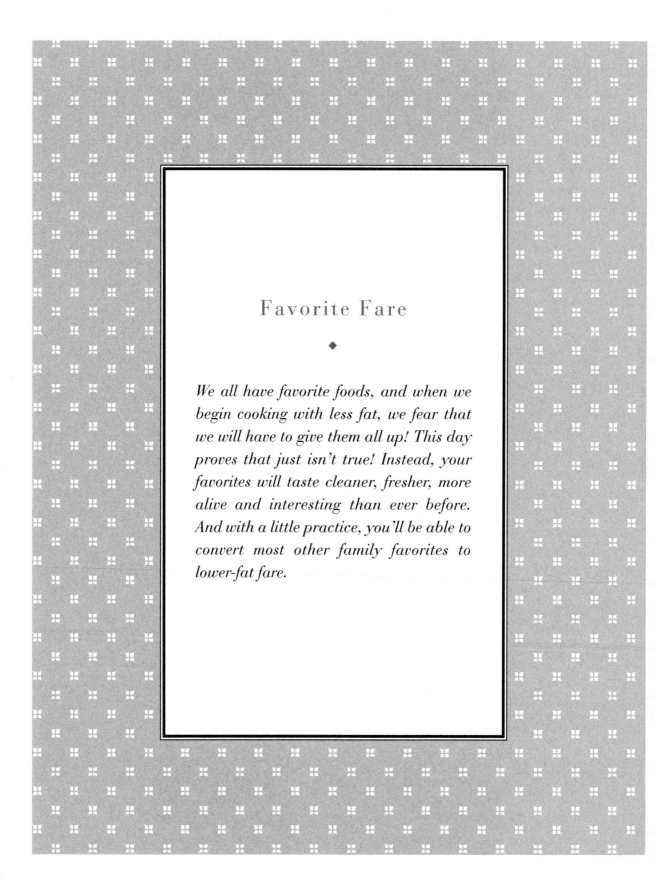

Favorite Fare

◆

We all have favorite foods, and when we begin cooking with less fat, we fear that we will have to give them all up! This day proves that just isn't true! Instead, your favorites will taste cleaner, fresher, more alive and interesting than ever before. And with a little practice, you'll be able to convert most other family favorites to lower-fat fare.

Friday
DAY 5

Fresh Orange Juice
Honeydew Smoothie*
Spicy Carrot Muffins*

◆

Creamy Chicken Salad*
Green Beans
Whole-wheat Roll
Peach Frozen Yogurt*

◆

Tomato and Arugula Salad*
Pasta Primavera Verde*
Country French Bread
Fresh Raspberries
with Vanilla Dreamy Cream*

Breakfast Menu

Foods (per serving)	Cal.	Carb. (g)	Prot. (g)	Chol. (mg)	Fat (g)/%	Sod. (mg)
Orange juice, 6 oz.	83.5	19.4	1.4	0	0.3/3	1.2
Honeydew Smoothie* (p.75)	157	41	3	0.5	0.3/2	42
Spicy Carrot Muffins*	172	30	2.5	12	5/26	268
Morning Snack						
Apple, 3½ oz.	59	15	0.2	0	0.4/6	0
Mini-rice cakes, 5	50	12	1	0	0/0	25

"Breakfast makes good memory."

RABELAIS

Spicy Carrot Muffins

If you like carrot cake, it will be hard to eat just one of these!

MAKES 18 MUFFINS

2½ cups all-purpose flour
1½ cups light brown sugar
2 teaspoons baking powder
1 teaspoon baking soda
1 teaspoon salt
2 teaspoons cinnamon
1 teaspoon ground ginger
½ teaspoon ground cloves
¼ cup canola oil
½ cup unsweetened applesauce
1 egg

¼ cup buttermilk
2 teaspoons vanilla extract
Two 2½-ounce jars baby food
    strained carrots
1 tablespoon minced orange zest
4 ounces unsweetened crushed
    pineapple, with juice
¾ cup loosely packed shredded
    coconut
3 tablespoons confectioners'
    sugar (optional)

1. Preheat the oven to 400° F. Lightly spray 18 standard-sized muffin tins with vegetable oil spray.

2. In a large bowl, combine the flour, sugar, baking powder, baking soda, salt, cinnamon, ginger and cloves. Add the oil, applesauce, egg, buttermilk, vanilla, strained carrots, orange zest and crushed pineapple with juice. Mix well. Stir in the coconut.

3. Fill the muffin cups two-thirds full. Bake for 5 minutes, reduce the temperature to 350° F. and bake for about 20 minutes longer, or until a toothpick inserted in the center of a muffin comes out clean. Turn the muffins out onto a wire rack. Serve warm or cooled and sprinkle lightly with confectioners' sugar, if desired. Store in an airtight container.

CAL. 172   CARB. 30G   PROT. 2.5G   CHOL. 12MG   FAT 5G/26%   SOD. 268MG
(ANALYZED PER MUFFIN)

MUFFIN TINS

Standard-sized muffin tins are 3 inches in diameter across the top and hold ½ cup of liquid. To cut the fat even more, use paper or foil liners rather than spraying the muffin tins with oil.

Lunch Menu

Foods (per serving)	Cal.	Carb. (g)	Prot. (g)	Chol. (mg)	Fat (g)/%	Sod. (mg)
Creamy Chicken Salad*	232	12	28	67	8.5/33	135
Green beans, steamed, 1 cup	96	13	3	0	0.4/3	11
Whole-wheat roll, 1	93	18	3	0	1.6/15	167
Peach Frozen Yogurt* (p. 108), ½ cup	124	26	5.6	0.6	0.1/1	140
Afternoon Snack						
Wickwood Gorp* (p. 300), ¼ cup	163	18	5	0.1	11/61	2

OVEN-POACHED CHICKEN BREAST EXPRESS

Poach chicken breasts lickety-split in the oven or the microwave. Place 2 whole chicken breasts—skinless, boneless and split in half—in a shallow baking dish. Add 1 cup broth or skim milk. Bake at 350°F., uncovered, for 30 minutes, turning once. Or microwave, covered tightly with plastic wrap, at full power for 8 minutes. Cool in the broth. Serve on a bed of rice or shred for salad, vegetable stew or potpie.

Creamy Chicken Salad

Here's old-fashioned creamy chicken salad goodness with only a smidgen of mayonnaise. We've cut the fat in half, without sacrificing taste at all.

85
◆

SERVES 2

*One 8-ounce chicken breast, boneless, skinless, cooked and
   shredded into bite-sized pieces*
¼ cup finely minced scallions, green part only
*8 ounces asparagus, steamed until tender, cut into ½-inch
   pieces (about 1½ cups)*
½ cup sliced water chestnuts
2 tablespoons sliced almonds, toasted (optional)
3 tablespoons Nonfat Blend (see page 298)
1 tablespoon mayonnaise
2 tablespoons finely minced fresh tarragon or dill
Freshly ground black pepper to taste

1. In a large mixing bowl, combine the chicken, scallions, asparagus, water chestnuts and almonds, if using.

2. In a small bowl, combine the Nonfat Blend, mayonnaise, tarragon and pepper and mix well. Add to the chicken and toss to coat. Taste and adjust the seasonings. Chill until serving.

CAL. 232   CARB. 12G   PROT. 28G   CHOL. 67MG   FAT 8.5G/33%   SOD. 135MG

Pasta Primavera Verde

This pasta dish is a standard at our house—although perhaps I should call it a vegetable dish: It's loaded with wonderful fresh veggies! I vary the green vegetables according to the season and it never becomes boring. And sometimes I add a tablespoon or two of Spinach Pesto (recipe at right) when I'm tossing the vegetables and pasta together.

SERVES 2

¼ pound dried Italian linguine
2 cups broccoli florets
¼ pound green beans, trimmed and cut into 1-inch pieces
¼ pound sugar snap peas or snow peas, stems removed
¼ pound asparagus, split lengthwise and cut in half
2 tablespoons finely minced fresh dill
2 tablespoons finely minced garlic
¼ cup finely chopped scallions, green part only
¼ teaspoon red pepper flakes
1 teaspoon olive oil
Salt and freshly ground black pepper

1. Bring 4 quarts of water to a rolling boil and cook the pasta for 8 to 10 minutes, until al dente.

2. Meanwhile, steam the broccoli and beans in a steaming basket set over 1 quart of simmering water for 4 to 6 minutes. Remove the broccoli and beans and set aside. Add the peas and asparagus to the steaming basket and steam for 3 to 4 minutes. Remove and set aside with the other vegetables. Reserve the steaming broth.

3. Drain the pasta and return it to the pot. Add the vegetables, dill, garlic, scallions, pepper flakes, oil and ½ to ¾ cup reserved steaming broth and heat over medium heat for 1 to 2 minutes, stirring to coat thoroughly. Season to taste with salt and pepper and serve immediately.

CAL. 338   CARB. 63G   PROT. 116G   CHOL. 0MG   FAT 4G/10%
SOD. 4MG

SPINACH PESTO

After summer is over, large quantities of basil can be hard to find, not to mention very expensive. This convenient alternative to the classic basil pesto brings the same great flavors together and can be used just as you would the original Genovese favorite.

MAKES 2½ CUPS

16 cups fresh spinach, washed, stems removed (from two 10-ounce packages)
½ cup low-fat, low-sodium chicken broth
1 cup grated Parmesan cheese
2 tablespoons minced garlic
1½ cups fresh basil, washed, stems removed
2 tablespoons extra-virgin olive oil

1. In a food processor fitted with the metal blade, puree the spinach a little at a time, alternating with the chicken broth until all is added and smooth.

2. Add the cheese, garlic, basil and oil and blend until smooth. Cover and refrigerate for up to 2 weeks.

Note: Parmesan cheese should always be aged Parmigiano-Reggiano—it promises the very best flavor for every gram of fat!

CAL. 24   CARB. 1.1G   PROT. 1.8G
CHOL. 2MG   FAT 1.5G/54%
SOD. 71MG (ANALYZED PER 1 TABLESPOON)

Tomato and Arugula Salad

I've not tired of this salad since I discovered it at Romeo Salta's in New York City in the late '60s. Romeo brought arugula from Italy for only three weeks each spring, and I was there as often as possible to savor it. Nowadays, it's easy to find arugula everywhere and very easy to grow yourself. And if someone else washes the sand from the arugula, I could eat this every day!

SERVES 2

2 cups arugula, washed and torn into bite-sized pieces
2 plum tomatoes, quartered lengthwise
2 thin red onion slices, separated
1 tablespoon Our House Dressing (see page 194)
1 ounce part-skim mozzarella, fresh buffalo mozzarella or
* smoked mozzarella, sliced into rounds*

In a large mixing bowl, toss the arugula, tomatoes and onion rings with the dressing. Divide between 2 small plates. Place a slice of mozzarella beside the salad and serve immediately.

CAL. 39   CARB. 7G   PROT. 2.1G   CHOL. 0MG   FAT 0.9G/35%   SOD. 48MG
(WITH PART-SKIM MOZZARELLA)

CAL. 80   CARB. 7G   PROT. 5G   CHOL. 11MG   FAT 4G/43%   SOD. 103MG
(WITH WHOLE-MILK MOZZARELLA)

87 ◆

VANILLA DREAMY CREAM

There's no fat in this dreamy-tasting dessert topping. I use it often!

MAKES ABOUT ½ CUP

½ cup nonfat cottage cheese
1 teaspoon vanilla extract
1 tablespoon sugar
Seeds from 1 vanilla bean

1. In a blender, process the cottage cheese until smooth.

2. In a small mixing bowl, combine the cottage cheese, vanilla, sugar and vanilla seeds and mix well. Refrigerate for at least 1 hour to allow the flavors to blend.

CAL. 23   CARB. 4G   PROT. 2G
CHOL. 0MG   FAT 0G/0%   SOD. 440MG
(ANALYZED PER 1 TABLESPOON)

Dinner Menu

FOODS (PER SERVING)	CAL.	CARB. (G)	PROT. (G)	CHOL. (MG)	FAT (G)/ %	SOD. (MG)
Tomato and Arugula Salad with whole-milk mozzarella*	80	7	5	11	4/43	103
Pasta Primavera Verde*	338	63	116	0	4/10	4
French bread, 2 slices	192	36	6	0	2/9	426
Raspberries, 1 cup	60	14	1	0	0.7/9	0
Vanilla Dreamy Cream*, 1 T.	23	4	2	0	0/0	440
EVENING SNACK						
Popcorn (air-popped), 2 cups	61	13	2	0	0.7/10	0.6
Today's Totals	**1985**	**341**	**185**	**91**	**38/17**	**1765**

Exercise Efforts

For a healthier lifestyle, you need to exercise thirty minutes or more at a time. Initially, the energy you burn is from carbohydrates. Fat is burned only after thirty minutes. The longer you exercise, the more fat you'll use up.

This chart, adapted from *The New England Journal of Medicine*, is based on the caloric expenditures of a 130-pound person during thirty minutes of exercise. If you're heavier, you'll burn more.

ACTIVITY	CALORIES BURNED IN 30 MINUTES	ACTIVITY	CALORIES BURNED IN 30 MINUTES
Sleeping	30	Bowling	168
Watching TV	30	Horseback riding	168
Standing	36	Walking downstairs	168
Desk work	60	Lawn mowing	172
Grocery shopping	84	Basketball	174
Walking 2 mph	87	Water skiing	180
Ping-Pong	96	Scrubbing floors	188
Washing the car	98	Shoveling snow	195
Window cleaning	104	Football	207
Folk dancing	105	Racquetball	225
Mopping floors	111	Squash	225
Baseball	117	Downhill skiing	240
Swimming	120	Cycling 13 mph	267
Cycling 5 mph	126	Canoeing	270
Golfing	129	Jogging 5 mph	270
Volleyball	129	Scuba diving	287
Hedge trimming	137	Chopping wood	290
Dancing (rock)	144	Cross-country skiing	294
Badminton	148	Jogging 7 mph	354
Walking 4 mph	156	Walking upstairs	438
Tennis	168		

Thirst Quenchers

It's easy to become happily addicted to a beverage and simply continue drinking it hour after hour. While few have fat, the calories add up and the sweetened ones stimulate your sweet tooth! Of course, the best thirst quencher of all is water. Top of my list!

12 OZ.	CAL.	FAT (G)	SOD. (MG)	CAFFEINE (MG)
Apple juice	160	0.4	10	0
Beer	140	0	17	0
Club soda	0	0	72	0
Cola	140	0.1	14	34
Cran-Raspberry juice	229	0.1	7	0
Diet cola	3	0	24	48
Ginger ale	115	0	24	0
Iced coffee	7	0.01	2	197
Iced tea	3	0	20	48
Lemon-Lime soda	143	0	9	0
Light beer	95	0	10	0
Orange juice	154	0.7	3	0
Perrier	0	0	3	0
Prune juice	242	0.1	14	0
Red wine	245	0	17	0
Tomato juice	58	0.2	438	0
Tonic water	115	0	13	0
Vegetable juice	65	0.3	378	0
Water	0	0	0	0
White wine	226	0	14	0

A Sparkling Spectrum

◆

Big flavors satisfy when you have a houseful to feed. They make our craving for fats evaporate—it's hard to ignore the intensity of thyme, lemon zest, sage, garlic and Parmesan. It's smart to keep ingredients with big flavors readily accessible in your pantry.

Saturday
DAY 6

Fresh Orange Juice

Seasonal Berries

Cinnamon French Toast* and
Pure Maple Syrup

Turkey Ham Slices

◆

Garden Green Salad with
Sherry Wine Vinegar Dressing*

Tawny Bean Soup*

Mandarin Oranges

◆

Summertime Bruschetta*

Osso Buco Bianco* with Orzo

Asparagus with Parmesan Shards

Braised Leeks*

Creamy Coffee Custard with
Chocolate Shavings*

Breakfast Menu

FOODS (PER SERVING)	CAL.	CARB. (G)	PROT. (G)	CHOL. (MG)	FAT (G)/%	SOD. (MG)
Orange juice, 6 oz.	83.5	19.4	1.4	0	0.3/3	1.2
Mixed berries, 1 cup	50	12	1	0	0.6/10	1.6
Cinnamon French Toast*	142	25	12	2.2	0.2/1	298
Maple syrup, 2 T.	105	27	0	0	1/1	4
Turkey ham, 2 oz.	60	1	9	35	2.5/38	660
MORNING SNACK						
Apple, 3½ oz.	59	15	0.2	0	0.4/6	0

Cinnamon French Toast

This makes the popular French toast of the '80s—made with challah, egg yolks and heavy cream and then browned in butter (with 80 percent of its calories from fat)—seem very much an indulgence.

SERVES 4

2 cups skim milk
½ teaspoon cinnamon
1 teaspoon vanilla extract
4 egg whites, lightly beaten
8 slices nonfat whole-wheat or
cracked-wheat bread
Syrup, lemon juice, confectioners'
sugar and fruit, for
serving (optional)

1. In a shallow mixing bowl, blend the milk, cinnamon and vanilla with a fork until foamy. Gradually add the egg whites. Pour into a large baking dish and lay the bread in the dish. Soak for 1 to 2 minutes.

2. Heat a nonstick skillet over medium-high heat. To make sure it is hot enough, sprinkle some drops of water in the pan; they should evaporate immediately. Using a spatula, place the bread in the pan. Fry for 2 to 3 minutes on each side, until golden brown. Serve immediately with syrup or sprinkled with lemon juice, confectioners' sugar and your favorite fruit, if desired.

CAL. 142   CARB. 25G   PROT. 12G   CHOL. 2.2MG   FAT 0.2G/1%   SOD. 298MG

92

"A good honest wholesome hungry breakfast."
WALTON

A CUP OF JOE

A great cup of java has never been so easy to come by—or as interesting as it is today. There's a whole new coffee jargon and coffee mania sweeping the country.

But remember: Only a robust brew ordered "black" is calorie-free. A *cafe latte* made with whole milk can have 250 calories and 13 grams of fat! Add whipped cream and it goes through the roof. Mocha drinks made with milk and chocolate syrup are worse—up to 320 calories and 24 grams of fat.

If you ask, most coffeehouses will make cappuccino with skim milk. You'll save untold thousands of calories.

Tawny Bean Soup

This is a most special bean soup. Glorious to look at, it evokes the colors of an autumn vista and is incredible to taste. Each bite shouts "more!"

SERVES 4

*2 cups plus 2 tablespoons
low-fat, low-sodium
chicken broth*
*3 small onions, coarsely
chopped (about 1 cup)*
*1 rib celery, diced (about
½ cup)*
*½ pound carrots, cut into
2-inch pieces*
*3 tablespoons finely minced
garlic*
*2 cups cooked or one 15-ounce
can red beans, drained*

*2 cups cooked or one 15-ounce
can white beans, cannellini
or navy, drained*
¼ cup brown or green lentils
¼ cup dry green split peas
2 cups beef broth
4 sprigs fresh thyme
4 bay leaves
8 sage leaves and stems
*¼ cup chopped Italian
parsley, for garnish*

1. In a medium-sized stockpot, heat 2 tablespoons broth over medium heat and sauté the onions, celery, carrots and garlic for 3 to 5 minutes, until the onions are translucent.

2. Add the beans, lentils, split peas, beef broth and the remaining chicken broth, thyme, bay leaves and sage. Bring to a boil, cover, reduce the heat and simmer for 1 hour. Uncover and cook for another 30 minutes, or until the peas and lentils are tender and the flavors are blended. Remove the thyme, bay leaves and sage.

3. Ladle into bowls and garnish with parsley. Serve immediately.

CAL. 406   CARB. 74G   PROT. 25G   CHOL. 0MG   FAT 2G/4%   SOD. 46MG

Lunch Menu

FOODS (PER SERVING)	CAL.	CARB. (G)	PROT. (G)	CHOL. (MG)	FAT (G)/%	SOD. (MG)
Salad greens, 1 cup	9.5	1.6	0.9	0	0.1/11	14
Sherry Wine Vinegar Dressing* (p. 121), 1 T.	16	0.6	0.15	0	1.7/84	75
Tawny Bean Soup*	406	74	25	0	2/4	46
Mandarin oranges, ½ cup	46	12	2	0	0.02/1	6

THE BEST BEANS

Valentine, Racquel, White Aztecs, Painted Ponies, Chocolate Runner, Wild Rice, Christmas, Snowcaps—they're legumes, beans with names as enchanting as their colors and unique flavors. One is slightly nutty. One tastes like wild rice. Another's blacker than any bean you've ever seen. They are a flavor adventure.

These are heirloom beans, grown by Elizabeth Berry on her ranch near Santa Fe. Although they are now more widely distributed than before—at Dean & DeLuca (New York City) and The Coyote Cafe General Store (Santa Fe)— you can write to Elizabeth directly for a catalog. Send $1.00 to Gallina Canyon Ranch, Box 706, Abiquiu, New Mexico 87510. The beans are as lovely in glass canisters as they are in your bean pot.

93

Osso Buco Bianco

Here's a lighter osso buco with the surprising taste of tarragon. The sauce is wonderful stirred into cooked white or brown rice or orzo. Try this garnished with gremolata.

SERVES 4

4 cross-cut sections veal shanks (about 2 inches thick and
   weighing approximately 2 pounds)
1 tablespoon all-purpose flour
8 plump cloves garlic, peeled and finely minced
1 pound baby carrots, peeled and cut into 1-inch lengths
1 cup dry white wine
1 cup beef broth
1 cup low-fat, low-sodium chicken broth
Six 6-inch sprigs fresh tarragon
1 tablespoon instant potato flakes (see Note)
Salt and freshly ground black pepper to taste
2 cups cooked rice or orzo, for serving (optional)
½ cup coarsely chopped Italian parsley

1. Preheat the oven to 375° F. Lightly spray a flameproof roasting pan with olive oil spray. Set the pan over medium-high heat. Add the veal shanks, sprinkle on both sides with the flour and brown for about 2 minutes on each side.

2. Add the garlic, carrots, wine, beef and chicken broths and tarragon. Cover and roast for 1 hour. Uncover and roast for about 30 minutes longer, until cooked through.

3. Remove the tarragon and the shanks from the roasting pan, covering the shanks with foil to keep warm. Defat the collected juices by skimming with a spoon or blotting with a paper towel. Set the roasting pan over medium-high heat and cook until the juices reduce to approximately 1 cup. When almost reduced, add the potato flakes, mix well and season to taste with salt and pepper. Serve the shanks with rice or orzo, topping both with a little sauce and garnishing with parsley.

NOTE: Martha White brand is my preference for potato flakes.

CAL. 255   CARB. 12G   PROT. 27G   CHOL. 86MG   FAT 6.6G/24%   SOD. 41MG

FRESH FLAVOR

Gremolata is an Italian seasoning mixture traditionally made with parsley, lemon zest and olive oil. Served at table as a topping for osso buco, it freshens the long-simmering stew with its bright flavor.

I find gremolata sparks a multitude of dishes—chicken stew, minestrone, asparagus soup, risotto, braised lamb shanks and more—even the simplest steamed green beans, asparagus or sugar snaps.

Sometimes I vary the herb—tarragon, mint, dill—sometimes the citrus. But the garlic and olive oil remain constant.

GREMOLATA

MAKES ABOUT
1 / 4 CUP

2 tablespoons minced fresh parsley
1 tablespoon minced lemon zest
2 teaspoons minced garlic
2 teaspoons olive oil

In a small bowl, combine the parsley, lemon zest and garlic. Drizzle in the olive oil, stirring.

CAL. 7.7 CARB. 0.28G PROT. 0.06G
CHOL. 0MG FAT 0.76G/84%
SOD. 0.46MG (ANALYZED PER TEASPOON)

Summertime Bruschetta

Summertime tomatoes with their wonderful juiciness are the best for topping grilled crusty peasant bread or sourdough baguettes.

MAKES 8 SLICES

4 ripe plum tomatoes, very finely diced
1 tablespoon finely minced garlic
¼ cup coarsely chopped fresh basil
2 tablespoons finely chopped Italian parsley
2 teaspoons lemon juice
Pinch of crushed red pepper flakes
Salt and freshly ground black pepper to taste
Eight ¼-inch-thick slices French or Italian bread
2 cloves garlic, halved

1. In a large mixing bowl, combine the tomato, minced garlic, basil, parsley, lemon juice, red pepper flakes and salt and pepper. Toss well and set aside for at least 3 hours.

2. Just before serving, grill or toast the bread and rub one side with garlic. Place a dollop of the tomato mixture on top of each one.

CAL. 141 CARB. 27G PROT. 5G CHOL. 0MG FAT 1.3G/8% SOD. 274MG
(ANALYZED PER SLICE)

95

Braised Leeks

I make these leeks in the microwave rather than braising them on top of the stove.

SERVES 4

1 pound leeks, cut in half lengthwise
2 teaspoons low-fat, low-sodium chicken broth
2 tablespoons brown sugar

1. Put the leeks in a glass dish and add the chicken broth. Cover tightly and microwave on high for 6 to 8 minutes.

2. Uncover, sprinkle with the brown sugar, cover, turning back a corner to vent, and then microwave for 2 minutes on high. Toss to coat and serve immediately.

CAL. 53 CARB. 13.1G PROT. 1.01G CHOL. 0MG FAT 0.23G/3% SOD. 31MG

Creamy Coffee Custard with Chocolate Shavings

One of my favorite flavor combinations—which I think originated with the café au lait flavor of Häagen-Dazs coffee ice cream and a little dab of fudge sauce. This satisfies me equally as well!

SERVES 4

4 egg whites
1 large egg
$^1\!/_2$ cup sugar
$^1\!/_4$ cup heavy cream
One 12-ounce can evaporated
    skim milk

2 tablespoons very strong
    brewed coffee, cooled
$^1\!/_2$ teaspoon vanilla extract
2 tablespoons dark chocolate
    shavings

1. Preheat the oven to 325°F.

2. In a mixing bowl, combine the egg whites, egg and sugar and stir gently until mixed. Whisk in the cream, evaporated skim milk, coffee and vanilla until the sugar dissolves.

3. Strain the custard into another bowl and pour into 4 individual 6-ounce custard cups. Place the cups in a large baking dish and add enough hot water to come halfway up their sides.

4. Bake for about 45 to 50 minutes, until the center of the custard is set and a knife comes out clean when inserted in the center. Cool in the water bath to room temperature. Cover and refrigerate for at least 2 hours. Serve topped with chocolate shavings.

CAL. 285   CARB. 40G   PROT. 12.2G   CHOL. 77MG   FAT 9G/28%   SOD. 175MG

96

"Be wiser than other people if you can; but do not tell them so."

LORD CHESTERFIELD

Dinner Menu

FOODS (PER SERVING)	CAL.	CARB. (G)	PROT. (G)	CHOL. (MG)	FAT (G)/%	SOD. (MG)
Summertime Bruschetta* (p. 95), 2 slices	282	54	10	0	2.6/8	558
Osso Buco Bianco*	255	12	27	86	6.6/24	41
Orzo, 1 cup	162	33	6	0	0.7/4	1
Steamed asparagus (6), with Parmesan shards, 2 T.	49	4	4	4.9	2/37	117
Braised Leeks*	53	13.1	1.01	0	0.23/3	31
Creamy Coffee Custard with Chocolate Shavings*	285	40	12.2	77	9/28	175
Today's Total	**2063**	**343**	**112**	**205**	**30/13**	**2029**

GLOBE-TROTTING
FROM YOUR PANTRY

It's easy to travel around the world with the things you have in your pantry and just a few extras. Sometimes you just need to rethink spice or herb combinations. Sometimes it's heightening an ingredient more than you normally would. Even just breaking old habits can make that plain old (but wonderful!) roasted chicken into an adventure!

FRENCH

* Dijon mustard
* Butter, cheese, cream, apples, carrots
* Onions, shallots, mushrooms, celery
* White or red wine, liqueurs
* Tarragon, thyme, parsley
* Olive oil, black olives, anchovies, capers
* Fennel seeds, garlic, tomatoes, lemon

MEDITERRANEAN

* Olive oil, white wine, seafood
* Garlic, onions, tomatoes, lemon, eggplant
* Oregano, mint, parsley, dill
* Feta cheese and lamb
* Raisins, black olives, pine nuts

SCANDINAVIAN

* Dill, chives, beets, onions, apples
* Red cabbage, turnips, potatoes
* Herring, shrimp, ham, salmon
* Dried fruit and horseradish
* Sour cream and butter, sweet mustard

GERMAN

* Egg noodles
* Sauerkraut, cabbage, onions, carrots, mushrooms
* Pork, beef, bacon, sausages
* Mustard, capers, pickles
* Caraway seeds

ITALIAN

* Olive oil, balsamic vinegar
* Parmesan, Pecorino, mozzarella and ricotta
* White and red wine
* Porcini mushrooms, onions, garlic, fennel
* Pasta, tomatoes, sun-dried tomatoes
* Sage, rosemary, basil, oregano, parlsey
* Dried red pepper flakes, black olives
* Sardines, pine nuts, anchovies, capers, raisins

SPANISH

* Red peppers, olives, oranges, garlic
* Seafood, sherry
* Paprika, saffron

A Cozy Sunday

◆

A lot of people, including me, count Sunday as their favorite day. It unfolds in a lazy way and meanders, according to many moods. Sometimes a big brunch and a light supper suffice, and for others, a midday family dinner is on the agenda. This is a day to schedule as you please and do those things that best nurture you.

Sunday
DAY 7

Fresh Orange Juice

Cool and Green Fruit Salad*

Easy Scrambled Eggs*

Sage Sausage Patties*

Very Berry Muffins*

◆

Beacon Club Broccoli Salad*

Spring Salmon Loaf with
Dilled White Sauce*

Green Green Beans*

French Bread

New German Chocolate Cake*

◆

Roasted Red Pepper Soup*

Tomato Mozzarella
Grilled Cheese*

Lime Frozen Yogurt*

Breakfast Menu

Foods (per serving)	Cal.	Carb. (g)	Prot. (g)	Chol. (mg)	Fat (g)/%	Sod. (mg)
Orange juice, 6 oz.	83.5	19.4	1.4	0	0.3/3	1.2
Cool and Green Fruit Salad*	158	41	1.9	0	0.8/4	25
Easy Scrambled Eggs*	115	1.2	12	107	2.5/30	169
Sage Sausage Patties*, 2	84	2	16	6	0.6/7	53
Very Berry Muffins*	172	33	2.7	9	3.3/17	179

Easy Scrambled Eggs

I don't like egg substitutes that are merely egg whites loaded with gums and coloring. My alternative solution to using whole eggs looks and tastes like them because I use them! Real eggs! I simply load up on the whites and am frugal when it comes to the yolks.

SERVES 4

10 large egg whites (about 1½ cups)
2 large whole eggs
2 tablespoons chopped fresh dill
Freshly ground black pepper to taste

1. In a mixing bowl, beat the egg whites and eggs until combined.

2. Spray a large nonstick skillet with vegetable oil spray and heat over medium-high heat. Pour the eggs into the pan, stirring with a spatula to prevent sticking, and cook for 1 to 2 minutes over medium-high heat. When they are almost done, add the dill. Cook for a little longer until set, sprinkle with pepper to taste and serve immediately.

CAL. 115   CARB. 1.2G   PROT. 12G   CHOL. 107MG   FAT 2.5G/30%   SOD. 169MG

EGGS EXPLAINED

	Cal.	Fat(g)/%	Chol. (mg)	Sat. Fat	Sod. (mg)
Regular large egg	75	5/60	215	2	63
Regular large egg yolk	63	5/72	215	2	48
Regular large egg white	16	trace/0	0	0	15
"Designer" eggs	72	5/63	215	2	64
Liquid egg substitute	25	0/0	0	0	80

100

"If you rest, you rust."
HELEN HAYES

EGGS

Although eggs once were considered a wholesome way to start the day, their saturated fat and cholesterol have eclipsed their nutritional value.

Most people are eating fewer than ever before, some substituting "designer eggs," others, egg substitutes. Both change the natural white/yolk ratio. Popular liquid egg substitutes are 99 percent egg whites, plus yellow coloring and guar gum added as a stabilizer. And they cost five times as much as real eggs.

"Designer eggs" are available under a variety of brand names. These "healthful" eggs are laid by chickens whose feed or environment has been altered. They are tasty, but their health benefits are dubious.

To me, it's a matter of balancing health with

flavor and good sense. And the flavor's in the yolk.

Substituting whites for whole eggs is fine in baking. But for breakfast, there's nothing like the real thing. My solution: Scramble five whites to one whole yolk in a nonstick pan. The taste is still there, and I won't have to worry about some future health study implicating the guar gum or yellow dye found in synthetic eggs.

Sage Sausage Patties

Ground turkey breast, which may be 99 percent fat free, is an admirable replacement for fattier beef, pork or turkey sausage, all of which may be loaded with fat.

MAKES TWELVE 2-INCH PATTIES

1½ pounds ground turkey breast

1 small onion, coarsely chopped

4 tablespoons finely chopped Italian parsley

1 tablespoon finely chopped fresh sage or 1 teaspoon dried

3 cloves garlic, peeled and finely minced

1 teaspoon ground ginger

1 teaspoon crushed red pepper flakes

½ teaspoon ground cloves

½ teaspoon freshly ground black pepper

1. In a large mixing bowl, combine all the ingredients and mix, using your fingers or 2 forks. Form into 12 patties, 2 inches in diameter and ¾ to 1 inch thick.

2. Arrange the patties in a large nonstick skillet. Cook over medium heat, turning once, for 12 to 17 minutes, until cooked through the center. Drain on paper towels and serve immediately.

CAL. 42   CARB. 1G   PROT. 8G   CHOL. 3MG   FAT 0.3G/7%   SOD. 26.5MG
(ANALYZED PER PATTY)

Cool and Green Fruit Salad

At Wickwood, the inn we own in Saugatuck, this is a menu favorite.

SERVES 4

½ honeydew melon, peeled, seeded and cut into chunks

1⅓ cups whole green grapes

2 kiwi, peeled and sliced

2 tablespoons frozen limeade concentrate

2 tablespoons minced fresh mint

⅓ cup blackberries, raspberries or a mixture of both

In a large mixing bowl, combine all the ingredients except the berries. Add the berries and mix gently. Serve slightly chilled.

CAL. 158   CARB. 41G   PRO. 1.9G   CHOL. 0MG   FAT 0.8/4%   SOD. 25MG

101

Very Berry Muffins

These muffins are winners! They are tender, lemony and can be filled with raspberries, blueberries or blackberries, or some of each.

MAKES 18 MUFFINS

2 cups sugar
¼ cup canola oil
1 teaspoon minced lemon zest
1 large egg
1 egg white, lightly beaten
½ cup unsweetened applesauce
1 cup Nonfat Blend (see page 298)

2½ teaspoons vanilla extract
2 teaspoons fresh lemon juice
2 cups all-purpose flour
1 tablespoon baking powder
1 teaspoon baking soda
1 pint fresh raspberries, blueberries, blackberries or a mixture of berries

1. Preheat the oven to 400°F. Lightly spray standard-sized muffin tins with vegetable oil spray.

2. In a large bowl, combine the sugar, oil and lemon zest. Add the egg and egg white and mix well. Add the applesauce and Nonfat Blend and stir well. Add the vanilla and lemon juice and stir.

3. Add the flour, baking powder and baking soda, stirring gently until completely blended. When the batter is smooth, gently fold in the berries, taking care not to overmix and break up the berries.

4. Fill the muffin cups three-quarters full and bake for 5 minutes. Reduce the temperature to 350°F. and bake for about 20 minutes, or until a toothpick inserted in the center of a muffin comes out clean. Allow to cool in the pan for one minute before turning the muffins out onto a wire rack to cool. Serve warm or at room temperature. Store in an airtight container as they can become sticky the next day—if there are any left.

NOTE: See page 84 for information on standard-sized muffin tins and on using paper liners.

CAL. 172   CARB. 33G   PROT. 2.7G   CHOL. 9MG   FAT 3.3G/17%   SOD. 179MG
(ANALYZED PER MUFFIN)

"Take your life in your own hands and what happens? A terrible thing: no one is to blame."

ERICA JONG

THE TASTE OF GREEN

We've noticed that parsley really does make green things taste greener.

We use it daily, tossing in a sprinkle of freshness, a dash of color and a last-minute sparkle of flavor to a dish. But have you really tasted parsley lately?

There are three kinds available: familiar curly parsley; the more pungent Italian, or flat-leafed, parsley; and Hamburg, rooted or turnip-rooted parsley, sold in specialty stores only in the late fall and winter. Both the root, which tastes a bit like celeriac, and the leaves of rooted parsley may be used.

And then there's cilantro, sometimes called Chinese parsley because of its appearance, but from an entirely different plant called coriander. Its lacy-looking leaves add fresh cooked flavor.

Last but best of all is chervil. Its tiny lacy leaves are the color and taste of the essence of spring. Find a source or grow it yourself.

Never, ever use these dried; after all, it's their freshness that adds the sparkle.

Lunch Menu

Foods (per serving)	Cal.	Carb. (g)	Prot. (g)	Chol. (mg)	Fat (g)/%	Sod. (mg)
Beacon Club Broccoli Salad*	147	20	4	0	7/41	42
Spring Salmon Loaf with Dilled White Sauce*	299	24	31	47	8.6/26	844
Green Green Beans*	96	13	3	0	0.4/3	11
French bread, 2 slices	192	36	6	0	2/9	426
New German Chocolate Cake*	223	39	3	6	6.9/27	87

Beacon Club Broccoli Salad

This is a favorite salad in Kalamazoo and has become the best way I know of to eat loads of broccoli.

SERVES 4

6 cups broccoli florets (1 to 1½ pounds)
½ cup coarsely chopped red onion
8 cherry tomatoes, halved
½ cup orange juice
3 tablespoons red wine vinegar
2 tablespoons light brown sugar
1 tablespoon finely minced orange zest
2 tablespoons olive oil

103
◆

1. Put the broccoli in a large steaming basket and steam over 1 inch of boiling water for 3 to 5 minutes, until tender but still crunchy. Drain and rinse immediately with cold water to stop the cooking. Drain, and transfer to a bowl and toss with the onion and tomatoes.

2. In a small bowl, combine the orange juice, vinegar, sugar and orange zest. Slowly whisk in the oil until well blended. Dress the broccoli with ⅓ cup of dressing and toss well. (Reserve the remaining dressing for future use.) Chill the salad for 1 hour before serving.

Cal. 147   Carb. 20g   Prot. 4g   Chol. 0mg   Fat 7g/41%   Sod. 42mg

Spring Salmon Loaf
with Dilled White Sauce

This is one of those "mom" dishes that bring back wonderful memories. Even my mom, June, who doesn't like "weeds" (herbs!) and was leery of my tampering with her white sauce, loved this. It may look like a production, but it really isn't.

SERVES 4

One 14¾-ounce can salmon, drained, bones removed, flaked
⅓ cup plain bread crumbs
2 tablespoons Nonfat Blend (see page 298)
¼ cup coarsely chopped onion
¼ cup coarsely chopped celery
½ cup finely minced Italian parsley
1 teaspoon finely minced lemon zest
1 teaspoon Dijon mustard
½ teaspoon Worcestershire sauce
1 to 2 dashes of Tabasco sauce
1 large egg white, lightly beaten
½ recipe Faux White Sauce (see page 305), without butter
2 tablespoons finely minced fresh dill
1 cup fresh or frozen peas, thawed

1. Preheat the oven to 350°F.

2. In a large mixing bowl, combine the salmon, bread crumbs, Nonfat Blend, onions, celery, parsley, lemon zest, mustard, Worcestershire sauce and Tabasco and mix well. Add the egg white and mix until blended. Lightly spray a small loaf pan with olive oil spray. Transfer the salmon mixture to the pan and press lightly into place. Bake for 30 to 45 minutes, or until set and lightly browned.

3. In a saucepan, combine the Faux White Sauce with the dill and peas and gently heat until just hot.

4. Invert the salmon onto a platter and cover with the sauce. Serve immediately.

CAL. 299   CARB. 24G   PROT. 31G   CHOL. 47MG   FAT 8.6G/26%   SOD. 844MG

104

GREEN GREEN BEANS

Parsley really does make green beans taste greener.

SERVES 4

2 pounds green beans, ends snapped
1 teaspoon finely minced garlic
3 tablespoons finely minced Italian parsley
Freshly ground black pepper to taste

1. Put the beans in a large skillet and cover with ½ inch of water. Cover and cook over medium-high heat for 4 to 6 minutes, until crisp-tender. Drain. You may have to do this in batches.

2. In a large bowl, toss the beans with the garlic, parsley and pepper.

CAL. 96   CARB. 13G   PROT. 3G
CHOL. 0MG   FAT 0.4G/3%
SOD. 11MG

New German Chocolate Cake

This is a wonderful light version of an old classic—in fact, so wonderful, it's hard to stop eating! Perhaps treat a neighbor so that you're not tempted to keep munching.

SERVES 24

CAKE

4 ounces German sweet
  chocolate, coarsely chopped
  ¹/₂ cup water
  2 cups all-purpose flour
  1 teaspoon baking soda
2 cups sugar
Two 2¹/₂-ounce jars strained
  baby food prunes
1 teaspoon vanilla extract
1 cup buttermilk
6 large egg whites, lightly beaten

FROSTING

¹/₂ cup sugar
4 teaspoons cornstarch
4 tablespoons unsalted butter
¹/₄ cup corn syrup
³/₄ cup evaporated skim milk
1 teaspoon vanilla extract
¹/₂ cup shredded coconut
²/₃ cup chopped pecans, toasted

1. Preheat the oven to 350°F. Spray a 15 × 10 × 2-inch baking pan with vegetable oil spray.

2. Make the cake: Combine the chocolate and water in a small saucepan and warm over low heat for 3 minutes, until melted and smooth. Set aside to cool slightly.

3. In a small bowl, combine the flour and baking soda. In a mixing bowl, mix the sugar and prunes. Add the vanilla and buttermilk and stir thoroughly. Add the chocolate and stir well.

4. In the mixing bowl of an electric mixer, beat the egg whites on medium speed until frothy. Fold into the prune mixture. Slowly add the flour mixture in quarter-cup amounts. Combine gently, slowly folding with a spatula, until smooth. Pour into the pan and bake for 25 minutes. Cool completely before frosting.

5. Make the frosting: In a medium saucepan, combine the sugar, cornstarch, butter, corn syrup, milk and vanilla and cook over medium heat until bubbling. Add the coconut and pecans, cool slightly and spread evenly on the cooled cake.

CAL. 223   CARB. 39G   PROT. 3G   CHOL. 6MG   FAT 6.9G/27%   SOD. 87MG

"The only way to get rid of a temptation is to yield to it."

OSCAR WILDE

105

Tomato Mozzarella Grilled Cheese

This warm, lush sandwich makes an old-fashioned butter-fried grilled sandwich seem too heavy. Everyone loves this, and the variations are endless!

SERVES 4

8 slices fat-free multi-grain bread
4 ounces part-skim mozzarella cheese, thinly sliced
2 small plum tomatoes, thinly sliced
2 small onions, thinly sliced
Freshly ground black pepper to taste
1/3 cup skim milk
2 egg whites

1. Place 2 slices of bread on a work surface and layer each with slices of the cheese, tomato and onion. Season with pepper and top each with another slice of bread. Repeat to make 4 sandwiches in all.

2. Lightly spray 2 nonstick skillets with olive oil spray and heat over medium-low heat.

3. In a mixing bowl, lightly beat the milk and egg whites with a fork. Gently coat each side of the sandwiches in the egg mixture by holding them in the bowl for 10 to 12 seconds on each side.

4. Cook the sandwiches for 3 to 4 minutes on each side, spraying the side that is up with olive oil spray before turning the sandwich. The bread will toast and the cheese melt as it becomes done. Serve immediately.

CAL. 201   CARB. 27G   PROT. 14G   CHOL. 21MG
FAT 6G/24%   SOD. 819MG

CALCIUM SOURCES

Adult needs range from 800 to 2000 milligrams of calcium a day, depending on age and factors such as pregnancy and post-menopausal status. To help you reach your goal, choose:

♦ Milk and milk products such as yogurt and cheese—the most concentrated sources

♦ Calcium-fortified orange juice

♦ Greens—turnip, kale, chard, bok choy

♦ Sardines and salmon, with the bones

♦ Tofu, if made with a calcium coagulant

♦ Fortified cereals

♦ Dried beans

♦ Cooked broccoli

♦ Oatmeal

♦ Figs

♦ Oranges

Roasted Red Pepper Soup

Smoky and ever so slightly spicy, this soup warms my heart.

SERVES 4

4 cups beef broth
3 red peppers, roasted and diced (about 1½ cups)
2 medium onions, halved and thinly sliced
(about 1 cup)
3 tablespoons lemon juice
1 tablespoon finely minced lemon zest
Pinch of cayenne
¼ teaspoon cinnamon
½ cup finely minced fresh cilantro

1. In a stockpot, combine the broth, peppers, onions, lemon juice, lemon zest, cayenne and cinnamon and bring to a boil over high heat. Reduce the heat and simmer, partially covered, for about 30 minutes, until thickened and full-flavored. Cool slightly.

2. In a food processor fitted with the metal blade, puree the soup. Alternatively, puree with an immersion blender. Return to the pot, add the cilantro and gently reheat. Serve immediately.

CAL. 52   CARB. 9G   PROT. 2G   CHOL. 0MG   FAT 0.2G/4%   SOD. 3.5MG

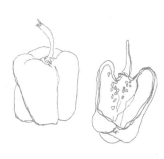

ROASTING PEPPERS

Roasting red, yellow, orange and purple bell peppers imbues them with a flavor that is smoky and intense—and a soft, rich, velvety texture.

To roast: Preheat the broiler. Cut the peppers in half, removing the seeds and membrane. For a more evenly charred skin, cut slits every 1 to 2 inches around the circumference of the peppers to allow them to lie flat. Place under the broiler, skin side up, 2 to 3 inches from the heat. Rotate until blackened all over, 8 to 12 minutes. Transfer the peppers to a paper or plastic bag, close and allow to sweat for 15 to 20 minutes. Remove and gently peel away the charred skin. Store covered and refrigerated for up to a week. Be sure to make use of the lovely, natural juices that collect.

Dinner Menu

FOODS (PER SERVING)	CAL.	CARB. (G)	PROT. (G)	CHOL. (MG)	FAT (G)/%	SOD. (MG)
Roasted Red Pepper Soup*	52	9	2	0	0.2/4	3.5
Tomato Mozzarella Grilled Cheese*	201	27	14	21	6/24	819
Lime Frozen Yogurt* (p. 109), ½ cup	208	47	7	1	0.1/0	158
Today's Totals	**2030**	**312**	**104**	**197**	**39/17**	**2818**

107

Fabulous Frozen Yogurts

Making frozen yogurt at home is fun and really so easy that it can almost be an everyday event. The great benefit of homemade is that you can really make it almost totally fat-free by using nonfat plain yogurt and nonfat cottage cheese. And you can make it so much better than the commercial brands because you control the quality and quantity of the ingredients. How many commercial brands use a pint of fresh raspberries or real vanilla beans for a quart of frozen yogurt?

Just remember to invest in an ice-cream maker that makes it easy on you. You'll save so much in the long run. Remember, too, to pack the frozen yogurt, just out of the machine, very tightly into a plastic container, smooth the top, spread plastic wrap across it and then close with the plastic top. This prevents crystallization.

My advice: Make small batches at a time—just enough for 24 to 48 hours. The fresher the yogurt, the better the flavor!

BLACKBERRY FROZEN YOGURT

MAKES 1 QUART

1 cup nonfat cottage cheese
3 cups fresh or frozen
  unsweetened blackberries
1 cup nonfat plain yogurt
1 cup sugar
2 teaspoons lemon zest

1. In a blender, process the cottage cheese until smooth.

2. In a large bowl, combine the blackberries with the other ingredients and mix well.

3. Transfer the mixture to an ice-cream machine and freeze according to the manufacturer's directions. Transfer to a container with a lid and let mellow in the freezer for 3 to 4 hours. Eat within 48 hours.

CAL. 140 CARB. 29G PROT. 6.3G
CHOL. 0.6MG FAT 0.4G/3%
SOD. 134MG (ANALYZED PER ½ CUP)

STRAWBERRY FROZEN YOGURT

MAKES 1 QUART

4 cups sliced fresh
  strawberries
1 cup sugar
2 cups nonfat plain yogurt
1 tablespoon vanilla extract
¼ cup Amaretto liqueur
  (optional)

1. In a large bowl, combine the strawberries, sugar, yogurt and vanilla and mix well.

2. Follow the directions in step 3 for Blackberry Frozen Yogurt. Just before the yogurt is done, add the Amaretto, if desired.

CAL. 159 CARB. 36G PROT. 4G
CHOL. 1MG FAT 0.4G/2% SOD. 48MG
(ANALYZED PER ½ CUP)

PEACH FROZEN YOGURT

MAKES 1 QUART

1 cup nonfat cottage cheese
2 cups fresh or canned
  peach puree
1 cup light brown sugar
1 tablespoon lemon juice
1 cup nonfat plain yogurt

1. In a blender, process the cottage cheese until smooth.

2. In a large bowl, combine the peach puree, brown sugar and lemon juice. Add the yogurt and cottage cheese and mix well.

3. Follow the directions in step 3 for Blackberry Frozen Yogurt.

CAL. 124 CARB. 26G PROT. 5.6G
CHOL. 0.6MG FAT 0.1G/1%
SOD. 140MG (ANALYZED PER ½ CUP)

CANTALOUPE FROZEN YOGURT

MAKES 1 QUART

1 cantaloupe, peeled and
  cut into chunks
Juice of 1 lemon
1 cup nonfat plain yogurt
½ cup sugar
1 teaspoon vanilla

1. In a food processor, fitted with a metal blade, puree the cantaloupe. Transfer to a large mixing bowl and add the remaining ingredients.

2. Follow the directions in step 3 for Blackberry Frozen Yogurt.

CAL. 91 CARB. 21G PROT. 2.4G
CHOL. 0.6MG FAT 0.2G/2% SOD. 30MG
(ANALYZED PER ½ CUP)

LIME FROZEN YOGURT

MAKES 1 QUART

1 cup nonfat cottage cheese
2 cups nonfat plain yogurt
1 cup lime juice
2 tablespoons lime zest
1½ cups sugar

1. In a blender, process the cottage cheese until smooth.

2. In a large bowl, combine the cottage cheese, yogurt, lime juice, lime zest and sugar and mix well.

3. Follow the directions in step 3 for Blackberry Frozen Yogurt.

CAL. 208 CARB. 47G PROT. 7G
CHOL. 1MG FAT 0.1G/0% SOD. 158MG
(ANALYZED PER ½ CUP)

RASPBERRY FROZEN YOGURT

MAKES 1 QUART

1 cup nonfat cottage cheese
2 cups fresh or frozen
  raspberry puree
1 cup nonfat plain yogurt
1 cup sugar
1 teaspoon vanilla

1. In a blender, process the cottage cheese until smooth.

2. In a large bowl, combine the cottage cheese, raspberry puree, yogurt, sugar, and vanilla and mix well.

3. Follow the directions in step 3 for Blackberry Frozen Yogurt.

CAL. 150 CARB. 32G PROT. 5.6G
CHOL. 0.6MG FAT 0.2G/2%
SOD. 134MG (ANALYZED PER ½ CUP)

CAFE AU LAIT FROZEN YOGURT

MAKES 1 QUART

1 cup nonfat cottage cheese
2 cups nonfat plain yogurt
1 cup sugar
¼ cup brewed coffee or
  espresso
2 teaspoons vanilla
2 tablespoons Kahlúa
  (optional)

1. In a blender, process the cottage cheese until smooth.

2. In a large bowl, combine the cottage cheese, yogurt, and sugar and mix well. Add the coffee to taste and then the vanilla and mix until smooth.

3. Follow the directions in step 3 for Blackberry Frozen Yogurt. When almost frozen, add the Kahlúa, if desired.

CAL. 153 CARB. 31G PROT. 7G
CHOL. 1MG FAT 0.0G/1% SOD. 157MG
(ANALYZED PER ½ CUP)

CHOCOLATE FRANGELICO FROZEN YOGURT

MAKES 1 QUART

1 cup nonfat cottage cheese
1 cup nonfat plain yogurt
½ cup sugar
1 teaspoon vanilla extract
1 vanilla bean, split and
  seeded
½ cup semisweet chocolate
  chips
¼ cup plus 1 tablespoon
  Frangelico liqueur

1. In a blender, process the cottage cheese until smooth.

2. In a large bowl, combine the cottage cheese, yogurt, sugar, vanilla and vanilla seeds and mix well.

3. Follow the directions in step 3 for Blackberry Frozen Yogurt. Just before the yogurt is done, stir in the chocolate chips and the Frangelico.

CAL. 137 CARB. 23G PROT. 6G
CHOL. 0.6MG FAT 3G/20%
SOD. 135MG (ANALYZED PER ½ CUP)

Cultural Crossings

◆

The past decade has exposed us all to wonderful foods from many cultures. The flavors amuse and intrigue. The key to enjoying these tastes is to re-create them with readily accessible ingredients and cooking methods that fit our lifestyles, while erasing the fat whenever and wherever possible. Yes! this is possible to do without losing the integrity of the dishes we've come to love.

Monday
DAY 8

Fresh Orange Juice

Old-Fashioned Oatmeal
with Skim Milk

Whole-wheat Toast

◆

Oriental Chicken Salad*

Seven-grain Roll

Fresh Sliced Strawberries and
Chocolate Chip Bites*

◆

Vegetable Soup

Black Bean Quesadillas* with
Pico de Gallo* and Creamy
Guacamole*

Savvy Spinach Salad*

New German Chocolate Cake*

Breakfast Menu

Foods (per serving)	Cal.	Carb. (g)	Prot. (g)	Chol. (mg)	Fat (g)/%	Sod. (mg)
Orange juice, 6 oz.	83.5	19.4	1.4	0	0.3/3	1.2
Oatmeal, ¾ cup	156	27	7	0	2.6/15	2
Skim milk, ½ cup	43	6	4	2	0.2/4	62
Whole-wheat toast, 1 slice	107	23	4	0	0.4/3	136
MORNING SNACK						
Raspberry Frozen Yogurt* (p. 109)	150	32	5.6	0.6	0.2/2	134

Lunch Menu

Foods (per serving)	Cal.	Carb. (g)	Prot. (g)	Chol. (mg)	Fat (g)/%	Sod. (mg)
Oriental Chicken Salad*	230	19	32	63	3.5/13	2102
Seven-grain roll, 1	93	18	3	0	1.7/15	167
Strawberries, 1 cup	50	12	1	0	0.6/11	1.6
Chocolate Chip Bites* (p. 141), 6	156	24	1.9	7.2	6.6/37	126

Oriental Chicken Salad

112

This is a cool, refreshing chicken salad chock-full of vegetables, laced with ginger and soy.

SERVES 2

1 whole boneless, skinless chicken breast (about 8 ounces)

1 tablespoon plus 2 teaspoons finely minced fresh ginger

5 tablespoons rice wine vinegar

¼ cup soy sauce

1 cup low-fat, low-sodium chicken broth

1 tablespoon finely minced garlic

1 teaspoon Dijon mustard

¼ cup hot water

4 cups mixed greens, such as watercress, Bibb and/or leaf lettuce, arugula and spinach

6 canned baby beets, quartered

10 thin slices cucumber

8 fresh green beans, julienned

2 tablespoons fresh cilantro, minced

1. In a small baking dish, arrange the chicken breast and top with 1 tablespoon ginger, 3 tablespoons rice wine vinegar,

Stuck on sugar?
Try something new!
Per tablespoon:

Honey
64 cal./0g fat

Molasses
54 cal./0g fat

Maple syrup
51 cal./0g fat

Raisins
27 cal./0g fat

Almonds
48 cal./4g fat

Walnuts
52 cal./5g fat

Coconut
26 cal./3g fat

Wheat Germ
27 cal./1g fat

Blueberries
5 cal./.03g fat

Strawberries
3 cal./.03g fat

Bananas
6 cal./.03g fat

Raspberries
4 cal./.04g fat

Dried figs
30 cal./.1g fat

Buttermilk
6 cal./0g fat

Nonfat yogurt
8 cal./0g fat

2 tablespoons soy sauce and the broth. Stir gently, cover and refrigerate to marinate overnight.

2. Preheat the oven to 400°F.

3. Bake the chicken in the marinade for 20 to 25 minutes, until the juices run clear when the meat is pierced with a fork. Allow to cool completely. When cool, shred into bite-sized pieces.

4. In a small bowl, combine the remaining 2 teaspoons ginger, 2 tablespoons vinegar and 2 tablespoons soy sauce with the garlic, mustard and hot water. Mix thoroughly.

5. In another bowl, toss the greens with 2 tablespoons of the dressing to coat. (Save the remaining dressing, refrigerated, for future use.) Divide the greens between 2 plates and top with the beets, cucumber, beans and chicken. Toss gently to combine, sprinkle with cilantro and serve immediately.

CAL. 230   CARB. 19G   PROT. 32G   CHOL. 63MG   FAT 3.5G/13%   SOD. 2102MG

Dinner

Creamy Guacamole

Finally, there's a guacamole that lets us dip into it with some abandon. Others can be 97 percent fat!

MAKES ABOUT 2 CUPS

¼ cup Nonfat Blend (see page 298)
½ avocado, peeled
½ cup finely chopped red onion
2 cups finely chopped tomatoes
1 tablespoon seeded and finely minced jalapeño

1 tablespoon finely minced garlic
2 tablespoons lime juice
¼ cup finely minced cilantro
1 tablespoon finely minced lime zest
Dash of Tabasco

In a blender or using an immersion blender, blend the Nonfat Blend and avocado until smooth. Transfer to a bowl, add the remaining ingredients and mix well. Cover with plastic wrap and refrigerate for at least 1 hour before serving.

CAL. 3   CARB. 0.4G   PRO. 0.1G   CHOL. 0MG   FAT 0.1G/30%   SOD. 0.6MG
(ANALYZED PER 1 TEASPOON)

113
◆

Black Bean Quesadillas

Layers of powerful flavors ooze together to make each bite delicious.

SERVES 2

$1/2$ cup cooked or canned black beans, drained
1 tablespoon finely minced garlic
1 teaspoon low-fat, low-sodium chicken broth
2 tablespoons finely minced fresh cilantro
$1/4$ cup low-fat goat cheese
$1/3$ cup nonfat cottage cheese
Salt and freshly ground black
    pepper to taste
2 large flour tortillas (about
    10 inches)
1 cup stemmed, coarsely chopped
    fresh spinach
$1/4$ cup finely minced red onion
$1/2$ cup salsa (mild, medium or hot)
$1/4$ cup grated part-skim mozzarella

1. Preheat the oven to 425°F. In a small bowl, combine the beans, garlic, broth and cilantro. Using a fork, crush the beans slightly and set aside.

2. In a blender or using an immersion blender, blend the goat cheese and cottage cheese until smooth. Season with salt and pepper and set aside.

3. Spread half of the bean mixture over each tortilla and top with half of the cheese mixture.

4. Sprinkle each tortilla with spinach, onion and salsa. Place one tortilla on a baking sheet and position the other on top of it. Sprinkle with mozzarella and bake for about 12 minutes, or until bubbling and heated through. Serve immediately.

CAL. 342   CARB. 50G   PROT. 20G   CHOL. 18MG   FAT 7.8G/20%   SOD. 620MG

PICO DE GALLO

Here's the salsa that disappears quickly.

MAKES 2 CUPS

$1^1/2$ cups coarsely chopped
    tomatoes
$1/4$ cup coarsely chopped
    onion
$1/4$ teaspoon sugar
1 seeded and finely minced
    jalapeño
1 tablespoon plus 2
    teaspoons fresh lime juice
$1/2$ cup finely minced fresh
    cilantro

In a large mixing bowl, combine all of the ingredients. Cover and chill for at least 1 hour before serving.

CAL. 1.5 CARB. 0.4G PROT. 0.05G
CHOL. 0MG FAT 0G/0% SOD. 10MG
(ANALYZED PER 1 TABLESPOON)

Savvy Spinach Salad

This is as satisfying as ever because the spinach is still combined with the eggs, mushrooms and now turkey ham for a slightly smoky flavor. Missing are bacon, egg yolks (cholesterol) and loads of oil (read fat). Give it a try—I think you'll be surprised at how fresh it tastes.

SERVES 2

4 cups cleaned, stemmed and torn (into bite-sized pieces)
*   fresh spinach*
1 pound mushrooms, stemmed and quartered
½ cup fresh alfalfa or other sprouts
4 hard-boiled egg whites, coarsely chopped
8 scallions, green part only, coarsely chopped
1 ounce turkey ham, julienned (about ¼ cup)
2 tablespoons White Wine Dressing (see page 118)

In a large bowl, toss the spinach, mushrooms, sprouts, egg whites, scallions and turkey ham. Chill for at least 1 hour before serving. Just before serving, add the dressing and toss to coat the leaves. Serve immediately.

CAL. 234   CARB. 34G   PROT. 30G   CHOL. 7.6MG   FAT 3.9G/15%   SOD. 94MG

115

> *"Cuisine is when things taste like themselves."*
> CURNONSKY

EAT YOUR SPINACH

Popeye's beat-em-to-the-punch power source has become a modern-day magic bullet. Eat lots of this dark leafy green loaded with carotenoids and other nutrients to lower your risk of cancer and heart attack. Nobody's given us a magic number, but a cup a day can't hurt.

Dinner Menu

FOODS (PER SERVING)	CAL.	CARB. (G)	PROT. (G)	CHOL. (MG)	FAT (G)/%	SOD. (MG)
Vegetable soup, 1 cup	128	19	14.4	0	0/0	224
Black Bean Quesadillas*	342	50	20	18	7.8/20	620
Pico de Gallo*, ¼ cup	6	1.6	0.2	0	0/0	40
Creamy Guacamole*, 3 T.	27	3.6	0.9	0	0.9/30	5.4
Savvy Spinach Salad*	234	34	30	7.6	3.9/15	94
New German Chocolate Cake* (p. 105)	223	39	3	6	6.9/27	87
Today's Totals	**2029**	**328**	**128**	**107**	**37/16**	**3802**

S A L A D   B A R   S M A R T S

It should be a healthy eater's dream come true—a tempting array of fresh fruits, greens and vegetables—a lush green oasis in a fat-filled world.

Look again: Everything's swimming in mayonnaise, oil or sour cream. There are cold cuts, bacon, olives and artichoke hearts marinated in oil and dressings all loaded with fat. It's a mine field.

Don't skip the salad bar but have the restraint of a saint. It can sabotage the healthiest intentions.

	CAL.	FAT (G)		CAL.	FAT (G)
Avocado, 1 T.	9	1	Orange Dressing*, 1 T.	9	0
Blue cheese dressing, 1 T.	77	8	Pesto Dressing*, 1 T.	17	2
Croutons, 1 T.	11	1	Pine nuts, ½ oz.	80	9
Cucumber slices, 6	12	0	Raisins, 1 T.	27	0
Feta Dressing*, 1 T.	16	1	Ranch dressing, 1 T.	55	6
French dressing, 1 T.	67	6	Real bacon bits, 1 T.	154	15
Fresh tomatoes, 2	40	0	Red onion, 1 T.	10	0
Green beans, 1 T.	8	0	Red wine vinegar, 1 T.	1	0
Green peas, 1 T.	9	0	Roquefort Dressing*, 1 T.	9	0
Greens, 1 cup	10	0	Russian dressing, 1 T.	76	8
Honey dressing, 1 T.	50	3	Shredded Cheddar cheese, 1 T.	25	2
Italian dressing, 1 T.	69	7	Tarragon-Buttermilk Dressing*, 1 T.	7	0
Lemon Dressing*, 1 T.	17	2	Vegetable "bacon" bits, 1 T.	27	2
Lemon juice, 1 T.	4	0	Vinaigrette, classic, 1 T.	69	7
Olives, black, 3	36	3			
Olives, green, 3	21	2			

SASSY SALAD DRESSINGS

Drowning wonderful fresh salad greens with a heavy oil-based or fatty dairy dressing is a common mistake. It can increase your fat intake faster than you can imagine.

Luckily, over the years, I've evolved to where I like my dressings to rely on flavors other than oil. Sometimes I use just a squeeze of lemon or lime juice to wake up the greens. Sometimes I want more intriguing flavors.

All of these dressings have big, intense flavors and so just a tablespoon sprayed or splashed on a cup of greens is delicious. Some of the fat percentages may look high. But check the grams; they're quite low. And remember, you're tossing the dressing over lots of good things.

TOMATO-BASIL DRESSING

MAKES ABOUT ⅔ CUP

⅔ cup buttermilk
2 teaspoons tomato paste
1 tablespoon finely minced
    fresh basil
2 teaspoons finely minced
    garlic
Freshly ground black pepper
    to taste
1 large plum tomato, finely
    chopped
Salt to taste (optional)

In a blender, blend the buttermilk, tomato paste, basil, garlic and pepper until smooth. Stir in the tomatoes. Season with salt, if desired.

Transfer to a jar with a tight-fitting lid and refrigerate until ready to use. Whisk before using.

CAL. 9 CARB. 1G PROT. 0.6G
CHOL. 0.5MG FAT 0.2G/16%
SOD. 24MG (ANALYZED PER 1
TABLESPOON)

WATERCRESS DRESSING

MAKES ABOUT ½ CUP

1 cup watercress
2 scallions, coarsely chopped
1 tablespoon white wine
    vinegar
2 tablespoons low-fat,
    low-sodium chicken broth
1 teaspoon lemon juice

1 teaspoon finely minced
    lemon zest
1 tablespoon hot water
Salt and freshly ground
    black pepper to taste
    (optional)

In a blender, blend the ingredients until smooth. Transfer to a jar with a tight-fitting lid and refrigerate until ready to use. Whisk before using.

CAL. 2.6 CARB. 0.5G PROT. 0.2G
CHOL. 0MG FAT 0.01G/4% SOD. 11MG
(ANALYZED PER 1 TABLESPOON)

WHITE WINE DRESSING

MAKES ABOUT ½ CUP

2 teaspoons finely minced
   orange zest
3 tablespoons orange juice
2 tablespoons white wine
   vinegar
2 teaspoons soy sauce
½ teaspoon Dijon mustard
2 teaspoons sesame oil
1 teaspoon brown sugar
Salt and freshly ground
   black pepper to taste
   (optional)

In a small bowl, combine
the ingredients. Cover and
refrigerate until needed.
Whisk before using.

CAL. 17 CARB. 1.5G PROT. 0.13G
CHOL. 0MG FAT 1.2G/62%
SOD. 93.4MG (ANALYZED PER
1 TABLESPOON)

LEMON DRESSING

MAKES ABOUT ⅓ CUP

1 tablespoon lemon juice
½ teaspoon finely minced
   lemon zest
¼ teaspoon prepared
   horseradish
2 tablespoons hot water
½ teaspoon sugar
2 tablespoons olive oil
Salt and freshly ground
   black pepper to taste
   (optional)

In a small bowl, combine
the lemon juice, lemon zest,
horseradish, hot water and
sugar. Slowly drizzle in the
olive oil, whisking continually, to emulsify. Season
with salt and pepper, if
desired. Cover and refrigerate until ready to use.
Whisk before using.

CAL. 17 CARB. 0.4G PROT. 0.1G
CHOL. 0MG FAT 1.8G/92%
SOD. 0.3MG (ANALYZED PER
1 TABLESPOON)

PESTO DRESSING

MAKES ABOUT ⅔ CUP

3 tablespoons Spinach
   Pesto (see page 86)
3 tablespoons white wine
   vinegar
¼ cup hot water
1 tablespoon olive oil
Salt and freshly ground
   black pepper to taste
   (optional)

In a small bowl, combine
the pesto, vinegar and
water. Slowly drizzle in the
olive oil, whisking continuously, to emulsify. Season
with salt and pepper, if
desired. Cover and refrigerate until ready to use.
Whisk before using.

CAL. 17 CARB. 0.5G PROT. 0.4G
CHOL. 0.4MG FAT 1.5G/80%
SOD. 0.2MG (ANALYZED PER
1 TABLESPOON)

CREAMY PESTO DRESSING

MAKES ABOUT ⅔ CUP

⅔ cup buttermilk
2 tablespoons Spinach
   Pesto (see page 86)
Salt and freshly ground
   black pepper to taste
   (optional)

In a blender, blend the
ingredients until smooth.
Transfer to a jar with a
tight-fitting lid and refrigerate until ready to use.
Whisk before using.

CAL. 9 CARB. 0.9G PROT. 0.7G
CHOL. 0.8MG FAT 0.3G/32%
SOD. 16MG (ANALYZED PER
1 TABLESPOON)

118

SALAD DRESSINGS ...

MANGO CHUTNEY DRESSING

MAKES ABOUT ¾ CUP

⅔ cup nonfat plain yogurt
2 tablespoons mango
   chutney
Salt and freshly ground
   black pepper to taste
   (optional)

In a blender, blend the
ingredients until smooth.
Transfer to a jar with a
tight-fitting lid and refrigerate until ready to use.
Whisk before using.

CAL. 9 CARB. 1G PROT. 0.8G
CHOL. 0.2MG FAT 0.03G/3%
SOD. 10MG (ANALYZED PER
1 TABLESPOON)

FETA DRESSING

MAKES ABOUT ¾ CUP

⅔ cup buttermilk
1 teaspoon finely minced
   garlic
1 tablespoon lemon juice
1 teaspoon finely minced
   lemon zest
3 tablespoons crumbled feta
   cheese
Salt and freshly ground
   black pepper to taste
   (optional)

In a blender, blend the
ingredients until smooth.
Transfer to a jar with a
tight-fitting lid and
refrigerate until ready to
use. Whisk before using.

CAL. 16 CARB. 1G PROT. 1G
CHOL. 3.9MG FAT 0.9G/51%
SOD. 57MG (ANALYZED PER
1 TABLESPOON)

COOL CUCUMBER DRESSING

MAKES ABOUT 1 CUP

⅔ cup nonfat plain yogurt
½ cup peeled and chopped
   cucumber
1 teaspoon finely minced
   garlic
Freshly ground black
   pepper to taste
1 teaspoon lemon juice
2 tablespoons finely minced
   fresh dill
Salt to taste (optional)

In a blender, blend the
ingredients until smooth.
Transfer to a jar with a
tight-fitting lid and refrigerate until ready to use.
Whisk before using.

CAL. 5.4 CARB. 0.7G PROT. 0.4G
CHOL. 0.2MG FAT 0.01G/1% SOD. 7MG
(ANALYZED PER 1 TABLESPOON)

TARRAGON-BUTTERMILK DRESSING

MAKES ABOUT ⅔ CUP

⅔ cup buttermilk
1 teaspoon grated onion
1 teaspoon finely minced
   garlic
Freshly ground black
   pepper to taste
1 teaspoon dried tarragon
Salt to taste (optional)

In a blender, blend the
ingredients until smooth.
Transfer to a jar with a
tight-fitting lid and refrigerate until ready to use.
Whisk before using.

CAL. 7 CARB. 0.9G PROT. 0.6G
CHOL. 0.5MG FAT 0.14G/18%
SOD. 16MG (ANALYZED PER
1 TABLESPOON)

AND STILL MORE

ROQUEFORT DRESSING

MAKES ABOUT ²/₃ CUP

²/₃ cup buttermilk
1 teaspoon dry white wine
1 tablespoon crumbled
  Roquefort cheese
Salt and freshly ground
  black pepper to taste
  (optional)

In a blender, blend the ingredients until smooth. Transfer to a jar with a tight-fitting lid and refrigerate until ready to use. Whisk before using.

CAL. 9 CARB. 7G PROT. 7G
CHOL. 1MG FAT 0.4G/36%
SOD. 29MG (ANALYZED PER
1 TABLESPOON)

ORANGE-GINGER DRESSING

MAKES ABOUT ³/₄ CUP

2 teaspoons finely minced
  fresh ginger
1 teaspoon finely minced
  garlic
6 tablespoons red wine
  vinegar
2 tablespoons orange juice
¼ cup hot water
2 teaspoons olive oil
Salt and freshly ground
  black pepper to taste
  (optional)

In a small mixing bowl, combine the ginger, garlic, vinegar, orange juice and water. Slowly drizzle in the olive oil, whisking continuously, until emulsified. Season with salt and pepper, if desired. Cover and refrigerate until ready to use. Whisk before using.

CAL. 13 CARB. 1.7G PROT. 0.1G
CHOL. 0MG FAT 0.9G./54%
SOD. 13MG (ANALYZED PER
1 TABLESPOON)

TARRAGON-DIJON DRESSING

MAKES ABOUT ³/₄ CUP

¼ cup white wine vinegar
1 teaspoon finely minced
  garlic
6 tablespoons hot water
1 teaspoon Dijon mustard
2 tablespoons finely minced
  fresh tarragon
2 teaspoons olive oil
Salt and freshly ground
  black pepper to taste
  (optional)

In a small bowl, combine the vinegar, garlic, water, mustard and tarragon. Slowly drizzle in the olive oil, whisking continuously, until emulsified. Season with salt and pepper, if desired. Cover and refrigerate until ready to use. Whisk before using.

CAL. 11 CARB. 0.6G PROT. 0.07G
CHOL. 0MG FAT 0.9G/77%
SOD. 13MG (ANALYZED PER
1 TABLESPOON)

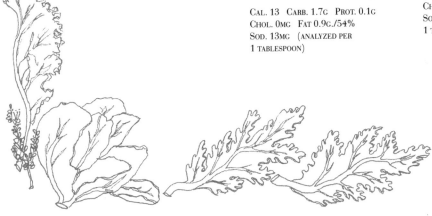

SALAD DRESSINGS

ORANGE-BASIL DRESSING

MAKES ABOUT 1/3 CUP

2 tablespoons orange juice
1/4 cup white wine vinegar
2 tablespoons finely minced
   fresh basil
1 teaspoon finely minced
   garlic
1 teaspoon finely minced
   orange zest
Salt and freshly ground
   black pepper to taste
   (optional)

In a blender, blend the
ingredients until smooth.
Transfer to a jar with a
tight-fitting lid and refrigerate until ready to use.
Whisk before using.

CAL. 3.4 CARB. 0.7G PROT. 0.05G
CHOL. 0MG FAT 0.01G/3%
SOD. 0.09MG (ANALYZED PER
1 TABLESPOON)

SHERRY WINE VINEGAR DRESSING

MAKES ABOUT 1/3 CUP

2 tablespoons sherry wine
   vinegar
3 tablespoons hot water
2 teaspoons capers

1 tablespoon olive oil
Salt and freshly ground
   black pepper to taste
   (optional)

In a small bowl, combine
the vinegar, water and
capers. Slowly drizzle in the
olive oil, whisking continuously, to emulsify. Season
with salt and pepper, if
desired. Cover and refrigerate until ready to use.
Whisk before using.

CAL. 16 CARB. 0.6G PROT. 0.15G
CHOL. 0MG FAT 1.7G/84%
SOD. 75MG (ANALYZED PER
1 TABLESPOON)

ORANGE DRESSING

MAKES 1 SCANT CUP

2/3 cup nonfat plain yogurt
1/4 cup orange juice
1 tablespoon lemon juice
1 teaspoon finely minced
   orange zest
1 teaspoon honey
Salt and freshly ground
   black pepper to taste
   (optional)

In a blender, blend the
ingredients until smooth.
Transfer to a jar with a
tight-fitting lid and refrigerate until ready to use.
Whisk before using.

CAL. 12 CARB. 2G
PROT. 0.8G CHOL. 0.2MG
FAT 0.04G/3% SOD. 11MG
(ANALYZED PER 1 TABLESPOON)

ORANGE-BALSAMIC DRESSING

MAKES ABOUT 1 CUP

1/2 cup orange juice
1/2 cup balsamic vinegar
1 tablespoon finely minced
   garlic
1/4 teaspoon freshly ground
   black pepper
2 tablespoons sugar
1 tablespoon finely minced
   orange zest
Salt to taste (optional)

In a small bowl, combine
the ingredients. Cover and
refrigerate until ready to
use. Whisk before using.

CAL. 12 CARB. 3G PROT. 0G
CHOL. 0MG FAT 0G/0% SOD. 0.4MG
(ANALYZED PER 1 TABLESPOON)

Balancing Act

◆

An insatiable curiosity is what drives most creative cooks. Every day offers endless possibilities for flavor combinations. The trick to feeling confident in the kitchen is first to imagine the taste of the dish you're trying to create, and then understand the taste of each ingredient at its peak of ripeness. Next, taste the ingredients as they cook and then again after each flavoring addition. Cooking with these ingredients soon becomes second nature and you will find yourself creating your very own taste sensations.

Tuesday
DAY 9

Cran-Raspberry Juice

English Muffin with
Honey and Peanut Butter

◆

Turkey, Tomato and Pesto Sandwich*

Chef's Salad

Crispy Pretzels

◆

Artichoke with Lemon Dipping
Sauce*

Salad Greens with Watercress
Dressing*

Tuscan Potatoes*

Grilled Veal Chops with
Roasted Garlic Puree*

Green Beans

Italian Bread

Honeydew Melon

Breakfast Menu

FOODS (PER SERVING)	CAL.	CARB. (G)	PROT. (G)	CHOL. (MG)	FAT (G)/%	SOD. (MG)
Cran-Raspberry Juice, 6 oz.	110	27	0	0	0/0	15
English muffin, 1, with peanut butter, ½ T., and honey, 1 T. (below)	231	44	7	0	5/19	240
Skim milk, ½ cup	43	6	4	2.2	0.2/4	62
MORNING SNACK						
Green grapes, 1 cup	114	29	1	0	0.9/7	3

The Peanut Butter Puzzle

	CAL.	CARB. (G)	PROT. (G)	CHOL. (MG)	FAT (G)/%	SOD. (MG)
HIGH-FAT PEANUT BUTTER BREAKFAST						
English muffin	120	25	4	0	1/8	200
1 T. honey	64	17	0.7	0	0/0	1
1 T. chunky peanut butter	94	4	4	0	8/77	78
Total	**279**	**46**	**9**	**0**	**9/29**	**279**
PREFERRED PEANUT BUTTER BREAKFAST						
English muffin with 1 T. honey and ½ T. peanut butter mixed with ½ T. water	231	44	7	0	5/19	240
PEANUT BUTTER ANALYSIS						
1 T. chunky unsalted	94	4	4	0	8/77	43
1 T. smooth	94	3	4	0	8/77	76
1 T. smooth unsalted	96	3	4	0	8/75	43
1 T. natural	94	3	4	0	8/77	96
1 T. natural unsalted	94	3	4	0	8/77	28

Turkey, Tomato and Pesto Sandwich

You won't even think about the "missing" mayonnaise here!!

S E R V E S   2

1 tablespoon Nonfat Blend (see page 298)
1 tablespoon Spinach Pesto (see page 86)
4 slices nonfat French bread
2 red bell peppers, roasted and sliced
*   into strips (see page 107)*
2 ounces fresh turkey breast slices
1 large plum tomato, thinly sliced
1 cup torn green leaf lettuce

In a small bowl, combine the Nonfat Blend and Spinach Pesto until smooth. Spread evenly over the bread. Layer the red peppers, turkey, tomato and lettuce on 2 slices. Top with the remaining bread slices and serve.

CAL. 266   CARB. 44G   PROT. 16G   CHOL. 14MG   FAT 3.3G/11%   SOD. 466MG

125
◆

PEANUT BUTTER AND HONEY

My favorite breakfast treat was always a toasted English muffin thickly spread with peanut butter and a drizzle of honey. But when I saw the nutritional analysis, I was shocked!

Now I stretch the peanut butter over two English muffin halves by mixing ½ tablespoon of warm water into ½ tablespoon of chunky peanut butter in a small bowl. It sounds odd, but it works to cut the fat.

On the opposite page is a look at that shocking nutritional analysis, which caught my eye, followed by the preferable alternative. I've then listed the nutritional profile of peanut butters in general.

Lunch Menu

FOODS (PER SERVING)	CAL.	CARB. (G)	PROT. (G)	CHOL. (MG)	FAT (G)/%	SOD. (MG)
Turkey, Tomato and Pesto Sandwich*	266	44	16	14	3.3/11	466
Chef's Salad						
Salad greens, 2 cups	19	3.2	1.8	0	0.2/11	28
Red onion, 3 slices	6.8	1.4	0.4	0	0.07/4	1.0
Cucumber, ½ cup	7.5	0.9	1.6	0	0.07/2	29
Monterey Jack, 1 oz.	105	0.2	7	25	8.5/73	152
Tomatoes	26	5.7	1	0	0.04/1	11
3 olives, ripe	15	0.9	0	0	1.2/72	105
Turkey ham, 1 oz.	30	0.5	4.5	17.5	1.3/38	330
Pretzels, 1 oz., low-sodium	110	22	4	0	0/0	340
AFTERNOON SNACK						
Carrots, 2 oz.	24	6	0.6	0	0.1/2	69
Celery, 2 oz.	9	2	0.4	0	0.1/10	49

Lemon Dipping Sauce

This is great served as a replacement for lemon-butter sauce for dipping asparagus, artichokes or green beans.

MAKES ABOUT ⅓ CUP

2 tablespoons low-fat, low-sodium
   chicken broth
3 tablespoons lemon juice
1 teaspoon finely minced lemon
   zest
1 teaspoon unsalted butter, melted
1 teaspoon olive oil

Whisk together the broth, juice and zest. Slowly add the butter and oil, continually whisking until emulsified. Serve at room temperature.

CAL. 18   CARB. 0.9G   PROT. 0.1G   CHOL. 2MG   FAT 1.7G/79%   SOD. 14.2MG
(ANALYZED PER 1 TABLESPOON)

126
◆

Grilled Veal Chops
with Roasted Garlic Puree

SERVES 2

Two 6- to 8-ounce loin veal chops, about 1 inch thick
2 tablespoons balsamic vinegar
1 tablespoon Roasted Garlic
   Puree (see page 298)

1. Preheat the grill or broiler.

2. Brush the chops on both sides with the vinegar. Grill or broil about 3 inches from the heat for 2 to 3 minutes on each side. Top each chop with ½ table-spoon Roasted Garlic Puree, which will melt from the heat of the chop. Serve immediately.

CAL. 280   CARB. 1.7G   PROT. 43G   CHOL. 172MG
FAT 10.2G/26%   SOD. 156MG

THE OIL OF CHOICE

Evidence continues to mount in favor of olive oil. A monounsaturated fat, it has a role in lowering total blood and LDL cholesterol and maintaining HDL cholesterols—all of which decrease the risk of heart attack. And a recent survey in Greece* showed that women who consumed olive oil and lots of fruits and vegetables had a lower risk of breast cancer.

A study of American and Canadian women linked a diet high in saturated fats and low in vegetables to a higher risk of ovarian cancer.

*Harvard School of Public Health—Dr. Dimitrious Trichopoulos

Tuscan Potatoes

This recipe is a classic that is usually tossed with loads of olive oil, which is truly unnecessary; a light coating will do.

SERVES 2

1 pound small red new potatoes
1 tablespoon finely minced garlic
1 teaspoon olive oil
¼ cup minced stemmed fresh mint
Kosher or sea salt and freshly ground black pepper to taste

1. Preheat the oven to 350°F.

2. Scrub the potatoes, place in a shallow roasting pan and roast for 1 hour. While still hot, halve or quarter any that are not bite-sized.

3. Immediately transfer the hot potatoes to a medium bowl. Toss with the garlic, oil, mint and salt and pepper. Taste and adjust the seasonings. Serve immediately or at room temperature.

CAL. 201   CARB. 42G   PROT. 4G   CHOL. 0MG   FAT 2.5G/11%   SOD. 13MG

> *"Eating an artichoke is like getting to know someone really well."*
> WILLI HASTINGS

IT'S ALL IN ZEST

Citrus skin is loaded with aromatic oils. Use a zester to skim the flavorful, colorful peel and leave the bitter pith behind. A utensil with fine tiny holes, the zester can easily be held in one hand while the other rotates the fruit.

Dinner Menu

FOODS (PER SERVING)	CAL.	CARB. (G)	PROT. (G)	CHOL. (MG)	FAT (G)/%	SOD. (MG)
Artichoke, 1 whole	60	13	4	0	0.2/2	114
Lemon Dipping Sauce*, 2 T.	36	1.8	0.2	4	3.4/79	28.4
Salad greens, 1 cup	9.5	1.6	0.9	0	0.1/11	14
Watercress Dressing* (p. 117), 1 T.	2.6	0.5	0.2	0	0.1/4	11
Tuscan Potatoes*	201	42	4	0	2.5/11	13
Grilled Veal Chops with Roasted Garlic Puree* (p. 298)	280	1.7	43	172	10.2/26	156
Green beans, 1 cup	22	1	1	0	0.2/8	2
Italian bread, 1 slice	96	18	3	0	1/10	213
Honeydew melon, ¼	80	19	1	0	0.2/2	22
Today's Totals	**1904**	**291**	**107**	**234**	**39/18**	**2563**

Food on the Run

◆

Time is our most precious commodity. Key to today's cooking is that marketing be easy and recipes can be done in short order. Flavors should be intense, so that when you finish, you feel satisfied but never overstuffed. This approach leaves time for the truly important things in your life.

Wednesday
DAY 10

Fresh Orange Juice
Cinnamon Toast*
Fruit Yogurt
Great Granola*

◆

White Lightning Chicken Chili*
Crisp Breadsticks
Red Berries Fruit Salad*

◆

Seasonal Green Salad with
Cool Cucumber Dressing*
Spicy Shrimp Pasta*
Parmesan Toast*
A Perfectly Ripened Pear
and Parmesan

Breakfast Menu

FOODS (PER SERVING)	CAL.	CARB. (G)	PROT. (G)	CHOL. (MG)	FAT (G)/%	SOD. (MG)
Orange juice, 6 oz.	83.5	19.4	1.4	0	0.3/3	1.2
Cinnamon Toast* (p. 57), 2	130	4	28	0	0/0	182
Fruit yogurt, 6 oz.	180	33	8	10	1.5/8	105
Great Granola* (p. 64), 2 T.	141	28	3.6	0	2.3/16	28

Bread Spreads

Bread essentially becomes new when you do not automatically smear it with butter. Its texture, flavor and crunchy crust all take on a new dimension. Next time, taste the bread before you spread.

ONE TABLESPOON	CAL.	FAT (G)/%
Olive oil	119	14/100
Butter	102	12/100
Mayonnaise	99	11/100
Cream cheese	101	10/89
Chunky peanut butter	94	8/77
Neufchâtel cream cheese	38	3/71
Mustard	11	0.7/57
Apple butter	32	0.1/3
Blended nonfat cottage cheese	10	0/0
Honey	64	0/0
Raspberry jam	36	0/0
Salsa	2	0/0

Lunch Menu

FOODS (PER SERVING)	CAL.	CARB. (G)	PROT. (G)	CHOL. (MG)	FAT (G)/%	SOD. (MG)
White Lightning Chicken Chili*	455	50	52	88	5.5/11	165
Breadsticks, 2	160	26	12	0	4/22	420
Red Berries Fruit Salad*	116	28	1.4	0	0.8/6	3
AFTERNOON SNACK						
Apple, 3½ oz.	59	15	0.2	0	0.4/6	0
Peanut butter, 1 T.	94	3	4	0	8/77	22

130

BREAD ALONE

At one time in America, if you wanted good bread, you had to bake it yourself. Luckily, as we've gotten busier, great local bakeries have sprung up everywhere. The bakery shelf has become a complex place: white, rye, oat bran, sourdough, French, Italian, challah, whole-grain, multi-grain, cracked wheat, stone-ground—it's a dizzying array.

But just because all breads are complex carbohydrates doesn't mean they're equally good for you. Look for whole wheat or some other whole-grain or multi-grain as the first ingredient. That's the source of the real fiber— and the real benefit, not to mention great texture and flavor. Low-fat, nonfat, low-sodium and low-sugar are also high priorities.

RED BERRIES FRUIT SALAD

Strawberries laced with lemon and orange become more intensely flavored and juicier, requiring less sugar to bring out their lusciousness.

SERVES 2

1½ pints strawberries, cleaned and cut into halves
1 tablespoon frozen lemonade concentrate
1 teaspoon frozen orange juice concentrate
1 tablespoon plus 1 teaspoon sugar
3 ounces raspberries, for garnish

1. Place the strawberries in a bowl, setting aside ¼ cup of strawberries.

2. In a blender, blend the lemonade and orange juice concentrates, sugar and the reserved ¼ cup strawberries until smooth. Pour the strawberries in the bowl, top with sauce and garnish with raspberries.

CAL. 116 CARB. 28G PROT. 1.4G
CHOL. 0MG FAT 0.8G/6% SOD. 3MG

"Honest bread is very well—it's the butter that makes temptation."
JERROLD

White Lightning Chicken Chili

This is a most flavorful and satisfying chili, sparked by the flavors of the Southwest: garlic, chili peppers, cumin and the fresh zing of limes and cilantro.

SERVES 2

1½ cups plus 2 tablespoons low-fat, low-sodium chicken broth
¾ cup chopped onion
2 teaspoons minced garlic
2 teaspoons minced jalapeño
½ teaspoon dried oregano
Pinch of cayenne
½ teaspoon ground cumin
Pinch of ground cloves
2 cups cooked or canned Great Northern white beans, drained
1 tablespoon lime juice
8 ounces skinless, boneless chicken breast, poached and shredded into bite-sized pieces (see page 85)
2 tablespoons chopped fresh cilantro or dill
1 tablespoon grated Parmesan cheese

1. In a medium soup pot, heat 2 tablespoons broth over medium-high heat. Add the onion and sauté for about 5 minutes, until translucent. Add the garlic, jalapeño, oregano, cayenne, cumin and cloves. Sauté, stirring occasionally, for about 3 minutes, until fragrant.

2. Add the beans, lime juice and remaining 1½ cups broth and bring to a brisk simmer. Reduce the heat and simmer gently, covered, for 30 minutes. Add the chicken, adjust the seasonings, and heat through.

3. Add the cilantro and stir gently. Ladle into soup bowls, garnish with Parmesan cheese and serve immediately.

CAL. 455 CARB. 50G PROT. 52G CHOL. 88MG FAT 5.5G/11%
SOD. 165MG

131
◆

Spicy Shrimp Pasta

Generally in this dish, shrimp and linguine swim in a sea of olive oil, but for this moist and very tasty pasta, I use just one teaspoon of olive oil—enough to deepen the flavors and satisfy completely.

SERVES 2

¼ pound dried Italian linguine
¾ cup low-fat, low-sodium chicken broth
8 large shrimp, peeled and halved lengthwise
2 tablespoons finely minced garlic
2 plum tomatoes, chopped (about 1 cup)
⅛ to ¼ teaspoon crushed red pepper flakes, or to taste
1 teaspoon olive oil
2 tablespoons finely minced fresh Italian parsley

1. In a large saucepan, bring 4 quarts of water to a boil and cook the pasta for 8 to 10 minutes, until tender but firm to the bite.

2. Meanwhile, heat 2 tablespoons of the chicken broth in a large skillet over medium-high heat and add the shrimp and 1 table-spoon garlic. Sauté for 1 to 2 minutes, add the tomatoes and season with red pepper flakes. Cook for 1 minute longer, until the shrimp are firm and pink.

3. Add the remaining broth, the oil, parsley and the remaining 1 tablespoon garlic and stir.

4. Drain the pasta and add it to the sauce. Toss thoroughly and serve immediately.

CAL. 304   CARB. 52G   PROT. 15G   CHOL. 47MG   FAT 4G/11%   SOD. 65MG

Dinner Menu

FOODS (PER SERVING)	CAL.	CARB. (G)	PROT. (G)	CHOL. (MG)	FAT (G)/%	SOD. (MG)
Salad greens, 1 cup	9.5	1.6	0.9	0	0.1/11	14
Cool Cucumber Dressing* (p. 119), 1 T.	5.4	0.7	0.4	0.2	0.01/1	7
Spicy Shrimp Pasta*	304	52	15	47	4/11	65
Parmesan Toast*, 2 slices	154	16	8	10	6/39	410
Pear, 1	98	25	0.7	0	0.7/6	1
Parmesan cheese, 1 oz.	56	0.5	6	10	4/60	232
Today's Totals	**2046**	**303**	**141**	**165**	**38/17**	**1661**

PARMESAN TOAST

These are crisp, crunchy, habit-forming and perfectly delightful with soups and salads. Be as spicy as you dare.

MAKES 24 SLICES

Twenty-four ¼-inch-thick slices Italian or French bread
2 tablespoons canola oil
Crushed red pepper flakes to taste
1½ cups fresh Parmesan shards (see page 67)

1. Set the bread out to dry overnight on baking sheets.

2. Preheat the oven to 500° F. Lay the bread on foil-covered baking sheets. Lightly brush each slice with oil and sprinkle with red pepper flakes. Cover with cheese. Bake for 1 minute.

3. Smooth the partially melted cheese with a knife and bake for 1 minute more, or until the cheese just begins to bubble. Cool before serving.

CAL. 77   CARB. 8G   PROT. 4G
CHOL. 5MG   FAT 3G/39%
SOD. 205MG (ANALYZED PER SLICE)

Five Fruits a Day

FRUITS	AMOUNT	CAL.	VIT.A	VIT.C	POTASS.	FIBER
Asian pear	1	95		x	x	x
Apple, with skin	1	81		x	x	x
Apricots	4	101	x	x	x	x
Bananas	1	105	x	x	x	x
Blackberries	1 cup	74		x	x	x
Blueberries	1 cup	82		x		x
Cantaloupe	¼	57	x	x	x	
Cherries, sweet	1 cup	104	x	x		x
Figs	1	37	x	x		x
Grapefruit, red or pink	½	37	x	x		
Grapes, green	30	90		x	x	x
Honeydew melon	¼	80		x	x	
Kiwi	1	46		x	x	x
Mango	½	68	x	x		x
Nectarines	1	67	x	x	x	x
Oranges	1	62	x	x	x	x
Papaya	1	117	x	x	x	x
Peaches	1	37	x	x	x	x
Pears	1	98		x	x	x
Pineapple	1 cup	77		x	x	x
Plums	1	36	x	x	x	x
Pomegranates	1	104	n/a	x	x	x
Raspberries	1 cup	61		x	x	x
Rhubarb, cooked	1 cup	42		*		n/a
Star fruit	1	42	x	x	x	n/a
Strawberries	1 cup	45		x	x	x
Tangerines	1	37	x	x	x	x
Watermelon	1 cup	50	x	x	x	x

x = contains at least 10% of the RDA
n/a = not available

FIVE FRUITS A DAY

(AVERAGE NUMBER OF CALORIES PER SERVING)

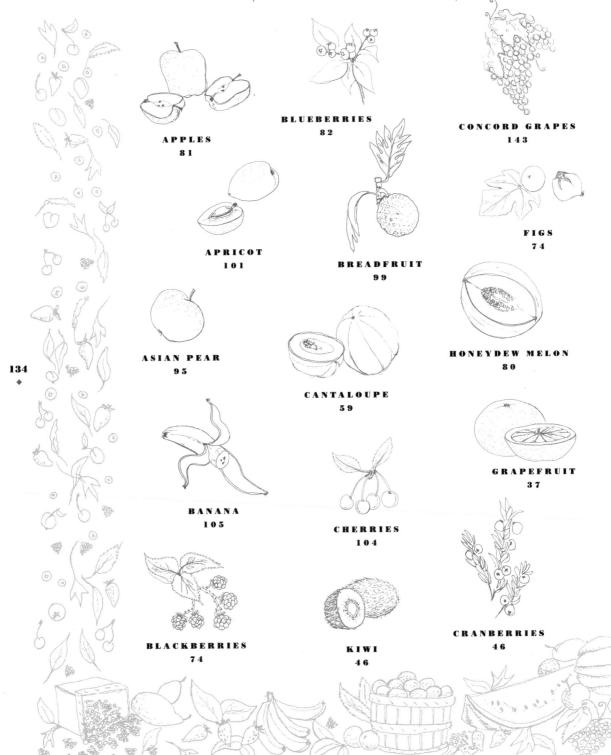

APPLES
81

BLUEBERRIES
82

CONCORD GRAPES
143

APRICOT
101

BREADFRUIT
99

FIGS
74

ASIAN PEAR
95

CANTALOUPE
59

HONEYDEW MELON
80

BANANA
105

CHERRIES
104

GRAPEFRUIT
37

BLACKBERRIES
74

KIWI
46

CRANBERRIES
46

134
◆

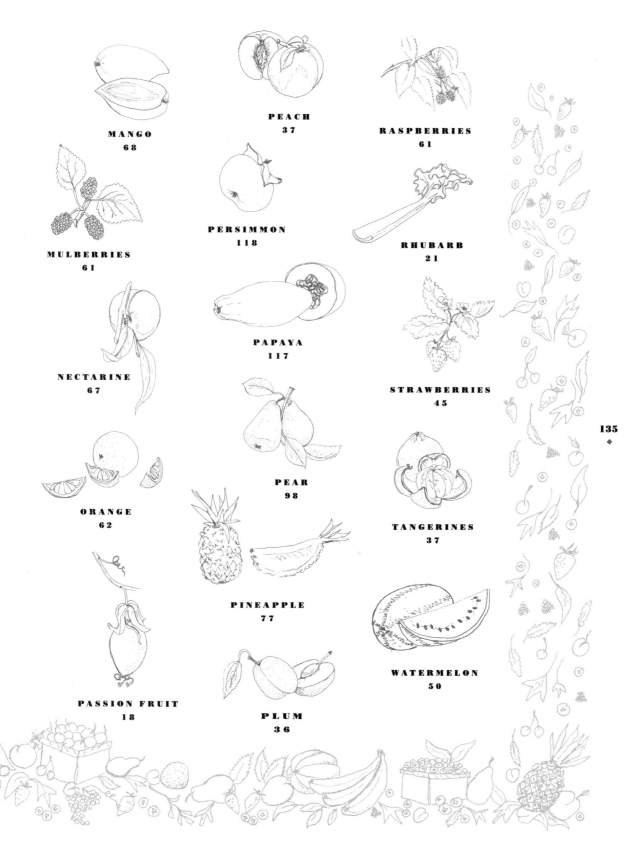

MANGO
68

PEACH
37

RASPBERRIES
61

MULBERRIES
61

PERSIMMON
118

RHUBARB
21

NECTARINE
67

PAPAYA
117

STRAWBERRIES
45

ORANGE
62

PEAR
98

TANGERINES
37

PASSION FRUIT
18

PINEAPPLE
77

PLUM
36

WATERMELON
50

135
♦

Good Fun, Great Food

Having people over for a bite during the week used to seem overwhelming, but now that casualness is chic, it's much easier. Just fix your own favorites and add a few special touches for friends. By doing what comes naturally, entertaining really conveys your most personal style, and you can do it all with the back of your hand.

Thursday
DAY 11

Strawberry Smoothie*
Great Granola* with Skim Milk
Whole-wheat Toast

◆

Hot and Sour Soup*
Caesar Salad with Pepper Croutons*
French Bread

◆

Gazpacho Salad*
Broiled Lamb Chop
One-Two-Three Potatoes*
Asparagus Spears with Parmesan
Shards
Creamy Warm Berries*
and Chocolate Chip Bites*

Breakfast Menu

Foods (per serving)	Cal.	Carb. (g)	Pro. (g)	Chol. (mg)	Fat (g)/%	Sod. (mg)
Strawberry Smoothie* (p. 74)	204	49	3	0	0.2/5	4
Great Granola* (p. 64), ½ cup	282	56	7	0	5/16	57
Skim milk, ½ cup	43	6	4	2	0.2/4	62
Whole-wheat toast, 1 slice	107	23	4	0	0.4/3	136
MORNING SNACK						
Orange juice, 6 oz.	83.5	19.4	1.4	0	0.3/3	1.2

Lunch Menu

Foods (per serving)	Cal.	Carb. (g)	Prot. (g)	Chol. (mg)	Fat (g)/%	Sod. (mg)
Hot and Sour Soup*	102	18	4	0	0.4/3	392
Caesar Salad with Pepper Croutons* (p. 79)	218	29	16	14	6.5/25	546
French bread, 1 slice	96	18	3	0	1/9	213
AFTERNOON SNACK						
Spinach Dip* (p. 162), 2 T.	24	18	3	0.6	0.2/6	96
Carrots, baby, ¼ lb.	43	9	1	0	0.6/12	40

"I don't wait for moods. You accomplish nothing if you do that. Your mind must know it has got to get down to earth."

PEARL S. BUCK

138

Hot and Sour Soup

This Sichuan favorite, loaded with big flavor, is really quite easy
to make at home. It's also a great base to which you may add
a variety of interesting Chinese greens.

SERVES 4

4 cups low-fat, low-sodium chicken broth
1 ounce dried mushrooms (porcini or shiitake)
1½ tablespoons rice wine vinegar
6 tablespoons dry sherry
1½ tablespoons soy sauce
¼ to ½ teaspoon crushed red pepper flakes
1 tablespoon finely minced garlic
1½ teaspoons finely minced ginger
4 ounces fresh button mushrooms, stemmed and quartered
*One half 15-ounce can bamboo shoots, drained and finely
    julienned (about ½ cup)*
2 tablespoons cornstarch

- *2 tablespoons water*
- *5 large scallions, green parts only, chopped (about ½ cup)*
- *½ cup firm tofu, cut into ¼-inch cubes (optional)*

1. In a small saucepan, bring 1 cup of the chicken broth to a boil over medium-high heat. Add the dried mushrooms, cover, remove from the heat and let the mushrooms plump for 1 hour. Drain, reserve the soaking liquid and chop the mushrooms fine.

2. In a large stockpot, combine 3 cups of the broth, vinegar, sherry, soy sauce, red pepper flakes to taste, garlic, ginger and reserved mushroom soaking liquid. Bring just to a boil over medium-high heat, reduce the heat and simmer, uncovered, for 15 to 20 minutes, until the flavors blend. Add the chopped mushrooms, button mushrooms and bamboo shoots and simmer for about 15 minutes longer, until the bamboo shoots are tender.

3. In a small bowl, dissolve the cornstarch in the water and stir until smooth. Stir into the soup to thicken it slightly. Add the scallions and tofu, if desired, heat through and serve immediately.

CAL. 102   CARB. 18G   PROT. 4G   CHOL. 0MG   FAT 0.4G/3%   SOD. 392MG

139
◆

GREAT GREENS

The variety of greens available in the United States seems to multiply from day to day. Don't let them intimidate you. Pass them up and you'll miss all the fun!

When in doubt, take a leafy stranger home for dinner. Toss some into a simple salad. To taste it warm, sauté a bit in olive oil and chicken broth. Stir-fry. Wilt it as a bed for fish or simmer it in soup.

Bok choy: This has white stems and green leaves—both are delicate and edible. Look for baby bok choy.

Chinese cabbage: Barrel-shaped napa and more elongated michihili are mild and crunchy.

Choy sum: Slightly bitter, the stems are more tender than the leaves. The tiny yellow flowers are edible, too.

Mizuna: It means "water vegetable" because the stalks are very juicy. Use baby leaves in salads; mature ones are better cooked.

Green mustard: There are many varieties, with leaves of different shapes. The flavor is always pungent.

Red mustard: The flavor is similar to hot wasabi.

Pea shoots: These are the tendrils and top few leaves of the snow pea plant. The delicate pea flavor comes through raw, steamed or stir-fried.

Tatsoi: This is a ground-hugging member of the bok choy family, with thick dark green leaves that grow like rose petals. Slightly bitter, it's great raw. It adds sparkle to soups when tossed in at the last minute.

Gazpacho Salad

By leaving the Spanish soup chunky, I have created a salad filled with zippy flavor—an idea borrowed from the original *Settlement Cookbook.*

SERVES 4

2 small cucumbers, sliced very thin
4 scallions, white bulb and 3 inches of green,
*   coarsely chopped*
4 plum tomatoes, cut into bite-sized pieces
1 orange or yellow bell pepper, seeds and
*   membrane removed, diced (about*
*   ½ cup)*
¼ cup finely minced Italian parsley
2 tablespoons finely minced garlic
1 cup low-sodium tomato juice
2 teaspoons red wine vinegar
Dash of Tabasco sauce
Salt and freshly ground black pepper to
*   taste*
4 cups dark green leaves, such as spinach, watercress or
*   arugula, washed, stemmed and dried*

1. In a medium-sized bowl, combine the cucumbers, scallions, tomatoes, pepper and parsley and toss lightly.

2. In a small bowl, combine the garlic, tomato juice, vinegar and Tabasco and mix with a fork. Season with salt and pepper.

3. Drizzle the dressing over the salad and toss well. Divide the greens among 4 salad plates, top with the dressed vegetables and serve immediately.

CAL. 70   CARB. 15G   PROT. 4G   CHOL. 0MG   FAT 0.6G/7.7%   SOD. 194MG

ONE-TWO-THREE POTATOES

These crispy potatoes are loaded with golden garlic and require no effort at all! I love these!

SERVES 4

1 pound small russet
*   potatoes, quartered*
1 tablespoon plus 1
*   teaspoon olive oil*
¼ cup finely minced garlic
2 tablespoons chopped
*   fresh parsley*
Salt and freshly ground
*   black pepper to taste*

1. Preheat the oven to 375°F.

2. Place the potatoes in a 9 × 12-inch baking dish and toss with the oil. Roast for 25 minutes, stirring several times. Add the garlic, toss and cook for 5 to 10 minutes, until the garlic is tender and beginning to brown.

3. Toss with the parsley, season with salt and pepper and serve immediately.

CAL. 153   CARB. 26G   PROT. 3G
CHOL. 0MG   FAT 4.6G/27%
SOD. 10MG

CHOCOLATE CHIP BITES

These are chock-full of crunch and chocolate flavor—but not loaded with calories, cholesterol or fat.

MAKES ABOUT 175 COOKIES

1 cup packed light brown sugar
3/4 cup granulated sugar
1/2 cup canola oil
1 large egg
2 large egg whites
2 1/4 cups all-purpose flour
1 teaspoon baking soda
1 teaspoon salt
1 1/2 cups semisweet chocolate chips

1. Preheat the oven to 375°F. Lightly spray 2 baking sheets with vegetable oil spray.

2. In the mixing bowl of an electric mixer set on medium-high speed, cream the sugars, oil, egg and egg whites until smooth. Add the flour, baking soda and salt and mix on medium speed until blended. Stir in the chocolate chips.

3. Drop the dough in 1/2-teaspoon amounts 1 inch apart on the sheets. Bake for 7 to 9 minutes, or until lightly brown. Cool on wire racks. Repeat until all the dough is used.

CAL. 26 CARB. 4G PROT. 0.32G
CHOL. 1.2MG FAT 1.1G/37%
SOD. 21MG (ANALYZED PER COOKIE)

Creamy Warm Berries

Berries laced with cream and sugar are warmed ever so gently.

SERVES 4

6 tablespoons nonfat sour cream
3 tablespoons packed light brown sugar
2 cups fresh mixed berries, such as
    strawberries (quartered), raspberries and
    blackberries

1. Preheat the broiler.

2. In a bowl, combine the sour cream and brown sugar. Add the berries and toss gently to coat.

3. Cut two 15-inch-long pieces of aluminum foil and stack on top of each other. Make a basket by rolling the edges of the foil up and over. Pour the berries onto the foil. Broil for 2 to 3 minutes 6 inches from the heat source, or until bubbling. Serve immediately.

NOTE: You can broil the berries in a shallow broiling pan instead of the aluminum foil basket.

CAL. 66   CARB. 16G   PROT. 2G   CHOL. 0MG   FAT 0.3G/4%   SOD. 18MG

Dinner Menu

FOODS (PER SERVING)	CAL.	CARB. (G)	PROT. (G)	CHOL. (MG)	FAT (G)/%	SOD. (MG)
Gazpacho Salad*	70	15	4	0	0.6/7.7	194
Broiled lamb chop, 4 oz.	245	0	34	108	11/40	95
One-Two-Three Potatoes*	153	26	3	0	4.6/27	10
Asparagus spears, 6, with Parmesan shards, 1 T.	49	4	4	4.9	2/37	117
Breadsticks, 2	160	26	12	0	4/22	420
Creamy Warm Berries*	66	16	2	0	0.3/4	18
Chocolate Chip Bites*, 2	52	8	0.64	2.4	2.2/37	42
EVENING SNACK						
Popcorn (air-popped), 2 cups	61	13	2	0	0.7/10	0.6
Today's Totals	**2056**	**353**	**108**	**132**	**41/18**	**2399**

All-American Favorites

◆

Crisp, clean-tasting American food favorites always taste great. They seem to taste fresh and new each time we take a bite. They're like old friends; they just wear well.

Friday
DAY 12

Fresh Orange Juice

Shredded Wheat or Your Favorite
Cereal with Skim Milk

Banana Muffins*

◆

Forty-Carat Carrot Soup*

A Great Tuna Salad Sandwich*

Crisp Waldorf Salad*

Fresh Strawberries

◆

Tomato and Basil Pizza*

Great Greens with Pesto Dressing*

Breadsticks

Cantaloupe Frozen Yogurt*

Breakfast Menu

Foods (per serving)	Cal.	Carb. (g)	Prot. (g)	Chol. (mg)	Fat (g)/%	Sod. (mg)
Orange juice, 6 oz.	83.5	19.4	1.4	0	0.3/3	1.2
Shredded Wheat, 1 cup	170	41	5	0	0.5/0.3	0
Skim milk, 1 cup	86	12	8	4	0.4/4	124
Banana Muffin*	140	27	1.3	0.1	3.3/21	171
MORNING SNACK						
Orange, 1	62	16	1	0	0.2/3	0
Graham crackers, 2 whole	120	25	2	0	1.5/11	210

Banana Muffins

These light and moist banana muffins are great right out of the oven.

MAKES 18 MUFFINS

*3 ripe bananas, mashed
  (about 1¹/₃ cups)*
1 cup sugar
¹/₄ cup canola oil
*1 cup unsweetened
  applesauce*

1¹/₂ cups cake flour
¹/₂ cup all-purpose flour
2 teaspoons baking soda
1 teaspoon baking powder
3 tablespoons buttermilk
1 tablespoon vanilla extract

1. Preheat the oven to 400°F. Lightly spray standard-sized muffin tins with vegetable oil spray.

2. In a large bowl, combine the bananas, sugar, oil and applesauce. Add the flours, baking soda and baking powder and mix just until blended. Add the buttermilk and vanilla and stir gently; do not overmix.

3. Fill the muffin cups two-thirds full and bake for 5 minutes. Reduce the temperature to 350°F. and bake for 15 to 20 minutes, or until a toothpick inserted in the center of a muffin comes out clean. Turn the muffins out onto wire racks to cool completely.

NOTE: See page 84 for information on standard-sized muffin tins and on using paper liners.

CAL. 140   CARB. 27G   PROT. 1.3G   CHOL. 0.1MG   FAT 3.3G/21%
SOD. 171MG   (ANALYZED PER MUFFIN)

"Life is like a banana, to be peeled and savored."
DONNA "BANANA" LEONARD

144

Foods (per serving)	Cal.	Carb. (g)	Prot. (g)	Chol. (mg)	Fat (g)/%	Sod. (mg)
Forty-Carat Carrot Soup*	87	17	3	0	0.3/3	28
A Great Tuna Salad Sandwich*	225	24	18	27	7.7/29	496
Crisp Waldorf Salad*	244	52	5	3	4/14	69
Strawberries, ½ cup	25	6	0.5	0	0.3/11	0.8
AFTERNOON SNACK						
Wickwood Gorp* (p. 300), ¼ cup	163	18	5	0.1	11/61	2

OPEN-FACE TUNA MELT

SERVES 4

Tuna salad mixture
4 slices nonfat multi-grain bread
2 ounces part-skim mozzarella cheese, thinly sliced

1. Preheat the broiler.

2. Divide the tuna salad among the bread slices and cover evenly with the mozzarella. Broil for 3 to 5 minutes, until the cheese is bubbling and golden. Serve immediately.

CAL. 218 CARB. 15G PROT. 20G
CHOL. 32MG FAT 9.6G/39%
SOD. 454MG

*"We all live
in suspense,
from day to day,
from hour to hour;
in other words,
we are the hero of
our own story."*
MARY McCARTHY

A Great Tuna Salad Sandwich

This never grows old and always tastes fresh. Sometimes I add green grapes or chunks of pineapple or cantaloupe to create an entrée salad. If you prefer, use low-fat mayonnaise—and cut your fat even more! It is your taste call.

SERVES 4

One 6-ounce can solid white tuna, packed in water,
*   drained*
½ cup coarsely chopped red onion
2 tablespoons Nonfat Blend (see page 298)
2 tablespoons mayonnaise
1 tablespoon sweet pickle relish
2 hard-boiled egg whites, coarsely chopped (about ½ cup)
Freshly ground black pepper to taste
8 slices nonfat multi-grain bread, toasted, if preferred
4 large lettuce leaves, such as Bibb or romaine, or
*   several arugula leaves*

In a bowl, combine the tuna, onion, Nonfat Blend, mayonnaise, relish, egg whites and pepper and mix well. Divide among 4 slices of bread and top each with a lettuce leaf. Top each with another slice of bread and serve immediately.

CAL. 225 CARB. 24G PROT. 18G CHOL. 27MG FAT 7.7G/29% SOD. 496MG

145

DRESSING BASES FOR CREAMY SALADS

Once you try to reduce or eliminate mayonnaise, only your own taste buds can decide which of the following you would choose to spend your fat allowance on.

1 Tablespoon	Cal.	Fat(g)/%
Mayonnaise	99	11/100
Low-calorie mayonnaise	36	3/75
Fat-free mayonnaise	11	0/0
Nonfat Blend (see page 298)	9	0/0
Nonfat cottage cheese	9	0/0
Nonfat yogurt	8	0/0

Forty-Carat Carrot Soup

Deeply flavored and fresh at the same time—this soup is a winner!

146
◆

SERVES 4

4 cups low-fat, low-sodium chicken broth
1 small onion, coarsely chopped
2 teaspoons white rice
½ teaspoon curry powder
¾ teaspoon ground ginger
⅔ pound baby carrots, halved
⅛ teaspoon ground cloves
Salt and freshly ground black pepper to taste
1½ tablespoons finely minced fresh mint

1. In a stockpot, heat 2 tablespoons broth over medium heat. Add the onion and cook for 5 to 7 minutes, until tender. Add the rice, curry, ginger, carrots, cloves, salt and pepper and the remaining broth and bring to a boil over medium-high heat. Reduce the heat and simmer, partially covered, for about 30 minutes.

2. Cool slightly and then puree with an immersion blender or in a food processor fitted with a metal blade. (You may have to puree the soup in batches.)

3. Return the soup to the pot, add the mint and heat gently. Adjust the seasonings and serve immediately.

CAL. 87   CARB. 17G   PROT. 3G   CHOL. 0MG   FAT 0.3G./3%   SOD. 28MG

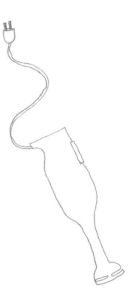

IMMERSION BLENDER

The smoothness of creamed soup varies with the equipment you use to puree it. An upright blender is smoothest, but it usually requires you to puree the soup in several batches.

A food processor makes a coarser puree, even when solids are pureed first before the liquids are added.

The immersion blender, which lets you puree right in the pot, is the easiest of all. Long available in France, it's finally made its way here. The puree is somewhat coarser, too. But the hand-held blender is fun to use and cleanup is a snap!

Many convenient commercially made foods contain a hidden liability: trans-fatty acids. These are created when hydrogen is pumped into vegetable oil under pressure to solidify it. They increase risk factors for cardiovascular disease by raising blood cholesterol levels.

Hydrogenated fats give foods longer shelf life and allow food manufacturers to use cheaper ingredients. You won't find the phrase "trans-fatty acids" on the label. Instead, look for the term "partially hydrogenated oils and fats"—and when you see it, put the package back on the shelf. You'll find them in:
◆ Cereals ◆ Margarine ◆ Mayonnaise ◆ Instant soup ◆ Tortillas ◆ Chips ◆ Snack foods ◆ Crackers ◆ Dressings and sandwich spreads ◆ Ready-to-bake pizza ◆ Egg rolls, fish sticks and other fried foods ◆ Ready-to-bake biscuits ◆ Rolls and croissants ◆ Frozen pies ◆ Cakes ◆ Cupcakes ◆ Slim shakes ◆ Snack bars ◆ Bread stuffing ◆ Rice dishes ◆ Instant potato products ◆ Vegetable shortening for baking ◆ Dairy substitutes, such as coffee whiteners and "whipped toppings"

Crisp Waldorf Salad

I tend to make this fairly often and keep it on hand in the fridge. It can be served as dessert or for breakfast (really!), for lunch or as a snack. Make it and watch it disappear.

SERVES 4

½ cup golden raisins
½ cup apple juice or rum
2 tablespoons low-fat sour cream
½ cup Nonfat Blend (see page 298)
1 teaspoon finely minced lime zest
1 teaspoon lime juice
2 teaspoons honey
2 tablespoons finely minced fresh mint
*1 sweet red apple, such as Red Delicious or McIntosh,
  cored and chopped*
*1 tart green apple, such as Granny Smith, cored and
  chopped*
1 cup red grapes
1 cup green grapes
½ cup coarsely chopped celery
2 tablespoons coarsely chopped walnuts, toasted

1. In a small bowl, combine the raisins and apple juice and set aside to plump for about 1 hour.

2. In another bowl, combine the sour cream, Nonfat Blend, lime zest, lime juice, honey and mint and stir until well blended. Set aside.

3. In a large bowl, combine the apples, grapes, celery and walnuts. Drain the raisins and add to the bowl. Add the dressing and toss to coat. Cover and refrigerate until ready to serve.

NOTE: To accelerate plumping the raisins, combine them with the apple juice in a microwave-safe container and microwave on high power for 1½ minutes. Set aside to cool while preparing the rest of the salad.

CAL. 244   CARB. 52G   PROT. 5G   CHOL. 3MG   FAT 4G/14%   SOD. 69MG

147
◆

FUSION COOKING

The '90s are one of the most exciting times ever to be cooking. We've discovered ingredients from around the world, mastered different cooking techniques and learned to achieve faraway tastes right here at home.

The key to attaining this waterfall of flavors is to keep a few essential ingredients in your pantry for each country's cooking and then to substitute ingredients from your local market for those that are perishable and difficult to find. With these flavors at your fingertips, you can accomplish cross-culture cooking anytime you like.

AMERICAN

- Carrots, cabbage, corn, celery, onions
- Peas, parsley, squash
- Allspice, cinnamon, cloves, nutmeg
- Marjoram, sage
- Chicken, turkey, bacon, beef, ham
- Clams, salmon, shrimp
- Worcestershire, barbecue and Tabasco sauces

SOUTHEAST ASIAN

- Pork, beef, shrimp, crab
- Chilies, cayenne, garlic, scallions
- Cilantro, lime juice, bean sprouts
- Anchovy paste, coconut, tomato paste
- Peanuts, rice noodles, mung bean paste noodles

CAJUN

- Shrimp, crab, chicken
- Celery, garlic, scallions
- Okra, onions, bell peppers
- Thyme, garlic salt, cayenne pepper

JAPANESE

- Buckwheat and rice noodles
- Seafood, shiitake mushrooms, miso
- Soy sauce, rice vinegar, sesame oil
- Ginger, scallions, Daikon, cucumbers

TEX-MEX

- Black beans, corn
- Canned and fresh green chilies
- Garlic, onions, tomatoes, cilantro
- Chili powder, oregano, cumin, lime juice
- Flour tortillas

MIDDLE EASTERN

- Olive oil, olives
- Tomatoes, cucumbers
- Lentils, chickpeas, ground lamb
- Raisins, pine nuts, walnuts
- Garlic, onions, lemons, parsley, mint
- Allspice, cinnamon, cloves, cumin
- Yogurt, sesame paste (tahini), phyllo

CHINESE

- Black beans, chili paste with garlic
- Garlic, ginger, scallions
- Five-spice powder or anise seed
- Sesame oil, dry sherry, hoisin sauce
- Cilantro

PIZZAS

Tortilla pizza toppings are limited only by your imagination:

♦ Onion Confit (see page 299), olives and Parmesan shards

♦ Wild mushrooms, sage and fontina and Parmesan cheeses

♦ Arugula, prosciutto and mozzarella cheese

♦ Tomato sauce, roasted eggplant brushed with balsamic vinegar, minced olives and Parmesan shards

♦ Tomato sauce, plum tomato slices, capers, tuna, black olives, basil and shredded mozzarella cheese

♦ Crumbled soft goat cheese, julienned leeks, smoked salmon slivers, fresh dill and a drizzle of olive oil

♦ Grated Gruyère cheese, scallops, roasted garlic cloves, lemon zest and shredded Parmesan cheese

♦ Spinach Pesto (see page 86), slivered skim-milk mozzarella cheese, minced garlic, basil and fresh tomato slices

♦ Fontina cheese slivers, crumbled goat cheese, broccoli florets, peas, artichoke hearts, minced scallions, minced garlic and Parmesan shards

Tomato and Basil Pizza

Pizza is one of the easy places to run into trouble with fat. One way to avoid this is to make the pizza yourself—and with crisped flour tortillas, it's so easy!

SERVES 4

2 large flour tortillas (about 10 inches)
6 tablespoons Roasted Tomato Pizza Sauce
  (see page 303)
¼ cup finely minced fresh basil leaves
4 plum tomatoes, thinly sliced
2 teaspoons finely minced garlic
½ cup grated part-skim mozzarella cheese

1. Preheat the oven to 450°F. Line a baking sheet with aluminum foil.

2. Place the tortillas on baking sheets and bake for 1 minute, until crisp.

3. Spread the sauce evenly over the tortillas, leaving a ½-inch border, and sprinkle each with the basil. Top each with a single layer of tomato slices. Sprinkle each with garlic and then cheese and bake for 10 to 12 minutes, until the crust is crisp and golden. Serve immediately.

CAL. 157   CARB. 22.2G   PROT. 7.3G   CHOL. 8.2MG   FAT 4.7G/26%
SOD. 265MG

149

Dinner Menu

FOODS (PER SERVING)	CAL.	CARB. (G)	PROT. (G)	CHOL. (MG)	FAT (G)/%	SOD. (MG)
Tomato and Basil Pizza*	157	22.2	7.3	8.2	4.7/26	265
Salad greens, 2 cups	19	3.2	1.8	0	0.2/11	28
Pesto Dressing* (p. 118), 2 T.	34	1	0.8	0.8	3/80	0.4
Breadsticks, 2	160	26	12	0	4/22	420
Cantaloupe Frozen Yogurt* (p. 109), ½ cup	91	21	2.4	0.6	0.2/2	30
EVENING SNACK						
Popcorn (air-popped), 2 cups	61	13	2	0	0.7/10	0.6
Today's Totals	**1928**	**344**	**77**	**44**	**43/20**	**1848**

ONION CONFIT PIZZA

Classic flavors of Italy mingle atop a tortilla "pizza" crust. This is one of my favorites!

SERVES 2

1 large flour tortilla (about 10 inches)
1 tablespoon crumbled Gorgonzola
*   cheese*
2 tablespoons nonfat cottage cheese,
*   blended until smooth*
2 tablespoons low-fat, low-sodium
*   chicken broth*
1 cup fresh spinach, washed, dried,
*   stemmed and finely chopped*
1 tablespoon finely minced garlic
¾ cup Rich Onion Confit (see page 299)
Freshly ground nutmeg to taste
2 tablespoons golden raisins
2 tablespoons pine nuts (optional)

1. Preheat the oven to 450° F. Line a baking sheet with aluminum foil. Place the tortilla on the baking sheet and bake for 1 minute, until crisp.

2. In a bowl, combine the Gorgonzola and cottage cheese, stir and set aside.

3. In a saucepan, heat the broth over medium heat, add the spinach and garlic and cook for 2 to 3 minutes, until the spinach wilts.

4. Spread the cheese mixture on the tortilla, leaving a ½-inch border, and top with the Onion Confit. Gently spread the spinach and garlic over the onion and sprinkle with the nutmeg, raisins and pine nuts, if using. Bake for 10 to 12 minutes, until the tortilla is crisp and golden. Serve immediately.

CAL. 238   CARB. 35G   PROT. 10.6G
CHOL. 12.5MG   FAT 6.8G/25%   SOD. 561MG

PRIMAVERA PIZZA

Never has this classic been quicker!

SERVES 2

1 large flour tortilla (about 10 inches)
3 tablespoons Roasted Tomato Pizza
*   Sauce (see page 303)*
½ cup coarsely chopped zucchini
1 cup broccoli florets, broken into small
*   pieces*
½ cup stemmed and quartered
*   mushrooms*
2 scallions, coarsely chopped
*   (approximately 2 tablespoons)*
¼ cup grated part-skim mozzarella
*   cheese*

1. Preheat the oven to 450° F. Line a baking sheet with aluminum foil. Place the tortilla on the baking sheet and bake for 1 minute, until crisp.

2. Spread the sauce over the tortilla, leaving a ½-inch border, and scatter with the vegetables. Sprinkle with the cheese and bake for 10 to 12 minutes, until crisp and golden. Serve immediately.

CAL. 174   CARB. 25G   PROT. 10G   CHOL. 8MG
FAT 4.9G/24%   SOD. 275MG

PIZZAZZ

"SAUSAGE" AND MUSHROOM PIZZA

I make this for my husband, who likes his pizza the old-fashioned way—and guess what? He doesn't even know I use turkey!

SERVES 2

1 large flour tortilla (about 10 inches)
3 tablespoons Roasted Tomato Pizza Sauce (see page 303)
1/2 cup crumbled Spicy Turkey Sausage (see page 301)
1 cup stemmed and quartered mushrooms
1 small onion, sliced into thin rings (approximately 1/2 cup)
1 tablespoon finely minced garlic (optional)
1/4 cup grated part-skim mozzarella cheese

1. Preheat the oven to 450°F. Line a baking sheet with aluminum foil. Place the tortilla on the baking sheet and bake for 1 minute, until crisp.

2. Spread the sauce over the tortilla, leaving a 1/2-inch border, and arrange the sausage on top. Scatter with the mushrooms, onion and garlic, if using. Sprinkle with the cheese and bake for 10 to 12 minutes, until crisp and golden. Serve immediately.

CAL. 245   CARB. 27G   PROT. 23G   CHOL. 36MG
FAT 5.6G/20%   SOD. 264MG

CHICKEN SALAD PIZZA

This unusual pizza is a little higher in fat than others in the book, but it's incredibly delicious. Be brave—you'll be surprised how much everyone loves it.

SERVES 2

1 large flour tortilla (about 10 inches)
1 tablespoon Nonfat Blend (see page 298)
2 teaspoons mayonnaise
1 tablespoon finely minced fresh tarragon
4 ounces chicken breast, cooked and shredded (about 1 cup) (see page 85)
2 tablespoons coarsely chopped walnuts
Ten 3-inch-long Parmesan shards (see page 67)

1. Preheat the oven to 450°F. Line a baking sheet with aluminum foil. Place the tortilla on the baking sheet and bake for 1 minute, until crisp.

2. In a small bowl, combine the Nonfat Blend, mayonnaise and tarragon and mix well. Spread over the tortilla, leaving a 1/2-inch border, and arrange the chicken on top. Sprinkle with the walnuts and Parmesan shards and bake for 10 to 12 minutes, until crisp and golden and the cheese softens. Serve immediately.

CAL. 319   CARB. 18G   PROT. 24G   CHOL. 56MG
FAT 17G/47%   SOD. 337MG

Company's Coming

◆

Cooking with ease is most important when friends and family gather and are having fun—you don't want to be left out, stuck in the kitchen! The key is to plan a day with a repertoire of dishes that are packed with flavor and require no hovering. These dishes are either done quickly with little fuss or cooked slowly, blending their flavors beautifully. The weekend gives you time to braise, bake, roast, simmer or stew and have a good time. Time, too, to elicit plenty of kitchen helpers.

Saturday
DAY 13

Fresh Orange Juice
Hawaiian Fruit Salad*
Silver Dollar Corn Cakes*
Spicy Sausage Patties*

◆

Honey Mustard Beets*
Creamy Cucumber Salad*
Green Minestrone with Pesto*
Multi-grain Country Bread

◆

Simple Black Bean Salsa* and
Roasted Pepper Dip*
with Tortilla Chips*

Fresh Spring Greens with
Tarragon-Dijon Dressing*

Spicy Tomato and Sausage Lasagna*

Tiramisù Cake*

Breakfast Menu

Foods (per serving)	Cal.	Carb. (g)	Prot. (g)	Chol. (mg)	Fat (g)/%	Sod. (mg)
Orange juice, 6 oz.	83.5	19.4	1.4	0	0.3/3	1.2
Hawaiian Fruit Salad*	76	19	2	0	0.3/4	13
Silver Dollar Corn Cakes*	255	57	3.7	27	2.4/8	189
Spicy Sausage Patties*, 2	29	0.4	6.2	12.2	0.4/11	18
Morning Snack						
Apple, 3½ oz.	59	15	0.2	0	0.4/6	0

Silver Dollar Corn Cakes

During corn season, I frequently make these corn cakes for Sunday breakfast. I load the batter with more fresh corn than it seems it could possibly hold, and then add even more to heated maple syrup. These cook best when they're small.

SERVES 8

1½ cups pure maple syrup
2 cups fresh or frozen corn
  kernels
½ cup cornmeal
2 tablespoons all-purpose flour

½ teaspoon baking soda
¼ teaspoon salt
1½ teaspoons canola oil
¾ cup buttermilk
1 large egg, lightly beaten

1. In a small saucepan, heat the maple syrup and 1 cup of the corn kernels over low heat for 10 to 15 minutes, until the corn is tender and the mixture is heated through.

2. In a bowl, combine the cornmeal, flour, baking soda and salt. Stir in the oil, buttermilk and egg until just combined. Gently fold in the remaining 1 cup corn kernels.

3. Lightly spray a nonstick skillet with vegetable oil spray and heat over medium heat until a few drops of water, scattered on the pan, evaporate quickly. Drop 1 tablespoon of the batter for each cake into the skillet and cook for 1 minute per side, or until lightly golden. Spoon the warm maple syrup and corn over the cakes and serve.

CAL. 255   CARB. 57G   PROT. 3.7G   CHOL. 27MG   FAT 2.4G/8%   SOD. 189MG

"Have you seen a red sunset drip over one of my cornfields?"
CARL SANDBURG

Don't let your sweet tooth take over when you cut fat. While sugar's worst proven harm is tooth decay, it also affects mood swings, hypoglycemia, diabetes, the progression of gallstones and heart disease.

If not the true culprit, it's an accomplice, filling you up with calories instead of good food. When more than 9 percent of calories come from sugar (the American average is 20 percent), vitamin and mineral intake usually comes up short.

The cycle between over-indulging in sugar and sugar cravings is a vicious one. The same goes for sugar substitutes. So the next time you drink diet soda all day and can't understand why you crave a candy bar, switch to water. You'll see your sugar cravings diminish and your moods level out.

Hawaiian Fruit Salad

Lace pale yellow and orange fruits with a pinch of mint, crystallized ginger, cinnamon or vanilla.

SERVES 8

1 large cantaloupe, peeled, seeded and cut into chunks
1 large papaya, peeled and cut into chunks (about 2 cups)
One 14-ounce can mandarin oranges, plus juice
1 tablespoon chopped macadamia nuts (optional)

Place all ingredients in a salad bowl and toss to combine. Serve immediately or cover and refrigerate until ready to serve.

CAL. 76   CARB. 19G   PROT. 2G   CHOL. 0MG   FAT 0.3G/4%   SOD. 13MG

Spicy Sausage Patties

MAKES ABOUT THIRTY-SIX 1½-INCH PATTIES

1 sweet red pepper, stemmed, seeded and roasted
½ cup tightly packed fresh cilantro leaves
½ cup tightly packed fresh Italian parsley leaves
½ cup tightly packed shredded romaine lettuce
⅛ to ¼ teaspoon crushed red pepper flakes to taste
2 teaspoons crushed dried oregano
½ teaspoon salt
⅛ teaspoon freshly ground black pepper
⅛ teaspoon ground cumin
⅛ teaspoon ground cloves
1 pound lean ground turkey

1. In a food processor fitted with a metal blade, combine all of ingredients except the turkey and process until almost smooth. Scrape the mixture into a bowl. Add the turkey and, using your hands, mix to distribute it evenly. Cover and refrigerate for at least 2 hours to let the flavors blend.

2. Spray a nonstick skillet lightly with vegetable oil spray and heat over medium heat. Form the mixture into 1½-inch patties and cook for 3 to 5 minutes, turning once, until browned.

CAL. 14.5   CARB. 0.2G   PROT. 3.1G   CHOL. 6.1MG   FAT 0.2G/11%   SOD. 9MG
(ANALYZED PER PATTY)

Lunch Menu

FOODS (PER SERVING)	CAL.	CARB. (G)	PROT. (G)	CHOL. (MG)	FAT (G)/%	SOD. (MG)
Honey Mustard Beets*	156	27	3	0	5.5/29	579
Creamy Cucumber Salad*	14	3	1.1	0.1	0.1/5	9
Green Minestrone with Pesto*	142	19	11	5.6	2.8/17	575
Multi-grain bread, 2 slices	228	44	6	16	4/14	136
AFTERNOON SNACK						
Fruit yogurt, 6 oz.	180	33	8	10	1.5/8	105

Honey Mustard Beets

I love oven-roasted fresh beets, but to beat the clock I will use canned in a pinch.

SERVES 8

8 cups thinly sliced cooked or canned beets, drained
¾ cup finely minced fresh chives
½ cup finely minced fresh Italian parsley
2 tablespoons plus 2 teaspoons Dijon mustard
½ cup honey
4 teaspoons balsamic vinegar
Freshly ground black pepper to taste
½ cup walnut pieces, toasted

1. In a large bowl, combine the beets, chives and parsley.

2. In another bowl, combine the mustard, honey and vinegar and stir until smooth. Toss with the beet mixture to coat and then season with pepper. Sprinkle with walnuts. Set aside for 1 to 2 hours at room temperature before serving to give flavors time to blend.

NOTE: To toast walnut pieces and other nuts, spread them on a baking sheet and bake in a preheated 350°F. oven for 5 to 8 minutes, until lightly browned and fragrant. Stir 2 to 3 times during toasting. Transfer to a plate to cool.

CAL. 156   CARB. 27G   PROT. 3G   CHOL. 0MG   FAT 5.5G/29%   SOD. 579MG

156

"Travel light in life— take only what you need: a loving family, good friends, simple pleasures, someone to love, and someone to love you . . . enough to eat, enough to wear, . . . and a little more than enough to drink for thirst is a dangerous thing!"
—ANONYMOUS

Green Minestrone with Pesto

If you have pesto on hand in the freezer, this tasty soup can be cooked in a jiffy. And it's an easy soup to vary, depending on what's in the fridge or on your mind.

SERVES 8

6¼ cups low-fat, low-sodium chicken broth
2 onions, halved and thinly sliced (approximately 2 cups)
2 tablespoons finely minced garlic
2 small zucchini, halved lengthwise and
cut into 1-inch chunks (approximately 1½ cups)
1½ cups frozen lima beans
1½ cups shredded savoy cabbage
1½ cups fresh snow peas or sugar snap peas
1½ cups fresh or frozen green peas
6 scallions, green parts only, coarsely chopped
4 tablespoons Spinach Pesto (see page 86)
½ cup finely minced fresh Italian parsley
½ cup Parmesan shards (see page 67)

1. In a large stockpot, heat ¼ cup broth over medium heat and cook the onions and garlic for 2 to 3 minutes, stirring, until softened. Add the zucchini and remaining 6 cups broth, cover, reduce the heat to low and simmer for 15 minutes.

2. Add the lima beans and cabbage, cover and simmer for 5 minutes. Add the snow peas, green peas, scallions and Spinach Pesto, stir and cook for about 3 minutes longer, or until the snow peas are cooked but still crunchy. Add the parsley, stir and ladle into bowls. Top each bowl with 3 Parmesan shards and serve immediately.

CAL. 142   CARB. 19G   PROT. 11G   CHOL. 5.6MG   FAT 2.8G/17%   SOD. 575MG

**CREAMY
CUCUMBER SALAD**

SERVES 8

¼ cup nonfat plain yogurt
*2 tablespoons nonfat sour
cream*
2 teaspoons lemon juice
*4 teaspoons finely minced
fresh mint*
*4 cups very thinly sliced
cucumber*

In a small mixing bowl, combine the yogurt, sour cream, lemon juice and mint and mix well. Add the cucumber and toss. Cover and refrigerate for 1 hour before serving to allow flavors to blend.

CAL. 14   CARB. 3G   PROT. 1.1G
CHOL. 0.1MG   FAT 0.1G/5%
SOD. 9MG

Simple Black Bean Salsa

This quick and simple salsa is absolutely addictive. I make it all the time—and if I'm out of cooked beans, I'd rather make it with canned than not at all. Serve it with chips, fajitas or tortillas.

MAKES ABOUT 2 CUPS

2 cups cooked or canned drained black beans
¼ cup finely minced fresh cilantro
1 tablespoon finely minced garlic
1 tablespoon seeded and finely minced jalapeño
1 tablespoon low-fat, low-sodium chicken broth

In a large bowl, combine the ingredients and stir with a fork, slightly mashing the beans. Serve immediately or cover and refrigerate until ready to serve.

CAL. 10   CARB. 2G   PROT. 0.8G   CHOL. 0MG   FAT 0.05G/4%   SOD. 115MG
(ANALYZED PER TABLESPOON)

Spicy Tomato and Sausage Lasagna

This looks long and involved, but it actually pulls together in short order. And everyone always loves lasagna.

SERVES 8

1 pound lean ground turkey
1 onion, coarsely chopped (about 1 cup)
2 tablespoons finely minced garlic
2 tablespoons low-fat, low-sodium beef broth
1 teaspoon paprika
¼ teaspoon cayenne
¼ teaspoon crushed red pepper flakes
1½ cups nonfat cottage cheese
1 cup nonfat plain yogurt
⅛ teaspoon grated nutmeg
Salt and freshly ground black pepper to taste

TORTILLA CHIPS

These are so easy to make and so much better when they are your own and are served warm from the oven with salsa or your favorite dip.

MAKES 24 CHIPS

4 large flour tortillas
(about 10 inches),
each cut into 6 wedges

1. Preheat the oven to 275°F.

2. Lay the tortilla wedges on 2 baking sheets and bake for about 20 minutes, turning every 5 minutes. Cool on wire racks.

CAL. 18   CARB. 4G   PROT. 0.5G
CHOL. 0MG   FAT 0G/0%   SOD. 56MG
(ANALYZED PER CHIP)

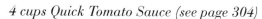

4 cups Quick Tomato Sauce (see page 304)
3 tablespoons tomato paste
9 cooked, drained lasagna noodles
2 cups firmly packed, coarsely chopped fresh spinach
3 tablespoons finely minced fresh oregano
½ cup finely minced fresh basil
2 cups grated part-skim mozzarella cheese

TURKEY ALL YEAR

Turkey's evolved from a holiday bird to a healthy staple. Lower in fat than chicken, it has a more robust flavor. And more cuts are currently available than you might imagine.

Ground turkey can be 99 percent fat free. But watch the labels—it can also be as fatty as hamburger. I have my butcher grind turkey breast meat for me so I know it's truly "lean."

A 3-ounce serving of turkey breast is only 134 calories and provides 67 percent of the USRDA for protein. Thank heavens. Turkey once a year was never enough.

1. Preheat the oven to 350° F. Lightly spray a shallow 9 × 13-inch baking dish with olive oil spray.

2. In a skillet, cook the turkey, onion, garlic and broth over medium heat for about 5 minutes, until the turkey is lightly browned. Season with paprika, cayenne and red pepper flakes. Set aside.

3. In a blender, process the cottage cheese and yogurt until smooth. Season with nutmeg and salt and pepper. Set aside

159
◆

4. In a saucepan, cook the Quick Tomato Sauce and tomato paste over medium heat, uncovered, for 15 to 18 minutes, stirring until thick and smooth. Add the turkey mixture and stir to blend.

5. Spread about ¼ cup sauce in the baking dish and top with 3 noodles. Top with a third of the cottage cheese mixture and a third of the spinach, and sprinkle with a third of the herbs, ½ cup mozzarella and a third of the remaining sauce. Lay 3 more noodles on top. Repeat the layers twice more, ending with mozzarella on top. Bake for 1 hour, until the sauce bubbles and the cheese begins to brown. Cool for 15 to 20 minutes before serving.

CAL. 324   CARB. 34G   PROT. 35G   CHOL. 46MG   FAT 6G/17%   SOD. 859MG

Tiramisù Cake

This is such a delightfully easy way to make tiramisù that the Italian dessert can be served frequently. After all, it has a third of the fat of the classic version.

SERVES 8

One 8-inch homemade or store-bought angel food cake
¾ cup nonfat cottage cheese
1½ cups cold brewed coffee
5 tablespoons Amaretto or Frangelico liqueur (optional)
1 cup mascarpone cheese
2 tablespoons skim milk
3 tablespoons confectioners' sugar
2 ounces bittersweet chocolate

160
♦

1. Using a serrated knife, cut the angel food cake horizontally into 4 equal layers.

2. In a blender, process the cottage cheese until smooth.

3. In a bowl, combine the coffee and 3 tablespoons liqueur, if desired. In another bowl, whisk the remaining 2 tablespoons liqueur, if desired, with the cottage cheese, mascarpone, skim milk and sugar.

4. In a shallow 8 × 8-inch baking dish, arrange 2 of the layers of cake, tearing it into pieces so that it covers the bottom of the dish.

5. Sprinkle half of the coffee mixture evenly over the cake and top with half the cheese mixture, spreading it evenly.

THE MEASURING HABIT

When cooking just for us, I used to pride myself in not really measuring. Except, of course, for baking. I've always felt that the flavors of raw ingredients can vary so much—even within a season or a region—that the only way to cook was to taste the food along the way. It might be a spoonful from the pot, a salad before it's dressed, a roast's pan juices as they calmly collect.

I still cook this way. But now that I prepare low-fat recipes, I've been shocked to realize just how big that first hunk of butter sometimes was and how much olive oil my twist of the wrist added at the beginning of some dishes.

When you follow these recipes and see how we've moistened our foods, make sure that you note how far a teaspoon of oil or a tablespoon of butter goes in adding flavor at the end of cooking.

My advice: get out your measuring spoons and stop eyeballing fats.

6. Arrange the remaining 2 layers of cake on top of the mascarpone, tearing it into pieces so that it covers the cheese. Sprinkle with the remaining coffee mixture and then top with the remaining cheese.

7. Using a vegetable peeler, grate the chocolate over the top of the cake. Cover loosely with aluminum foil and refrigerate at least 24 hours. Bring to room temperature before serving.

NOTE: If not using the optional liqueur, increase the coffee amount to 2 cups. Angel food cakes have varying amounts of air in them and therefore they absorb liquids in varying times and amounts. You want tiramisù to be very moist—so slightly adjust the coffee/liqueur amounts as you work.

CAL. 306   CARB. 46G   PROT. 10.9G   CHOL. 15.3MG   FAT 8.2G/23%   SOD. 522MG

"True life is lived when tiny changes occur."
LEO TOLSTOY

Dinner Menu

FOODS (PER SERVING)	CAL.	CARB. (G)	PROT. (G)	CHOL. (MG)	FAT (G)/%	SOD. (MG)
Simple Black Bean Salsa*, ¼ cup	40	8	3.2	0	0.2/4	460
Roasted Pepper Dip* (p. 162), 2 T.	18	1.8	3	0	0/1	90
Tortilla Chips*, 6	108	24	3	0	0/0	336
Salad greens, 2 cups	19	3.2	1.8	0	0.2/11	28
Tarragon-Dijon Dressing* (p. 120), 1 T.	11	0.6	0.07	0	0.9/77	13
Spicy Tomato and Sausage Lasagna*	324	34	35	46	6/17	859
Tiramisù Cake*	306	46	10.9	15.3	8.2/23	522
Today's Totals	**2048**	**354**	**99**	**132**	**33/15**	**3933**

DELIGHTFUL DIPS

LEMON-PEPPER DIP

MAKES ABOUT 1 CUP

1 cup nonfat cottage cheese
3 tablespoons finely minced
  fresh dill
1 teaspoon finely minced
  lemon zest
½ teaspoon lemon juice
½ teaspoon freshly ground
  black pepper

In a blender, process the
cottage cheese until smooth.
Transfer to a bowl, add the
dill, lemon zest, lemon
juice and pepper and mix
well. Cover and refrigerate
for 1 to 2 hours before
serving to allow the flavors
to blend.

CAL. 3 CARB. 0.2G PROT. 0.6G
  CHOL. 0MG FAT 0G/0%
    SOD. 18MG (ANALYZED PER
  TEASPOON)

SPINACH DIP

MAKES ABOUT
1 ½ CUPS

1 cup nonfat cottage cheese
3 tablespoons nonfat plain
  yogurt
1 cup frozen spinach,
  thawed and squeezed
  of excess water
1 teaspoon finely minced
  garlic
1 tablespoon grated
  Parmesan cheese
Freshly ground nutmeg to
  taste
Freshly ground black
  pepper to taste

In a blender, process the
cottage cheese until smooth.
Transfer to a bowl, add the
yogurt, spinach, garlic,
Parmesan cheese, nutmeg
and pepper and mix well.
Cover and refrigerate for 1
to 2 hours before serving to
allow the flavors to blend.

CAL. 4 CARB. 0.3G PROT. 0.5G
CHOL. 0.1MG FAT 0.03G/6%
SOD. 16MG (ANALYZED PER TEASPOON)

ROASTED PEPPER DIP

MAKES ABOUT
1 ¼ CUPS

1 cup nonfat cottage cheese
1 red or orange bell pepper,
  roasted, seeded and
  peeled (see page 107)
1 teaspoon finely minced
  garlic
Dash of cayenne or
  Tabasco sauce to taste

In a blender, process the
ingredients until smooth.
Cover and refrigerate
for 1 to 2 hours to allow the
flavors time to blend.

CAL. 3 CARB. 3G PROT. 0.5G
CHOL. 0MG FAT 0/1%
SOD. 15MG (ANALYZED PER TEASPOON)

ROQUEFORT DIP

MAKES ABOUT 1¼ CUPS

1 cup nonfat cottage cheese
3 tablespoons crumbled
 Roquefort cheese

In a blender, process the
cottage cheese until smooth.
Transfer to a bowl, add the
Roquefort and stir well
until tinged lightly with
pale green from the cheese.
Cover and refrigerate for 1
to 2 hours before serving to
allow the flavors to blend.

CAL. 4 CARB. 0.2G PROT. 0.6G
CHOL. 0.3MG FAT 0.1G/27%
SOD. 20MG (ANALYZED PER TEASPOON)

PESTO DIP

MAKES ABOUT 1 CUP

1 cup nonfat cottage cheese
2 tablespoons Spinach
 Pesto (see page 86)

In a blender, process the
cottage cheese until smooth.
Transfer to a bowl, add the
Spinach Pesto and mix
well. Cover and refrigerate
for 1 to 2 hours before
serving to allow the flavors
to blend.

CAL. 4 CARB. 0.2G PROT. 0.7G
CHOL. 0MG FAT 0.045G/10%
SOD. 18MG (ANALYZED PER TEASPOON)

SHRIMP DIP

MAKES ABOUT 1½ CUPS

1 cup nonfat cottage cheese
1 cup cooked large shrimp,
 cut into chunks (about
 14 shrimp)
1 tablespoon lemon juice
2 tablespoons finely minced
 fresh dill
1 to 2 dashes of Tabasco
 sauce

In a blender, process all the
ingredients until almost
smooth. Cover and refrigerate for 1 to 2 hours before
serving to allow the flavors
to blend.

CAL. 3.4 CARB. 0.2G PROT. 0.6G
CHOL. 2MG FAT 0.01G/4%
SOD. 15MG (ANALYZED PER TEASPOON)

SUN-DRIED TOMATO DIP

MAKES ABOUT 1½ CUPS

1 cup nonfat cottage cheese
¼ cup oil-packed drained
 sun-dried tomatoes
1 tablespoon finely minced
 scallions, green part only
1 teaspoon finely minced
 garlic
1 teaspoon tomato paste
2 tablespoons crumbled
 feta cheese

In a blender, process the
cottage cheese, tomatoes,
scallions, garlic and tomato
paste until smooth. Transfer to a bowl, add the feta
and mix well. Cover and
refrigerate for 2 hours
before serving to give the
flavors time to blend.

CAL. 4 CARB 0.3G PROT. 0.5G
CHOL. 0.4MG FAT 0.14G/30%
SOD. 18MG (ANALYZED PER TEASPOON)

CRAB DIP

MAKES ABOUT 1½ CUPS

1 cup nonfat cottage
 cheese
1 cup cooked crabmeat
½ cup finely chopped
 scallions, green part only
¼ teaspoon Worcestershire
 sauce
½ teaspoon bottled cocktail
 sauce

163

In a blender, process the
cottage cheese until smooth.
Transfer to a bowl, add the
crabmeat, scallions,
Worcestershire sauce and
cocktail sauce and mix.
Cover and refrigerate for 1
to 2 hours before serving to
allow the flavors to blend.

CAL. 4 CARB. 0.2G PROT. 0.7G
CHOL. 1.6MG FAT 0.03/7%
SOD. 17MG (ANALYZED PER TEASPOON)

Country Cooking

◆

Rustic country cooking brings with it naturally robust earthy flavors that mesmerize. The luncheon portion of this menu sets the pace for a long, long walk afterwards, taking that country place in your heart with you, or immersing yourself in the one that may already surround you.

Sunday
DAY 14

Cantaloupe Smoothie*

Oven Puff with Fresh Fruit*

Turkey Ham Slices

◆

Broccoli with Lemon-Pepper Dip*

Fresh Greens with Our House
Dressing*

Country-Roasted Chicken with
Green Beans and Potatoes*

Breadsticks

Satin Smooth Crème Brûlée*

◆

Tomato and Arugula Salad*

Chicken and Spinach Soup*

Country French Bread

Passion Fruit Papaya Frozen Yogurt*

Breakfast Menu

Foods (per serving)	Cal.	Carb. (g)	Prot. (g)	Chol. (mg)	Fat (g)/%	Sod. (mg)
Cantaloupe Smoothie* (p. 74)	161	40	3	0	1/5	15
Oven Puff with Fresh Fruit*	208	36	10	90	3/13	89.5
Turkey ham, 3 oz.	90	1.5	13.5	52.5	3.8/38	990

Oven Puff with Fresh Fruit

A light puffy pancake, this is ideal filled with fresh fruit.

SERVES 4

2 large eggs
3 large egg whites
½ cup skim milk
1 tablespoon vanilla extract
½ cup all-purpose flour
Dash of salt
1 tablespoon lemon juice
½ to 1 tablespoon confectioners'
*   sugar*
4 cups mixed fresh fruit, such as
*   raspberries, sliced strawberries, blueberries, sliced*
*   nectarines, peaches or bananas*

1. Preheat the oven to 425°F. Spray a large ovenproof skillet with vegetable oil spray and heat in the oven.

2. In a bowl, whisk together the eggs, egg whites, milk and vanilla. Add the flour and salt and stir to combine. Pour into the hot skillet and bake for 15 to 20 minutes, until puffed and the edges are browned and crisp.

3. Lift from the skillet with a spatula. Sprinkle with lemon juice and sugar to taste. Mound the fresh fruit in the center and serve immediately.

CAL. 208   CARB. 36G   PROT. 10G   CHOL. 90MG   FAT 3G/13%   SOD. 89.5MG

"I am one who eats breakfast gazing at morning glories."
MATSUO BASHO

166

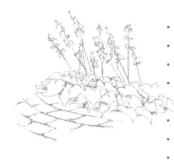

Lunch Menu

FOODS (PER SERVING)	CAL.	CARB. (G)	PROT. (G)	CHOL. (MG)	FAT (G)/%	SOD. (MG)
Broccoli, 1 cup	44	8	5	0	0.5/10	42
Lemon-Pepper Dip* (p. 162), 2 T.	18	1.2	3.6	0	0/0	108
Salad greens, 1 cup	9.5	1.6	0.9	0	0.1/11	14
Our House Dressing* (p. 194), 1 T.	18	2	0.1	0	1.2/58	31
Country-Roasted Chicken with Green Beans and Potatoes*	582	77	48.5	109	10.3/16	624
Breadsticks, 1	80	13	6	0	2/22	210
Satin Smooth Crème Brûlée*	291	44.5	12	77	7/22	178

Country-Roasted Chicken with Green Beans and Potatoes

This rustic, especially moist roasted chicken tastes delicious. Surrounded by roasted potatoes, loads of sweet, nutty roasted garlic and lightly browned green beans, this generous portion can be considered truly a feast.

167
◆

SKIN OFF!

Chicken and turkey can be cooked with their skin on with only a negligible amount of fat penetrating the meat itself. Keeping the skin on during cooking keeps the meat moist. In some dishes it's preferable; in others, it makes no difference.

Always remove the skin before eating. Of course if fat has collected, the pan juices need to be defatted.

When I cook with skin on, the recipe is analyzed *after* the skin has been removed.

SERVES 4

One 3-pound chicken, quartered, skin removed
Freshly ground black pepper
60 cloves garlic, peeled
2 pounds very small new potatoes,
  ¾ to 1 inch in diameter
4 cups low-fat, low-sodium
  chicken broth
½ teaspoon olive oil
¼ cup finely minced fresh mint
Kosher or sea salt
1½ pounds fresh green beans, trimmed

1. Preheat the oven to 400°F. Place the chicken, bone side down, in a shallow baking dish, sprinkle with pepper and surround with the garlic cloves. Roast for about 1½ hours. After 20 minutes, add

(continued on next page)

2 cups broth to the chicken and baste. After 45 minutes, add another 1¼ cups chicken broth and baste every 15 minutes until the juices run clear when thigh meat is pierced.

2. In another baking dish, arrange the potatoes and roast for about 45 minutes.

3. When the potatoes are fork-tender, toss immediately with the olive oil and mint. (If necessary, halve or quarter the potatoes into bite-sized pieces before tossing.) Season generously with salt and pepper.

4. Allow the chicken to rest for 5 to 10 minutes. Defat the pan juices by skimming with a spoon or blotting with paper towels. Keep warm.

5. In a large skillet, heat ½ cup of the remaining chicken broth and cook the beans, covered, for 4 to 5 minutes. Remove the lid, add the remaining ¼ cup broth and cook for 3 to 4 minutes longer, continually tossing the beans to prevent burning, until the beans are tender and lightly browned.

6. Divide the chicken, potatoes and beans among 4 plates, garnish with the garlic cloves and drizzle with the pan juices. Serve immediately.

CAL. 582   CARB. 77G   PROT. 48.5G   CHOL. 109MG   FAT 10.3G/16%   SOD. 624MG

"All human history attests that happiness for man— the hungry sinner! Since Eve ate apples, much depends on dinner."
AGPAGI BYPON

FEELING STRESSED?

Reach for a rice cake. What you eat affects not just your energy level but also your mood swings and the way you deal with pressure. Eating is just 25 to 30 grams of carbohydrates increases the level of a mood-regulating brain chemical called serotonin. So reach for a baked potato, a bagel, pretzels, low-fat tortilla chips, graham crackers or another food high in carbohydrates. You'll feel calmer, less stressed.

WALK TO THE MAX

A walker with hand weights may burn more fat calories than a faster walker without weights, even though they burn the same amount of calories.

If you warm up first, you'll burn even more fat. Just spend 5 to 10 minutes doing the exercise you're warming up for—in slow motion. The longer you intend to exercise, the longer you need to warm up. Then go at your own pace.

Satin Smooth Crème Brûlée

This classic has been reduced by almost 21 grams of fat and still is one of my favorites. Thank goodness I can enjoy it now without "the guilts."

SERVES 4

4 large egg whites
1 large egg
½ cup granulated sugar
¼ cup heavy cream
One 12-ounce can evaporated skim milk
1 tablespoon vanilla extract
1 whole vanilla bean, split, seeds removed
¼ cup packed light brown sugar

1. Preheat the oven to 350°F.

2. In the bowl of an electric mixer set on medium-high speed, combine the egg whites, egg and granulated sugar and beat well until combined. Slowly add the cream, evaporated skim milk and vanilla and beat on medium speed until smooth. Stir in the vanilla seeds and discard the pod.

169
◆

3. Strain into another bowl. Pour into four 6-ounce custard cups or ramekins. Place the cups into a large baking dish and add enough hot water to come halfway up the sides of the cups.

4. Bake for about 50 minutes, until the custard is set in the center and a knife inserted in the center comes out clean. Cool in the water bath. Cover and refrigerate for at least 2 hours.

5. Preheat the broiler. Sprinkle 1 tablespoon brown sugar evenly on top of each custard. Broil 3 to 4 inches from the heat for 2 to 3 minutes, until browned and bubbling. Remove and serve immediately.

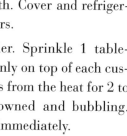

CAL. 291   CARB. 44.5G   PROT. 12G   CHOL. 77MG
FAT 7G/22%   SOD. 178MG

Chicken and Spinach Soup

This light Italian-inspired soup is great also as a first course or a light supper. It's even better when you have a little leftover chicken.

SERVES 4

8 ounces fresh spinach or arugula trimmed, well rinsed and dried
2 tablespoons finely minced fresh dill
5 cups low-fat, low-sodium chicken broth
Juice and zest of 2 lemons
6 ounces boneless, skinless chicken breast, julienned
Freshly ground black pepper to taste
¼ cup Parmesan shards (see page 67)
Freshly grated nutmeg to taste

1. Cut the spinach into very thin strips (chiffonade). Divide among 4 shallow soup or pasta bowls and top with the dill. Set aside.

2. In a saucepan, heat the chicken broth over medium heat and add the lemon juice and zest and the chicken. Cover and poach for 2 to 3 minutes, until the chicken is white and cooked through. Remove the chicken with a slotted spoon and divide evenly among the bowls.

3. Ladle the broth over the chicken and season with pepper. Top with the Parmesan shards and nutmeg and serve immediately.

CAL. 111   CARB. 5G   PROT. 15G   CHOL. 29MG   FAT 2.3G/21%   SOD. 165MG

170

ARUGULA

Emerald green, with an herby, slightly peppery flavor that intensifies as the leaves grow larger, arugula is one of my favorite leafy greens. Also called garden rocket or *roquette*, arugula is a member of the cabbage family and contains vitamins A and C and iron.

Among its virtues is a robust flavor that makes a salad a meal, much as spinach does. My all-time favorite mix is arugula, red onion, vine-ripened tomatoes and Our House Dressing (see page 194).

CHIFFONADE

Tossed and tangled, the slivered leaves of herbs and greens are as light and fluffy as chiffon. To make a chiffonade, wash and dry the leaves and remove the stems. Stack four or five leaves on top of each other, roll and slice thinly into strips, using a broad chef's knife.

Dinner Menu

Foods (per serving)	Cal.	Carb. (g)	Prot. (g)	Chol. (mg)	Fat (g)/%	Sod. (mg)
Tomato and Arugula Salad* (p. 87)	39	7	2.1	0	0.9/35	48
Chicken and Spinach Soup*	111	5	15	29	2.3/21	165
French bread, 2 slices	192	36	6	0	2/9	426
Passion Fruit Papaya Frozen Yogurt* (p. 295)	169	39.1	4.2	1.1	0.3/2	53.6
Evening Snack						
Popcorn (air-popped), 2 cups	61	13	2	0	0.7/10	0.6
Today's Totals	**2073**	**325**	**131**	**359**	**37/16**	**2994**

"Looks can be deceiving— it's eating that's believing."
—James Thurber

Simple Pleasures

◆

Taste buds cease to crave rich fatty foods when they are satisfied with bold flavors. And frequent little meals or nibbles ward off hunger and keep your energy peaked all day long. Don't hesitate if you want to try stretching the day's fare into smaller bites.

Monday
DAY 15

Fresh Orange Juice

Great Granola* with Yogurt

◆

Fresh Watercress and Tomato Salad
with Our House Dressing*

Peppered Tuna*

Rice with Tarragon and Toasted
Walnuts*

Country French Bread

Sparkling Fresh Raspberries

◆

Quick Black Bean Soup*

Roasted Pepper Quesadillas*

Salad Greens with Pesto Dressing*

A Bunch of Grapes

Breakfast Menu

Foods (per serving)	Cal.	Carb. (g)	Prot. (g)	Chol. (mg)	Fat (g)/%	Sod. (mg)
Orange juice, 6 oz.	83.5	19.4	1.4	0	0.3/3	1.2
Great Granola* (p. 64), ½ cup	282	56	7	0	5/16	57
Nonfat yogurt, ¼ cup	30	4	4	1	0/0	47

Lunch Menu

Foods (per serving)	Cal.	Carb. (g)	Prot. (g)	Chol. (mg)	Fat (g)/%	Sod. (mg)
Watercress, 2 cups	8	0.9	1.6	0	0/0	28
Cucumber and tomato slices	14	2.4	1.3	0	0.2/0.1	5
Our House Dressing* (p. 194), 1 T.	18	2	0.1	0	1.2/58	31
Peppered Tuna*	401	9	53	114	8/18	91
Rice with Tarragon and Toasted Walnuts*	219	43	6	0	2.4/10	286
French bread, 2 slices	192	36	6	0	2/9	426
Raspberries, 1 cup	61	14	1	0	0.7/9	0
Brown sugar, 1 T.	34	8	0	0	0/0	7
Balsamic vinegar, 1 T.	2	0.9	0	0/0	0	0
Afternoon Snack						
Apple, 3½ oz.	59	15	0.2	0	0.4/6	0

174

LOSING THE TASTE FOR FAT

Train your taste buds to prefer less fatty foods. Fruits will taste sweeter, turkey far more interesting. Curb your fat tooth for a while and fatty food suddenly tastes greasy and waxy, with an unappetizing texture. It lands in your stomach with a thud, masking the fresh flavors you've come to love.

Rice with Tarragon and Toasted Walnuts

I make this often, varying the rice, nuts and herbs—and it always tastes fresh. It matches perfectly with any fish, poultry or meat or completes an all-vegetable meal.

SERVES 4

1 cup white rice

2 cups low-fat, low-sodium chicken broth

1 cup coarsely chopped onion

2 tablespoons finely minced garlic

2 tablespoons coarsely chopped walnuts, toasted (see Note page 156)

1 tablespoon finely minced fresh tarragon

2 tablespoons finely minced fresh Italian parsley

SPARKLING FRUIT

When guests see me sprinkling balsamic vinegar on fruit, their eyes widen. But once they've tasted how it brings out natural fruit flavors, they're convinced. A few drops atop raspberries, strawberries, melons or peaches with a sprinkling of sugar is divine.

In a saucepan, combine the rice, chicken broth, onion and garlic and bring to a boil over high heat. Cover, reduce the heat and simmer for about 15 minutes, or until the rice is tender and the liquid is absorbed. Transfer to a bowl, add the walnuts, tarragon and parsley and toss well. Serve immediately.

CAL. 219   CARB. 43G   PROT. 6G   CHOL. 0MG   FAT 2.4G/10%   SOD. 286MG

Peppered Tuna

Here's a peppery tuna steak with a lovely red wine sauce that brings out tuna's truly meaty attributes.

SERVES 4

2 to 4 tablespoons cracked black peppercorns
Four 6-ounce yellowfin tuna steaks
Salt to taste
2 tablespoons unsalted butter
¼ cup minced garlic
2 tablespoons minced fresh tarragon
2 cups dry red wine

1. Preheat the broiler or prepare a charcoal or gas grill.

2. Press the cracked pepper into both sides of the tuna and season with a little salt. Broil or grill 4 inches from the heat for 4 to 6 minutes on each side, until opaque throughout (or rare in the center, if you prefer). Cover and keep warm.

3. In a small skillet, melt the butter over medium-high heat. Add the garlic and cook for 2 to 3 minutes, until lightly browned. Add the tarragon and wine, raise the heat and boil for 4 to 5 minutes, until reduced to ½ cup. Spoon the sauce over the tuna and serve immediately.

NOTE: To crack whole peppercorns, place them on a cutting board and, with the broad side of a chef's knife positioned on the peppercorns, pound the side of the knife several times with your open hand until the peppercorns crack into coarse pieces.

CAL. 401   CARB. 9G   PROT. 53G   CHOL. 114MG   FAT 8G/18%   SOD. 91MG

Quick Black Bean Soup

I make this soup the centerpiece of a menu often because it can be ready in under an hour and tastes terrific.

SERVES 4

1 teaspoon olive oil
4 plump cloves garlic, minced
1 red onion, diced
3 cups canned black beans,
*   with liquid*
2 ounces smoked pork, cut
*   into ¼-inch cubes*
1 teaspoon ground cumin
1 tablespoon finely minced
*   fresh oregano leaves*
1 bay leaf
Pinch of cayenne
2 tablespoons finely chopped
*   fresh Italian parsley*

3 tablespoons finely chopped
*   fresh cilantro*
Salt and freshly ground black
*   pepper to taste*
¼ cup dry sherry
½ red bell pepper, stemmed,
*   seeded and diced into*
*   ¼-inch pieces*
1 tablespoon packed light
*   brown sugar*
1 tablespoon lime juice
1 teaspoon minced lime zest
¼ cup nonfat cottage cheese
*   (optional)*

1. In a saucepan, heat the olive oil over low heat. Add the garlic and onion and cook for about 5 minutes, until the onion is tender.

2. Add the beans, pork, cumin, oregano, bay leaf, cayenne, 1 tablespoon each of parsley and cilantro and salt and pepper to taste. Simmer, uncovered, for 30 minutes.

3. Add the remaining parsley, 1 tablespoon cilantro, sherry, half the red bell pepper, brown sugar, lime juice and lime zest and simmer for another 10 minutes. Adjust the seasonings and serve hot, garnished with the remaining red pepper and cilantro.

4. In a blender, process the cottage cheese until smooth and spoon on top of the soup, if desired, before garnishing with the pepper and remaining cilantro.

NOTE: Smoked pork, often called smoked pork chops, is sold in many supermarkets. If you prefer, substitute turkey ham for the pork.

CAL. 234   CARB. 38G   PROT. 11.5G   CHOL. 6MG   FAT 3.8G/7.5%
SOD. 427MG

176

"Eliminate something superfluous from your life. Break a habit. Do something that makes you feel insecure."
PIERO FERRUCCI

EXERCISING

Current guidelines point to significant health benefits from only a half hour a day of moderately intense activity, such as gardening, walking and using the stairs. It all helps.

But it's also been proven that more is better. Increase activity and your HDL (good) cholesterol level will follow, which may very well protect you against heart disease.

Roasted Pepper Quesadillas

Quesadillas are really very simple to make at home.

SERVES 4

2 tablespoons Nonfat Blend (see page 298)
1 tablespoon Spinach Pesto (see page 86)
1 tablespoon minced seeded jalapeño
1/2 teaspoon crushed red pepper flakes
Freshly ground black pepper to taste
2 large flour tortillas (about 10 inches)
1/4 cup minced scallions, green part only
1/2 cup minced red onion
1/2 cup each roasted, peeled and diced red and
yellow bell peppers (see page 107)
1/2 cup shredded Monterey Jack cheese
1/2 cup shredded white Cheddar cheese
1 tablespoon chopped fresh cilantro

1. Preheat the oven to 450°F.

2. In a small mixing bowl, combine the Nonfat Blend, Spinach Pesto, jalapeño, red pepper flakes and black pepper and mix well.

3. Place the tortillas on a baking sheet sprayed with olive oil spray. Spread half the Nonfat Blend mixture on each, leaving a border.

4. Sprinkle the tortillas evenly with the scallions, onion, roasted peppers and cheeses. Sprinkle the cilantro on 1 tortilla and place the other tortilla on top of it. Bake for 8 to 10 minutes, until the cheese melts. Slice into wedges and serve warm.

CAL. 228   CARB. 20G   PROT. 11G   CHOL. 28MG   FAT 11G/45%   SOD. 173MG

Dinner Menu

FOODS (PER SERVING)	CAL.	CARB. (G)	PROT. (G)	CHOL. (MG)	FAT (G)/%	SOD. (MG)
Quick Black Bean Soup*	234	38	11.5	6	3.8/7.5	427
Roasted Pepper Quesadillas*	228	20	11	28	11/45	173
Salad greens, 1 cup	9.5	1.6	0.9	0	0.1/11	14
Pesto Dressing* (p. 118), 1 T.	17	0.5	0.4	0.4	1.5/80	0.2
Grapes, 1 cup	114	29	1	0	0.9/7	3
Today's Totals	**2006**	**300**	**106**	**149**	**38/17**	**1596**

◆ I use so many lemons and limes in my cooking that I keep them in a bowl on the kitchen counter. Otherwise, out of sight, out of mind.

◆ Peel or grate off the zest (the outermost peel) before juicing. Use it liberally.

◆ Lemons and limes at room temperature yield the most juice. Roll them on the counter, pressing firmly, before squeezing.

◆ Use lemon and lime juice freely to accentuate flavors in your cooking, from a spritz over raspberries or shrimp to a squeeze over broiled lamb chops.

◆ Keep white vegetables white by adding 2 tablespoons of lemon juice to the cooking water.

◆ Rub low-acid foods such as artichokes, bananas and peaches with lemon to heighten flavor and prevent browning.

◆ Freshen up dried herbs by chopping with lemon zest and parsley.

◆ Refrigerated, lemons will keep 6 weeks, limes 3 weeks. At room temperature, lemons last 2 weeks, limes 1 week.

177

Seasonal Serendipity

◆

The vast wealth of ingredients available in America allows many to know no season without suffering a loss of taste. They provide us with endless enjoyment at any time of the year, and with a well-stocked pantry you can create meals for a few.

Tuesday
DAY 16

Banana-Orange Smoothie*

Zucchini Muffins*

◆

Salad Greens with
Orange-Ginger Dressing*

Rosy Tomato Soup*

Cheddar Turkey Grilled Cheese*

◆

Watercress Salad with
Tarragon-Buttermilk Dressing*

Shrimp and Artichoke Pasta*

Strawberry Frozen Yogurt* atop
Fresh Raspberries

Crisp Biscotti with Dried Cherries*

Breakfast Menu

FOODS (PER SERVING)	CAL.	CARB. (G)	PROT. (G)	CHOL. (MG)	FAT (G)/%	SOD. (MG)
Banana-Orange Smoothie* (p. 74)	273	64	7	2	1/3	65
Zucchini Muffin*	210	41	2	0.1	5/20	434
Skim milk, ½ cup	43	6	4	2	0.2/4	62
MORNING SNACK						
Golden raisins, 2 oz.	171	45	2	0	0.3/1	7

"I do not know anyone who has got to the top without hard work. That is the recipe. It will not always get you to the top, but should get you pretty near."

MARGARET THATCHER

Zucchini Muffins

I often make muffin batter the night before I bake it. I fill the muffin cups and then bake the muffins early in the morning.

MAKES 12 MUFFINS

¼ cup canola oil
1½ cups sugar
1 teaspoon vanilla extract
2 cups grated zucchini
1½ cups cake flour
½ cup all-purpose flour
2 teaspoons baking soda

1 teaspoon baking powder
1 teaspoon salt
1 teaspoon cinnamon
1 teaspoon ground cloves
3 tablespoons buttermilk
½ cup unsweetened applesauce

1. Preheat the oven to 400°F. Lightly spray standard-sized muffin tins with vegetable oil spray.

2. In a large bowl, combine the oil, sugar and vanilla and stir until lightly thickened. Fold in the zucchini.

3. In a bowl, sift together the flours, baking soda, baking powder, salt, cinnamon and cloves. Add to the zucchini mixture and mix until just blended. Add the buttermilk and applesauce and stir just to blend. Do not overmix.

4. Fill the muffin cups three-quarters full. Bake for 5 minutes, reduce the temperature to 350°F. and bake for 15 to 20 minutes longer, or until a toothpick comes out clean. Turn the muffins out on a wire rack to cool. Serve warm or completely cool.

NOTE: See page 84 for information on muffin tins and using paper liners.

CAL. 210   CARB. 41G   PROT. 2G   CHOL. 0.1MG   FAT 5G/20%   SOD. 434MG
(ANALYZED PER MUFFIN)

FRESH START

Start every day with a fresh pick-me-up: lemon juice and water, in a ratio of one third to two-thirds. It's citrusy and cool in the summer, warm and soothing in the winter. I drink it as I'm getting dressed and my system perks right up, ready to greet the day.

180

Lunch Menu

Foods (per serving)	Cal.	Carb. (g)	Prot. (g)	Chol. (mg)	Fat (g)/%	Sod. (mg)
Salad greens, 1 cup	9.5	1.6	0.9	0	0.1/11	14
Orange-Ginger Dressing* (p. 120), 1 T.	13	1.7	0.1	0	0.9/54	13
Rosy Tomato Soup* (p. 78)	82	17	3.4	0	0.7/0.8	327
Cheddar Turkey Grilled Cheese*	263	24	20	55	11.8/38	855
AFTERNOON SNACK						
Snow peas, 1 cup	61	11	4	0	0.3/4	6
Pesto Dip* (p. 163), 2 T.	24	1.2	4.2	0	0.27/10	108

PROMISES

Make small promises to yourself about healthy new habits. Then keep them. Each is a small private victory, far more important than a public one.

Cheddar Turkey Grilled Cheese

Here's another warm and luscious sandwich. No one will feel deprived with this.

SERVES 2

2 teaspoons Dijon mustard
4 slices fat-free multi-grain bread
2 ounces white Cheddar cheese, thinly sliced
2 ounces turkey ham, thinly sliced
4 spinach leaves, washed, stemmed and dried
3 tablespoons skim milk
1 large egg white

1. Spread the mustard on 2 slices of bread and top each one with half the cheese, half the ham and 2 spinach leaves. Top with the remaining bread slices.

2. Lightly spray a nonstick skillet with olive oil spray.

3. In a shallow bowl, beat the milk and egg white together with a fork. Dip the sandwiches in the milk mixture, coating both sides by leaving them submerged for 10 to 12 seconds.

4. Cook the sandwiches in the skillet over medium-low heat for 3 to 4 minutes on each side, spraying the side that faces up briefly with olive oil spray before turning the sandwich. The sandwich will toast and the cheese will melt as it cooks. Serve immediately.

CAL. 263   CARB. 24G   PROT. 20G   CHOL. 55MG   FAT 11.8G/38%   SOD. 855MG

181

Crisp Biscotti with Dried Cherries

During the past twenty years, I've come to love biscotti. I prefer them not too dry, and so these have a smidgen of butter. Biscotti are commercially available but check labels; many have a lot of fat.

MAKES ABOUT 45 COOKIES

1 cup dried cherries
3 tablespoons Cran-Raspberry juice, orange juice or cider
4 tablespoons chilled unsalted butter, cut into pieces
1 cup sugar

2 large egg whites
2 cups all-purpose flour
2 teaspoons baking powder
¼ teaspoon salt
½ cup coarsely chopped toasted hazelnuts

1. Place the dried cherries in a large, microwave-safe bowl and stir in the Cran-Raspberry juice. Microwave for 1 to 2 minutes on high power, or until the fruit is soft. Cool to room temperature. Alternatively, soak the cherries in the juice for about 1 hour, until plumped and soft.

2. Preheat the oven to 325°F. Lightly spray 1 large baking sheet with vegetable oil spray.

3. In a food processor fitted with the metal blade, combine the butter and sugar and process until blended. Add the egg whites and process until smooth. Add the flour, baking powder and salt and pulse just until incorporated. Transfer to a bowl and add the drained cherries. Stir in the nuts until incorporated.

4. Divide the dough into 3 flattish logs about 12 inches long and 1½ inches wide. Lay the logs on the baking sheet about 2½ inches apart and bake for 25 to 30 minutes, until lightly browned. The logs will flatten slightly as they bake. Transfer the logs to a cutting board and cool for 10 to 15 minutes. Reduce the oven temperature to 275°F.

5. With a sharp knife, cut the logs diagonally into ½-inch-thick slices. Arrange the slices, standing upright, on the baking sheets and bake 15 to 25 minutes, or until the cut surfaces dry out slightly. Cool on wire racks to room temperature. Serve immediately or store in an airtight container.

CAL. 45   CARB. 10G   PROT. 0.6G   CHOL. 1.4MG   FAT 0.6G/11%   SOD. 55MG

182

VIN SANTO

In Italy, a glass of dry, velvety Vin Santo is the ultimate token of traditional hospitality. A strong amber wine, it's ordinarily reserved for important guests.

I don't take much stock in Very Important People. And I think the good things should be enjoyed—often. So Vin Santo at any old Tuesday dinner suits me fine. Just pour a glass and start dipping biscotti to your heart's content.

In Umbria and Tuscany, making Vin Santo is a venerable tradition. During the October grape harvest, selected bunches of Malvasia or Pulcinculo grapes are hung from the rafters to dry. Around Christmas, the raisins are pressed and the juice poured into a wooden keg to mingle with "la madre" (the wine "mother"). The kegs are placed under the eaves, where four to twenty years may pass before our sipping pleasure.

Shrimp and Artichoke Pasta

This is so pretty and delicious. Best of all, it's dinner in a jiffy.

SERVES 2

¼ pound linguine, cooked and ¼ cup cooking water reserved
2 tablespoons Spinach Pesto (see page 86)
2 tablespoons low-fat, low-sodium chicken broth
1 tablespoon finely minced garlic
8 large shrimp, peeled, deveined and halved lengthwise
½ cup frozen peas
12 frozen artichoke hearts, thawed and halved lengthwise
4 scallions, chopped, green parts only
¼ cup finely minced fresh Italian parsley
Salt and freshly ground black pepper to taste

1. Toss the pasta with the Spinach Pesto and keep it warm.

2. In a large skillet, heat the chicken broth over medium heat. Add the garlic and shrimp and cook for 1 to 2 minutes, until the shrimp is pink. Add the peas and artichokes, cover and cook for 1 to 2 minutes. Add the scallions and parsley, reduce the heat to low, add the pasta with pesto and reserved pasta cooking water and toss to coat evenly. Season with salt and pepper and serve immediately.

CAL. 192   CARB. 30G   PROT. 14G   CHOL. 48MG   FAT 2.3G/10%   SOD. 171MG

183
◆

Dinner Menu

FOODS (PER SERVING)	CAL.	CARB. (G)	PROT. (G)	CHOL. (MG)	FAT (G)/%	SOD. (MG)
Watercress salad, 2 cups	8	0.9	1.6	0	0/0	28
Tarragon-Buttermilk Dressing* (p. 119), 1 T.	7	0.9	0.6	0.5	0.14/18	16
Shrimp and Artichoke Pasta*	192	30	14	48	2.3/10	171
Breadsticks, 2	160	26	12	0	4/22	420
Strawberry Frozen Yogurt* (p. 108), ½ cup	159	36	4	1	0.4/2	48
Raspberries, 1 cup	60	14	1	0	0.7/9	0
Crisp Biscotti with Dried Cherries*, 2	90	20	1.2	2.8	1.2/11	110
EVENING SNACK						
Popcorn (air-popped), 2 cups	61	13	2	0	0.7/10	0.6
Today's Totals	**1887**	**353**	**84**	**112**	**31/15**	**2686**

AIR-POPPED POPCORN

Sometimes it seems the only time we use our microwave is to pop popcorn—until we found out this easy snack can be loaded with fat.

Take heart. The answer's still in the microwave. The Presto Power Pop air-pops popcorn in the microwave without any oil at all. Two cups have 61 calories and less than 1 gram of fat. Spritz on a little butter-flavored oil, add a tiny bit of butter or learn to love corn au naturel. Whichever, you're in control.

FISH SCHOOL

Even the most fatty fish and shellfish tend to have only as much fat as the leanest meat. Cold-water fish such as mackerel, sardines, salmon and tuna tend to have the most fat. Steer instead toward halibut, sole or haddock. Of course, the way you prepare it can add a little or a lot of fat.

3-OZ. SERVING	CAL.	FAT (G)/%	SAT. FAT (G)	CHOL. (MG)
Bass	106	3/25	0.8	65
Bluefish	135	5/33	1	65
Catfish	99	4/36	2	50
Clams, cooked	126	2/14	0.2	57
Cod	87	1/10	0.1	46
Crab, Alaskan king	83	1/11	0.1	45
Crayfish	75	1/12	0.2	113
Drumfish	130	5/35	1.2	70
Haddock	93	1/10	0.2	61
Halibut	111	3/24	0.4	35
Lobster	99	3/27	1.4	65
Mackerel	223	15/61	4	64
Monkfish	83	2/22	1	27
Mussels	146	4/25	0.7	48
Orange roughy	75	1/12	0.1	22

3-OZ. SERVING	CAL.	FAT (G)/%	SAT. FAT (G)	CHOL. (MG)
Oysters	69	2/26	0.9	85
Pompano	178	10/52	3.8	54
Perch	103	2/17	0.3	46
Pike	96	1/9	0.1	43
Red snapper	109	2/17	0.3	40
Salmon, canned	130	6/43	1.4	34
Salmon, fresh	156	6/35	1.4	48
Sardines in oil	184	11/54	2.4	121
Sardines in water	177	10/51	1.3	70
Scallops	91	3/30	0.5	27
Shrimp	84	1/9	0.3	166
Sole	100	1/9	0.3	58
Squid	117	4/31	0.9	239
Swordfish	132	4/27	1.2	43
Trout	128	5/39	1.4	59
Tuna, canned in water	99	1/9	0.2	26
Tuna, fresh	156	5/29	1.4	42
Whitefish	146	6/37	1	66

Source: Bowes & Churche's *Food Values of Portions Commonly Used,* Sixteenth Edition. Jean A. T. Pennington (Boston, Mass.: J. B. Lippincott Company, 1994).

FISH EXCHANGE

Fish that are similar in texture, taste and fat content can usually be cooked by the same method and with like flavorings. Selecting the freshest fish available from the market or wharf that day is the key.

THIN, DELICATE, FLAKY AND LEAN

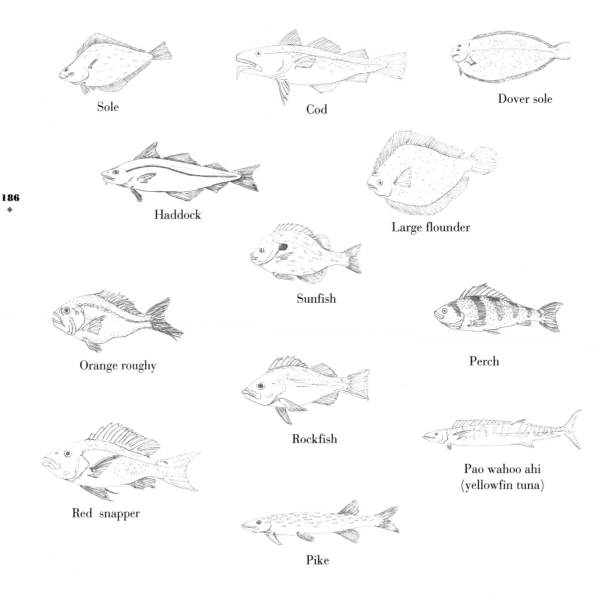

Sole

Cod

Dover sole

Haddock

Large flounder

Sunfish

Orange roughy

Perch

Rockfish

Red snapper

Pao wahoo ahi
(yellowfin tuna)

Pike

MEDIUM-FIRM, MEATY AND MODERATELY LEAN

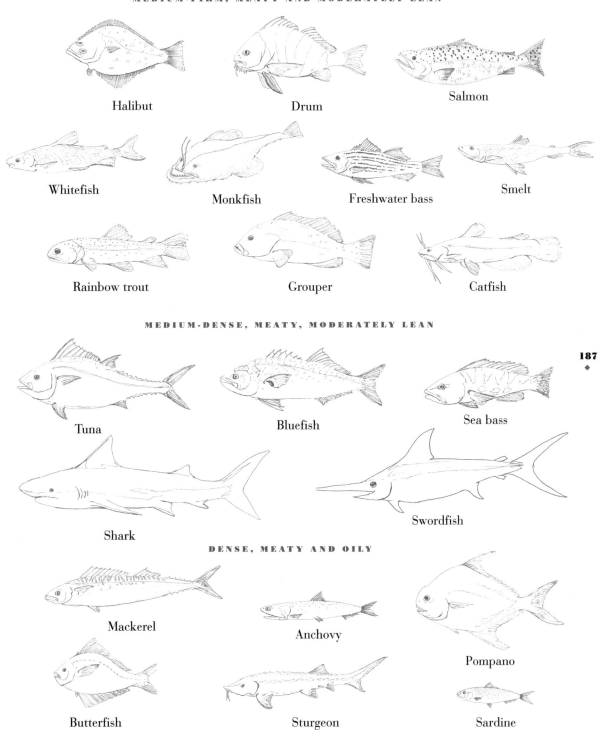

Halibut

Drum

Salmon

Whitefish

Monkfish

Freshwater bass

Smelt

Rainbow trout

Grouper

Catfish

MEDIUM-DENSE, MEATY, MODERATELY LEAN

Tuna

Bluefish

Sea bass

Shark

Swordfish

DENSE, MEATY AND OILY

Mackerel

Anchovy

Pompano

Butterfish

Sturgeon

Sardine

Smoky Flavors

Pork has been bred to be leaner over the years, but untrimmed it can be 38 to 50 percent fat. The pork tenderloin is the only naturally lean part of the pig. Untrimmed, it is 20 to 30 percent fat. Well trimmed, a tenderloin will be about 15 percent fat. And it must be trimmed very well to be 10 percent fat. If ham is very lean, baked and boiled it contains about 1 gram of fat per ounce, but it can contain up to 6 grams per ounce.

3-OZ.	CAL.	FAT (G)/%	SAT. FAT (G)	CHOL. (MG)
FRESH				
Center cut loin roast	165	6/33	2	66
Country-style ribs	210	13/54	5	79
Ham	187	9/45	3	80
Loin chops	172	7/36	3	70
Rib chops	186	8/40	3	69
Spareribs	340	26/69	10	103
Tenderloin	139	4/26	1	67
Wild boar	137	34/20	1	n/a
SMOKED				
Bacon (broiled)	584	55/85	3	468
Canadian bacon	45	2/40	1	28
Ham hock	93	7/68	3	38
Prosciutto	67	4/54	3	78
Turkey ham	90	3.8/38	1.5	52.5

Source: National Pork Producers Council, 1994. Food and Nutrition Consulting Services, Boston, Mass.

188

BUFFALO AND BEEFALO

Both are great alternatives to beef—not gamy-tasting, but the way great beef used to taste. Buy both in many supermarkets and butcher shops nationwide.

Beefalo is a breed that's three-eighths bison (buffalo) and five-eighths bovine (cattle). Bison's been bred with virtually every breed of cattle and the result looks like cattle. The meat of a beefalo is leaner, however, and has more protein, less fat and less cholesterol. Its finer texture cooks more quickly than beef. Both beefalo and buffalo have no fillers, tenderizers, pesticides, hormones or additives. And both are available in all of the cuts of regular beef. If you don't see either in the market, ask your butcher.

Here's the Beef: Veal, Buffalo and Venison

Beef is supposedly back, but in our household it is a very special treat. Lean meat does have a place in my cooking but it has become a flavor, not the focal point. We only need 40 to 60 grams of protein a day and a lean 3- to 4-ounce (90- to 120-gram) portion of beef more than fulfills that need.

Beef is 20 to 60 percent fat, but while you can't trim the marbleized fat, it will melt during cooking. Be sure to trim any separable fat before cooking. For leaner meats, try buffalo or venison sometime; you may be surprised at how terrific it is.

BEEF, 3-OZ.	CAL.	FAT (G)/%	SAT. FAT (G)	CHOL.(MG)
Beefalo	161	5/28	13	50
Brisket, flat part*	189	8/39	3	81
Buffalo	118	2/12	1	53
Chuck arm, pot roast*	183	7/35	3	86
Chuck or ground round	218	14/58	6	84
Elk	117	1/5	n/a	57
Eye round roast*	143	4/26	2	59
Flank steak	176	9/44	4	57
Round tip, roasted*	157	6/34	2	68
Sirloin steak*	165	6/33	2	76
T-bone steak	183	9/44	4	52
Tenderloin steak*	179	9/43	3	71
Top loin steak	176	8/41	3	65
Top round steak*(London broil)	153	4/25	1	71
Top sirloin*	166	6/33	2	70
Venison, farm	135	4/28	1	53
Venison, wild	127	1/8	n/a	99
VEAL, 3-OZ.				
Chop, loin cut*	149	6/36	2	90
Cutlet or roast	128	3/21	1	88
Ground, lean	140	7/40	3	88

* = leanest cuts of beef

Sources: The Meat Board, "Lessons on Meat" (Chicago, Ill.:National Livestock and Meat Board, 1991). *USDA Handbook* #8-10, 8-13, 8-17, Boston, Mass. Michigan State Cooperative Extension Services, 1993. Food and Nutrition Consulting Services, Boston, Mass.

Domestic and Wild Poultry

Chicken is lower in fat than beef. White meat is lower than dark. And more than half of the fat is in and around the skin. Frying doubles the fat, coating the chicken with flour and frying it triples the fat, and dipping it in batter increases the fat six times because it holds the fat in. That's what makes fried chicken so juicy. The really bad news is the cholesterol in chicken. It can have even more than some cuts of beef. And it has saturated fat, too. Stick with white meat, watch how you cook it and always remove the skin before eating.

3-OZ.	CAL.	FAT (G)/%	SAT. FAT (G)	CHOL. (MG)
CHICKEN				
Dark meat with skin	216	14/56	4	78
Dark meat without skin	176	8/42	2	80
Light meat with skin	191	6/29	2	72
Light meat without skin	148	4/23	1	73
TURKEY				
Dark meat with skin	190	10/46	3	77
Dark meat without skin	161	6/34	2	73
Light meat with skin	169	7/37	2	66
Light meat without skin	134	3/20	1	59
WILD TURKEY				
Light and dark with skin	139	1/5	0.2	55
GOOSE				
With skin	262	19/65	6	78
DUCK				
Domestic with skin	288	24/75	8	76
Domestic without skin	172	10/50	4	76
Wild mallard	130	2/12	2	0

PHEASANT

Domestic with skin	155	8/47	1	n/a
Domestic without skin	114	3/24	1	n/a
Wild with skin	126	1/4	0.4	45

PARTRIDGE

Gray	129	1/4	0.6	72
SQUAB	121	7/51	2	90
RABBIT	168	7/37	2	70

Sources: Bowes & Churche's *Food Values of Portions Commonly Used*, Sixteenth Edition. Jean A. T. Pennington (Boston, Mass.: J. B. Lippincott Company, 1994). Michigan Cooperative Eastern Services, 1993. Food and Nutrition Consulting Services, Boston, Mass.

 Lamb and Goat

You either love lamb or you don't. It happens to be my favorite meat. And if you eat lamb, you either like it pink or very well done. Regardless, it's among the fattiest of all meats. So when you indulge, buy the very best. Be aware of the amount you are eating and what you'll have to balance it out with––and then enjoy! And please try goat— it's delicious.

3-OZ.	CAL.	FAT (G)/%	SAT. FAT (G)	CHOL. (MG)
Goat	123	3/19	0.1	64
Loin lamb chop	185	8/40	3	80
Roast leg	250	18/64	7	83
Shank	208	4/19	2	91
Stew meat	158	6/35	2	77

Sources: The Meat Board, "Lessons on Meat" (Chicago, Ill.:National Livestock and Meat Board, 1991). Food and Nutrition Consulting Services, Boston, Mass.

Natural Nuances

◆

When you've gradually lowered fats, sugars and salt in your daily consumption, suddenly food's natural flavors seem to sparkle; they are fresher, crispier and more exciting. Now it's just a matter of preparing them with a little more creatively so that simple foods are truly special.

Wednesday
DAY 17

Tomato Juice

Raisin Bran or Your Favorite Cereal
with Skim Milk

◆

Watercress and Mandarin Orange
Salad with Our House Dressing*

Smoky Pea Soup*

Whole-wheat Roll

Fresh Strawberries

◆

Herbed Bruschetta*

Broiled Honey Salmon*

Hobo Potatoes*

Asparagus Spears with Parmesan
Shards

Green Beans

Peaches in Wine*

Foods (per serving)	Cal.	Carb. (g)	Prot. (g)	Chol. (mg)	Fat (g)/%	Sod. (mg)
Tomato juice, low-sodium, 6 oz.	29	7	1.3	0	0.1/3	17
Raisin Bran, 1 cup	170	43	4	0	1/5	300
Skim milk, 1 cup	86	12	8	4	0.4/4	124

Lunch

Our House Dressing

I've always preferred a dressing that is more acidic than oily. I keep this on hand to toss with greens and pasta, sprinkle on sandwiches or glaze vegetables, meats or poultry as they grill. Be sure to use balsamic vinegar from Modena, which is sharper when young and becomes sweeter, more caramelized and viscous as it ages. Don't worry about the hot water—it works.

194

MAKES ¾ CUP

2 teaspoons finely minced garlic
1 tablespoon Dijon mustard
½ cup balsamic vinegar
¼ cup hot water
1 tablespoon sugar
1 tablespoon olive oil
Salt and freshly ground black pepper to taste

1. In a small bowl, combine the garlic and mustard and mix well. Whisk in the balsamic vinegar, hot water and sugar. Taste the dressing; the sugar should take the edge off the vinegar.

2. Slowly add the olive oil, whisking continuously, until emulsified. Season with salt and pepper. Use immediately or cover and refrigerate.

CAL. 18   CARB. 2G   PROT. 0.1G   CHOL. 0MG   FAT 1.2G/58%   SOD. 31MG
(ANALYZED PER 1 TABLESPOON)

FIBER

We know we're supposed to eat more: 20 to 35 grams (according to the National Cancer Institute) a day.

It doesn't take a truck-load to achieve impressive results—a single cup of oat bran a day, or as much fiber as a cup and a half of beans, will do, along with a diet low in saturated fats and cholesterol. To boost your fiber intake:

◆ Choose whole-grain breads, cereals and crackers.

◆ Eat whole fruits instead of drinking juice.

◆ Eat at least 5 servings of fruits and vegetables each day.

◆ Add dried fruits to cookies, muffins, breads, rice, salads and puddings.

◆ Choose cereals with a minimum of 5 grams of fiber per serving.

◆ Choose fiber-rich snacks such as rice cakes, raw vegetables, popcorn and whole-grain crackers.

◆ Munch broccoli..

◆ Toss beans and peas into your salads.

◆ Eat a small low-fat bran muffin at 4:00 P.M.

◆ Keep an apple in your pocket for a quick snack.

Lunch Menu

Foods (per serving)	Cal.	Carb. (g)	Prot. (g)	Chol. (mg)	Fat (g)/%	Sod. (mg)
Watercress salad, 2 cups	8	0.9	1.6	0	0/0	28
Mandarin oranges, ¼ cup	23	6	1	0	0.01/1	3
Our House Dressing*, 1 T.	18	2	0.1	0	1.2/58	31
Smoky Pea Soup*	264	38	23	23	2/6	398
Whole-wheat roll, 1	93	18	3	0	1.6/15	167
Strawberries, 1 cup	50	12	1	0	0.6/11	1.6
AFTERNOON SNACK						
Brie, 2 oz.	190	0.2	12	56	15.8/75	356
Crackers, nonfat, 3	60	13	2	0	0/0	150

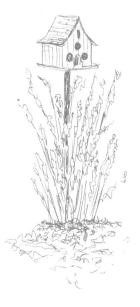

"Nature is pleased with simplicity. . . ."

ISAAC NEWTON

Smoky Pea Soup

One of the best things about split pea soup made with a ham bone is the smoky flavor. I reduced the fat and retained the deep smokiness by using turkey ham.

SERVES 6

195
◆

7 cups low-fat, low-sodium chicken broth

2 ribs celery, coarsely chopped (about ½ cup)

3 small onions, coarsely chopped (about 1 cup)

1 cup finely grated carrots

2 tablespoons finely minced garlic

1½ cups split peas

8 ounces turkey ham, cubed

¼ cup finely minced fresh Italian parsley

In a stockpot, heat ¼ cup chicken broth over medium heat and cook the celery, onion, carrots and garlic for about 10 minutes, until tender. Stir in the peas and ham and cook for 1 minute. Add the remaining 6¾ cups broth, bring to a boil, reduce the heat and simmer for about 1¼ hours, until the peas are tender. Serve immediately sprinkled with parsley.

CAL. 264   CARB. 38G   PROT. 23G   CHOL. 23MG   FAT 2G/6%   SOD. 398MG

Herbed Bruschetta

An Italian favorite you can create at home. This is a lovely tasting version of the Tuscan classic. In summer, this dish praises the glories of the tomato harvest. And if you use very ripe plum tomatoes, you can enjoy it during the remainder of the year, too.

MAKES 12 SLICES

¼ cup finely chopped fresh Italian parsley
¼ cup drained capers, chopped
2 teaspoons finely minced fresh tarragon
Salt and freshly ground black pepper to taste
1 tablespoon extra-virgin olive oil
1 large ripe tomato, finely diced
2 tablespoons finely minced fresh mint
Twelve ¼-inch-thick slices peasant bread or
  French bread

1. In a bowl, combine the parsley, capers, tarragon and salt and pepper. Add the oil and toss well. Set aside.

2. Put the tomato in another bowl and season with salt and pepper. Add the mint. Let stand at room temperature for at least 1 hour.

3. Toast or grill the bread slices.

4. Spread the oil mixture on the warm toast and top each with the tomato mixture. Serve immediately.

CAL. 91   CARB. 16G   PROT. 3G   CHOL. 0MG   FAT 1.8G/18%   SOD. 252MG
(ANALYZED PER SLICE)

"The right food always comes at the right time. Reliance on an out-of-season food makes the gastronomic year an endlessly boring repetition."
ROY ANDRIES DE GROOT

Hobo Potatoes

This campfire specialty is brought indoors without any butter!

SERVES 6

12 medium russet potatoes, washed and thinly sliced
3 medium red onions, thinly sliced, rings separated
2 tablespoons finely minced garlic
1½ teaspoons finely minced fresh tarragon or sage
Salt and freshly ground black pepper to taste

1. Preheat the oven to 350° F.

2. Lay 6 12 × 18-inch sheets of aluminum foil on the countertop and divide the potatoes, onion, garlic and herbs among the sheets. Season with salt and pepper.

3. Cover each with another sheet of foil and fold into 6 tight packages. Transfer to 2 baking sheets and bake for about 45 minutes, until the potatoes are fork-tender. Take care when opening the foil packages; the escaping steam is hot. Remove the potatoes to a serving plate and serve immediately.

CAL. 202   CARB. 46G   PROT. 5.5G   CHOL. 0MG   FAT 0.3G/1%   SOD. 16MG

HONEY

Honey has as many subtle flavors as there are flower growing places on earth. Flowers give honey its special ambrosia—linden, herbal, bramble, mimosa, chestnut, rosemary, fireweed, lilac, buckwheat, lavender or multifloral.

Americans favor clover, Australians eucalyptus, the French acacia and Canadians chestnut. The only way you'll find your favorite is to taste. A perfect sampling place, with more than 50 varieties: Les Abeilles, 21 Rue de la Butte-aux-Cailles 75013 Paris.

Broiled Honey Salmon

The slight sweetness of honey, the saltiness of soy and the dash of heat from the red pepper flakes intensify the extraordinary natural sweetness of the salmon.

SERVES 6

6 tablespoons honey
6 tablespoons soy sauce
2 pounds salmon fillet, skin on
¼ teaspoon crushed red pepper flakes
1 generous tablespoon minced fresh fennel fronds or
    Italian parsley

197

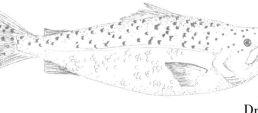

1. Preheat the broiler. Line a baking sheet with aluminum foil.

2. In a small bowl, combine the honey and soy sauce and mix well. Lay the salmon, skin side down, on the baking sheet. Drizzle a quarter of the sauce over the salmon. Sprinkle with the red pepper flakes and fennel and broil 2 inches from the heat source for 10 to 15 minutes, depending on the thickness of the salmon. Drizzle every 2 to 3 minutes with the remaining sauce until the salmon turns a deep mahogany, is opaque and flakes when pierced with a fork. Do not allow it to char. Serve immediately.

CAL. 392   CARB. 36G   PROT. 45G   CHOL. 114MG   FAT 7.6G/17%   SOD. 958MG

Peaches in Wine

At the peak of peach season, I just can't get enough and indulge in peach frozen yogurt, peach pie, peaches on granola, peach coffee cake and, best of all, the ripe, velvety orb itself, eaten out of hand, luscious juices dripping. My favorite dessert is perhaps the easiest of all. Serve this on the very hottest evening, amid the glitter of fireflies.

S E R V E S 6

4 cups sliced fresh peaches
2 cups dry white wine
3 tablespoons sugar
2 tablespoons finely minced fresh mint
½ cup Amaretto liqueur (optional)
Mint sprigs for garnish

In a glass bowl, combine the peaches, wine, sugar, mint and Amaretto, if desired. Cover and refrigerate for at least 6 hours. Garnish with mint sprigs before serving.

CAL. 201 CARB. 32G PROT. 1.3G CHOL. 0MG FAT 0.2G/1% SOD. 5MG

Out of sight, out of mind and out of reach works with most temptations:

◆ Don't buy them to begin with.

◆ If you do, put lethal snacks on a high shelf.

◆ Salted nuts—don't even start!

◆ Clean out the freezer. The ice cream probably has crystals anyway.

◆ A good friend is someone who will take the other half of the cake.

◆ When you bake, cut the recipes in half and buy smaller pans. Make tiny bite-sized cookies. They're more fun anyway.

◆ When you think of dessert, choose a fruit first, then make it special.

◆ Consciously choose your brief moment to indulge. Portion it out, eat slowly, and love every bite.

Dinner Menu

Foods (per serving)	Cal.	Carb. (g)	Prot. (g)	Chol. (mg)	Fat (g)/%	Sod. (mg)
Herbed Bruschetta*, 2 slices	182	32	6	0	3.6/18	504
Broiled Honey Salmon*	392	36	45	114	7.6/17	958
Hobo Potatoes*	202	46	5.5	0	0.3/1	16
Asparagus spears, 6, with Parmesan shards, 1 T.	49	4	4	4.9	2/37	117
Steamed green beans, ½ cup	23	5	1	0	0.2/6	1.9
Peaches in Wine*	201	32	1.3	0	0.2/1	5
Today's Totals	**2040**	**307**	**119**	**202**	**37/16**	**3178**

THE BIG CHEESES

There are numerous low-fat and nonfat cheeses on the market. Still, I'd rather enjoy the flavor of the real thing and just eat less of it. There are some low-fat types I'll use for cooking, such as part-skim mozzarella and Neufchâtel, but I usually use less of a more flavorful "real" cheese and stretch its flavor with nonfat cottage cheese or yogurt. It's totally up to your own taste levels. You'd be surprised how far the flavor of a little bit of real Roquefort will go, or a few shavings of Parmesan.

CHEESE, 1 OZ.	CAL.	FAT (G)/%	SAT. FAT (G)	CHOL. (MG)
American	106	9/76	6	27
Brie	95	8/76	n/a	28
Camembert	85	7/74	4	20
Cheddar	114	10/79	6	30
Cottage cheese, nonfat, ½ cup	70	0/0	0	10
Cream	99	10/91	6	25
Feta	75	6/72	4	25
Goat	76	6/71	5	71
Gruyère	117	9/69	5	31
Havarti	105	8/69	5	27
Mascarpone	62	5/73	3	15
Monterey Jack	106	9/76	n/a	25
Mozzarella, part-skim	72	5/63	3	16
Mozzarella, whole milk	80	6/68	4	22
Muenster	104	9/78	5	29
Neufchâtel	70	6/73	4	22
Parmesan, grated, 1 T.	28	2/64	1.2	5
Parmesan, whole milk	111	7/64	5	19
Ricotta, part-skim	39	2/46	2	9
Ricotta, whole milk	49	4/73	3	15
Romano	110	8/65	n/a	29
Roquefort	105	9/77	5	21
Swiss	107	8/67	5	26

Pure and Simply Delicious

◆

Cooking with the best fresh, natural ingredients you can find, lowering the fat and finding that you're wonderfully satisfied with the flavors can gradually and subconsciously convince you that you can eat all you want. The food tastes so great and is healthy, too, so why not have more? No. Watch your portions—you still need to be aware of the total calories consumed—otherwise you'll find yourself growing, even as your awareness does!

Thursday
DAY 18

Fresh Orange Juice
Winter Fruit Compote*
Multi-grain Cereal with Skim Milk

◆

Salad Niçoise*
Breadsticks
Cantaloupe Frozen Yogurt*

◆

Watercress and Red Onion Salad
with Orange Dressing*
One Thousand Spice Chicken*
Roasted Vegetable Melange*
Honeydew Melon and Lime

B r e a k f a s t   M e n u

FOODS (PER SERVING)	CAL.	CARB. (G)	PROT. (G)	CHOL. (MG)	FAT (G)/%	SOD. (MG)
Orange juice, 6 oz.	83.5	19.4	1.4	0	0.3/3	1.2
Winter Fruit Compote*	85	23	0.9	0.07	0.2/2	2
Multi-grain cereal, 1 cup	100	25	3	0/0	0	110
Skim milk, 1 cup	86	12	8	4	0.4/4	124
MORNING SNACK						
Grapes, 1 cup	114	29	1	0	0.9/7	3
Graham crackers, 2	120	25	2	0	1.5/11	210

L u n c h   M e n u

FOODS (PER SERVING)	CAL.	CARB. (G)	PROT. (G)	CHOL. (MG)	FAT (G)/%	SOD. (MG)
Salad Niçoise*	210	33	15	16	3.7/15	370
Breadsticks, 2	160	26	12	0	4/22	420
Cantaloupe Frozen Yogurt* (p. 109), ½ cup	91	21	2.4	0.6	0.2/2	30
AFTERNOON SNACK						
Apple, 3½ oz.	59	15	0.2	0	0.4/6	0
Muenster cheese, 2 oz.	209	0.6	13	54	17/73	356

Salad Niçoise

Here's a very special way to savor each of the tantalizing tastes of this famous salad from the South of France.

S E R V E S 4

4 small russet potatoes (about 10 ounces)
12 slices tomato
12 slices cucumber
2 tablespoons red wine vinegar
1 tablespoon sugar
2 tablespoons finely minced fresh
 Italian parsley
3 tablespoons hot water
1 teaspoon Dijon mustard
1 tablespoon white wine vinegar
Freshly ground black pepper to taste
12 ounces green beans, trimmed
1 tablespoon fresh oregano, finely minced

**W I N T E R   F R U I T
C O M P O T E**

This is always so nice to have on hand for breakfast, dessert or a snack.

S E R V E S 4

¾ cup unsweetened apple
 cider or pineapple juice
1 ounce pitted prunes
1 ounce dried cherries
1 ounce golden raisins
1 ounce dried apricots
2 whole cloves
One 1½-inch cinnamon
 stick
¼ cup water
Zest of 1 small orange

In a saucepan, combine the cider, prunes, cherries, raisins, apricots, cloves and cinnamon stick. Add the water, bring to a boil, reduce the heat and simmer for 30 minutes, until the fruit is plumped. Discard the cinnamon stick and cloves. Add the orange zest and set aside to cool. Serve immediately or cover and refrigerate until ready to serve. Bring to room temperature before serving.

CAL. 85   CARB. 23G   PROT. 0.9G
CHOL. 0.07MG   FAT 0.2G/2%
SOD. 2MG

**DON'T CLEAN
YOUR PLATE**

To eat less and break old
childhood habits:

♦ Start with a smaller
helping—and a smaller
plate. It'll help you alter
your daily diet immediately.

♦ Serve at the stove so you
don't take seconds.

♦ Always leave some food
on your plate. Forget the
little voice in your ear that
scolds about "starving
children" and contribute to
the hungry in a more direct
way.

♦ Eat only half a serving of
something high in fat. In
time, you'll be satisfied
with less.

♦ Eat slowly so your
body knows it's
satisfied before you
feel stuffed.

♦ If you're like me
and love to sit around
the table and chat, clear
off the food so you don't
end up nibbling on left-
overs.

1 tablespoon capers, drained
1 tablespoon lemon juice
2 teaspoons finely minced garlic
1 teaspoon finely minced lemon zest
1 tablespoon low-fat, low-sodium chicken broth
One 6½-ounce can white meat tuna in water, drained
4 lettuce leaves
Chopped parsley for garnish
8 niçoise olives (optional)

1. In a saucepan, cover the potatoes with cold water and bring to
a boil over high heat. Cook, uncovered, for 15 to 20 minutes, until
fork-tender. Drain and set aside to cool. Quarter when cool.

2. In a bowl, combine the tomato, cucumber, red wine vinegar
and sugar and toss to coat. Set aside and toss every 3 minutes for
15 minutes.

3. In another bowl, combine 1 tablespoon parsley,
2 tablespoons hot water, mustard, white wine
vinegar and pepper. Add to the potatoes, toss
well and set aside.

4. Put the beans in a steaming basket set over
1 inch of boiling water and steam over high heat
for 5 to 6 minutes, or until tender. Rinse under cool water
and set aside in a bowl.

5. In another bowl, combine the oregano, capers, lemon
juice, garlic, lemon zest, chicken broth and remaining
1 tablespoon hot water and mix well. Pour half over the beans.
Reserve the other half.

6. Put the tuna in a bowl, breaking it apart with a fork. Add the
remaining caper sauce and mix well.

7. Spoon the tuna on top of the lettuce leaves divided among
4 plates and arrange the green beans and potatoes next to the
tuna. Garnish each serving with tomato and cucumber slices.
Sprinkle with Italian parsley and garnish with olives, if desired.

CAL. 210   CARB. 33G   PROT. 15G   CHOL. 16MG   FAT 3.7G/15%   SOD. 370MG

Roasted Vegetable Melange

Too often, vegetables roasted in the oven are swimming in olive oil.
Just 2 teaspoons enriches the flavor—no need for another drop.

SERVES 4

1 zucchini, halved lengthwise and cut into ¾-inch chunks
2 cups broccoli florets
1 leek, thinly sliced (about 8 ounces)
½ pound asparagus, trimmed, if necessary, and cut into
  3-inch lengths
½ pound baby carrots, peeled and trimmed
12 shallots, peeled
20 cloves garlic
8 sprigs fresh thyme
2 teaspoons olive oil
1 cup low-fat, low-sodium chicken broth
½ pound cherry tomatoes
2 tablespoons finely minced fresh dill
¼ cup finely minced fresh Italian parsley
Salt and freshly ground black pepper to taste

204
◆

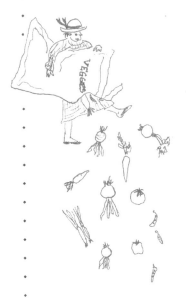

1. Preheat the oven to 350°F.

2. Arrange the zucchini, broccoli, leek, asparagus and carrots in
two 9 × 13-inch roasting pans. Divide the shallots, garlic, thyme,
oil and chicken broth between the pans and toss well.

3. Bake for 1½ hours, tossing every 15 minutes. Add the tomatoes and bake for 30 minutes longer. Season with the dill, parsley
and salt and pepper.

NOTE: This works well with quartered russet potatoes, frozen,
thawed peas and frozen, thawed artichoke hearts, too.

CAL. 171   CARB. 32G   PROT. 7.5G   CHOL. 0MG   FAT 3.7G/18%   SOD. 199MG

*"Don't go into a
restaurant for
something you can
do better at home."*
NICOLAS FREELING

One Thousand Spice Chicken

When I first tasted this chicken at Lola's in New York City, I couldn't believe cayenne was the only spice! The chicken *tastes* as though it's indeed seasoned with one thousand spices.

SERVES 4

2 large egg whites
½ teaspoon cayenne
½ cup toasted bread crumbs
  or Panko
One 3-pound chicken,
  skinless, cut into pieces

1. Preheat the oven to 450°F. Lightly spray a shallow roasting pan with vegetable oil spray.

2. In a shallow bowl, lightly beat the egg whites with a fork. Place the cayenne and crumbs in a plastic bag and shake well. Roll a few chicken pieces in the egg whites and then drop into the plastic bag and shake to coat. Repeat until all of the chicken is coated. Lay the chicken in the roasting pan, spray with a little vegetable oil spray and bake for about 35 minutes, until crispy.

205
◆

CAL. 367   CARB. 9G   PROT. 50G   CHOL. 146MG   FAT 12.7G/32%   SOD. 256MG

Dinner Menu

FOODS (PER SERVING)	CAL.	CARB. (G)	PROT. (G)	CHOL. (MG)	FAT (G)/%	SOD. (MG)
Watercress, 2 cups, with red onion slices, 3	24	4.5	2	0	0.1/4	29
Orange Dressing* (p. 121), 1 T.	12	2	0.8	0.2	0.04/3	11
One Thousand Spice Chicken*	367	9	50	146	12.7/32	256
Roasted Vegetable Melange*	171	32	7.5	0	3.7/18	199
Honeydew, ¼, with lime, 1 t.	80	19	1	0	0.2/2	22
Today's Totals	**1972**	**295**	**121**	**221**	**45/20**	**2143**

VEGETABLES	AMOUNT	CAL.	VIT. A	VIT. C	CALCIUM	FIBER
Alfalfa sprouts	1 cup	10	x	x	x	
Artichoke	1	60	x	x	x	
Asparagus	12	44	x	x	x	
Beets, cooked	1 cup	52		*		*
Broccoli, cooked	1 cup	24	x	x		*
Brussels sprouts cooked	1 cup	60	x	x		x
Cabbage, raw	1 cup	18		x		x
Carrot, raw	1	31	x	x		x
Cauliflower, cooked	1 cup	25		x		*
Celery, raw	1 stalk	6	x			
Corn, cooked	1 cup	133		x		x
Dandelion greens	1 cup	14	x	x	x	*
Eggplant, cooked	1 cup	26				x
Fennel, raw	1 cup	27		x	x	
Green beans, raw	1 cup	44	*	x		
Green peas, raw	1 cup	117	x	x		x
Green peppers, raw	1	28	*	x		
Kale, cooked	1 cup	42	x	x	x	x
Kohlrabi, cooked	1 cup	48		x		
Leek, cooked	1	32	x	x	x	x
Lettuce, Boston	1 cup	8	x	*		n/a
Lettuce, iceberg	1 cup	9	x	x		x
Lettuce, leaf	1 cup	10	x	*		

VEGETABLES	AMOUNT	CAL.	VIT. A	VIT. C	CALCIUM	FIBER
Lettuce, romaine	1 cup	8	x	x		
Mushrooms, raw	1 cup	42		*		*
Mustard greens, cooked	1 cup	28	x	x	x	x
Onions, raw	1 cup	60				*
Parsnips, cooked	1 cup	126		x		x
Potato, baked with skin	1	227	n/a	x		x
Radishes, raw	10	7		x		
Red pepper, raw	1	28	x	x		
Rutabaga, cooked	1 cup	58		x		*
Snow peas, cooked	1 cup	40		x	x	*
Spinach, raw	1 cup	12	x	x		*
Summer squash, cooked	1 cup	24	*	*		
Sweet potato, no skin	1	206	x	x		x
Swiss chard, cooked	1 cup	36	x	x	x	*
Tomato, raw	1	26	*	x		
Turnips, cooked	1 cup	28		x		x
Watercress	1 cup	4	x	x		x
Winter squash, cooked	1 cup	82	x	x		*

x = contains at least 10% of the RDA

* = contains at least 5 to 9% of the RDA

n/a = not available

Stop in for a Bite

◆

When meals are simple, it doesn't take much planning or preparation to expand one spontaneously so that folks can join you for dinner. And if they're those friends you open your kitchen door to, so much the better. It makes less work for you, and supper in the kitchen makes it all very cozy.

Friday
DAY 19

Pineapple Smoothie*

Oat Bran Muffins*

◆

Sunny Greek Salad*

Primavera Pizza*

Angel Food Cake with
Fresh Raspberries

◆

Broccoli with Lemon-Pepper Dip*

Hot and Sour Soup*

Salad Greens with
Orange-Balsamic Dressing*

Shrimp Fried Rice*

Herb Bread

Deep Dark Chocolate Custard*

Breakfast Menu

Foods (per serving)	Cal.	Carb. (g)	Prot. (g)	Chol. (mg)	Fat (g)/%	Sod. (mg)
Pineapple Smoothie* (p. 75)	224	52	6	2	1.4/5	66
Oat Bran Muffin*	133	34	3.9	0.9	1.9/10	315
Morning Snack						
Orange, 1	62	16	1	0	0.2/3	0

Oat Bran Muffins

These are the tastiest light bran muffins. You'll crave these because they're dense and crunchy—plus they keep well for several days!

MAKES 12 MUFFINS

½ cup dried cherries
¼ cup orange juice
1 cup cake flour
1¼ cups oat bran
2 teaspoons baking soda
2 teaspoons baking powder
¼ cup packed light brown sugar
2 tablespoons chopped almonds
1 cup buttermilk
1 cup fresh or canned drained crushed pineapple
½ teaspoon cinnamon
¼ teaspoon ground cloves
1 tablespoon grated orange zest

210

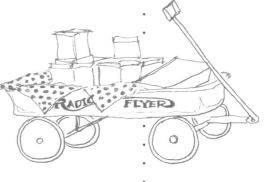

"The breakfast table is not a bulletin board for the curing of horrible dreams and depressing symptoms, but the place where a bright keynote for the day is struck."

B.G. Jeffries

WHY YOU NEED TO EXERCISE

Heart disease. Inactivity doubles your risk. Exercise reduces triglyceride levels and raises HDL (good) cholesterol. Vigorous exercise can even reverse the buildup of arterial plaque.

Stroke. A long-term study shows that inactivity increases your risk of stroke three-fold.

Osteoporosis. Weight-bearing exercise helps maintain bone density, decreasing the risk of fracture.

Cancer. Exercise appears to offer moderate protection against colon and breast cancer.

Hypertension. Exercise reduces blood pressure levels.

Diabetes. Adult-onset diabetes is less likely to develop in people who exercise.

1. Preheat the oven to 425°F. Lightly spray standard-sized muffin tins with vegetable oil spray.

2. In a small bowl, combine the cherries with the orange juice and set aside for about 1 hour to plump.

3. In a large bowl, combine the flour, oat bran, baking soda, baking powder, brown sugar and almonds and whisk to mix. Add the buttermilk, pineapple, cinnamon, cloves and orange zest and stir until just mixed. Do not overmix. Drain and add the plumped cherries, discarding the excess juice.

4. Fill the muffin cups two-thirds full and bake for 10 minutes. Reduce the temperature to 400°F. and bake for 5 minutes longer, or until a toothpick comes out clean. Turn the muffins out onto a wire rack to cool. Serve warm or cooled. Store in an airtight container.

NOTE: See page 84 for information on standard-sized muffin tins and using paper liners.

CAL. 133   CARB. 34G   PROT. 3.9G   CHOL. 0.9MG   FAT 1.9G/10%   SOD. 315MG
(ANALYZED PER MUFFIN)

211
◆

Sunny Greek Salad

This classic is always satisfying, even when made with far less olive oil than usual. The smidgen of feta is important, because this wouldn't be a Greek salad without it. Don't worry that the warm water will wilt the greens—it won't.

SERVES 4

8 cups mixed greens, such as Boston, Bibb or leaf lettuce
2 tablespoons lemon juice
¼ cup very warm water
2 tablespoons finely minced fresh oregano
2 small cucumbers, peeled and thinly sliced (about 40 slices)
2 large plum tomatoes, coarsely chopped
8 scallions, coarsely chopped, green part only
  (about ½ cup)
¼ cup capers
½ cup finely minced fresh Italian parsley
½ cup crumbled feta cheese
8 Kalamata olives

1. In a large mixing bowl, place the mixed greens. In a small bowl, combine the lemon juice, warm water and oregano and whisk well. Drizzle over the greens and toss thoroughly.

2. Divide the greens among 4 plates. Top each with cucumber, tomato, scallions, capers and parsley. Toss gently. Sprinkle the feta evenly over the salads and garnish each with 2 olives.

CAL. 99   CARB. 13G   PROT. 5.2G   CHOL. 12.6MG   FAT 3.8G/35%   SOD. 180MG

Lunch Menu

FOODS (PER SERVING)	CAL.	CARB. (G)	PROT. (G)	CHOL. (MG)	FAT (G)/%	SOD. (MG)
Sunny Greek Salad*	99	13	5.2	12.6	3.8/35	180
Primavera Pizza* (p. 150)	174	25	10	8	4.9/24	275
Angel food cake	103	22	4	0	0.1/1	126
Raspberries, 1 cup	61	14	1	0	0.7/9	0

TRUST YOUR TASTE

Recipes are just the bare bones. Good cooking comes from a spirit of adventure, trusting your instincts, taking risks.

Taste your ingredients. Fresh, natural flavors vary from one time to the next. That's what makes cooking fun. Learn what the anise flavor of tarragon really tastes like. Taste the arugula to find out how peppery it is today. Sample a strawberry to gauge the sweetness of this week's crop.

Add the most pungent flavorings a smidgen at a time. Taste. Add more if you like. Indulge in your favorites, adding more than the recipe calls for. Follow your personal tastes. It's your own signature, the spirit that makes my recipe into yours.

La Botte
28°.00

Shrimp Fried Rice

Usually loaded with oil, this version has only one teaspoon! Instead, each bite is loaded with flavor, making this the best I've ever had! If possible, cook the rice a day ahead of time or use left-over rice—this gives the rice time to dry out a little. Store cooked rice, covered, in the refrigerator.

SERVES 4

213
◆

1½ cups brown rice
2 tablespoons finely minced garlic
3 cups plus 2 tablespoons low-fat, low-sodium chicken broth,
 plus more if needed
½ teaspoon chopped fresh thyme leaves
1 teaspoon sesame oil
2 tablespoons finely minced fresh ginger
1 tablespoon finely minced lemon zest
⅓ cup finely minced shallots
½ pound medium shrimp, deveined, peeled and halved
¾ cup halved, thinly sliced onion
1 cup finely diced red bell pepper
2 cups coarsely chopped Chinese cabbage
1 cup bean sprouts
2 tablespoons soy sauce
2 tablespoons dry sherry
¼ cup finely minced fresh chives
2 large egg whites, lightly beaten
1 cup frozen green peas, thawed

(continued on next page)

1. In a saucepan, combine the rice, 1 tablespoon garlic, 3 cups chicken broth and the thyme and bring to a boil over high heat. Reduce the heat to low, cover and simmer for 45 to 55 minutes, until the rice is tender and the liquid absorbed.

2. In a wok or large skillet, heat the oil and remaining 2 tablespoons broth over high heat. Cook the remaining 1 tablespoon garlic, the ginger, lemon zest and shallots for 1 to 2 minutes, stirring, until tender. Take care not to burn. Add the shrimp and cook for 3 to 5 minutes, until pink. Add the onion, pepper, cabbage and sprouts and cook, stirring constantly, for 2 minutes. Add the soy sauce, sherry and more broth, if necessary, and toss for 1 minute. Add the chives and cooked rice and toss. Make a small hole in the center of the rice and pour in the egg whites; fold into the rice mixture. Fold in the peas and cook for 1 minute. Serve immediately.

CAL. 448   CARB. 74G   PROT. 27G   CHOL. 86MG   FAT 4.6G/9%   SOD. 1035MG

Deep Dark Chocolate Custard

This is a thick dark chocolate custard that is reminiscent of old-fashioned chocolate pudding.

SERVES 4

One 12-ounce can evaporated skim milk
3 tablespoons cocoa powder
4 large egg whites
1 large whole egg
½ cup sugar
¼ cup heavy cream
½ teaspoon vanilla extract
Vanilla Dreamy Cream (optional) (see page 87)

214

TIME: OUR GREATEST LUXURY

Everybody's going at breakneck speed, edging out activities like cooking and exercising in the process.

According to the Gallup Poll, one person in ten says they have no free time. Four in ten admit they're constantly rushed. Eight in ten say they sacrifice some career opportunities for family time.

We're living in the fastest, most time-conflicted era in history. The "overworked American" works the equivalent of one month more a year than his counterpart did twenty years ago. The free time left tends to get scheduled.

It's up to every one of us to prioritize our time, simplify our lives, look clearly at what is most important and make time for it.

Setting priorities is a continual process, not to be left for vacations, serious conversations or flights of fancy amid the clouds.

Every week, *first* schedule the things that are truly important in your life. Then schedule the stuff that has to get done. Next week, assess how you did.

1. Preheat the oven to 350°F.

2. In a small bowl, whisk together the milk and cocoa until smooth. In another bowl, combine the egg whites, egg and sugar and whisk well. Slowly whisk in the chocolate mixture, cream and vanilla.

3. Pour the mixture into four 6-ounce custard cups or ramekins. Put the cups in a roasting pan and add enough hot water to come halfway up the sides of the cups.

4. Bake for about 45 to 50 minutes, until the centers are set and a knife inserted in the center comes out clean. Cool in the water bath to room temperature. Cover and refrigerate for at least 2 hours. Serve with a dollop of Vanilla Dreamy Cream, if desired.

CAL. 280   CARB. 41G   PROT. 15G   CHOL. 77MG   FAT 8.2G/25%   SOD. 175MG

215
◆

Dinner Menu

Foods (per serving)	Cal.	Carb. (g)	Prot. (g)	Chol. (mg)	Fat (g)/%	Sod. (mg)
Broccoli, 1 cup	44	8	5	0	0.5/10	42
Lemon-Pepper Dip* (p. 162), 2 T.	18	1.2	3.6	0	0/0	108
Hot and Sour Soup* (p. 138)	102	18	4	0	0.4/3	392
Salad greens, 2 cups	19	3.2	1.8	0	0.2/11	28
Orange-Balsamic Dressing* (p. 121), 1 T.	12	3	0	0	0/0	0.4
Shrimp Fried Rice*	448	74	27	86	4.6/9	1035
Herb bread, 1 slice	93	18	3	0	1.7/15	167
Deep Dark Chocolate Custard*	280	41	15	77	8.2/25	175
EVENING SNACK						
Popcorn (air-popped), 2 cups	61	13	2	0	0.7/10	0.6
Today's Totals	**1993**	**355**	**89**	**187**	**30/14**	**2910**

Farmers' Market Feast

◆

An early morning trip to the farmers' market will plan your menus for you. Foods grown locally with a caring farmer's integrity just taste more like themselves. When the flavor is natural, it means you only need to encourage it gently when you're cooking to coax its optimum flavor.

Saturday
DAY 20

Fresh Orange Juice

Old-Fashioned Oatmeal with
Skim Milk and Brown Sugar

Fresh Strawberries

Cinnamon Toast*

◆

Roasted Vegetable Feast*

Country French Bread

Spicy Carrot Cake with
Cream Cheese Frosting*

◆

Shrimp Dip with Cucumber Slices*

Watercress Salad with
Our House Dressing*

Broiled Beef Tenderloin

Herbed Scalloped Potatoes*

Green Beans with
Roasted Red Peppers*

Café au Lait Frozen Yogurt*

Breakfast Menu

FOODS (PER SERVING)	CAL.	CARB. (G)	PROT. (G)	CHOL. (MG)	FAT (G)/%	SOD. (MG)
Orange juice, 6 oz.	83.5	19.4	1.4	0	0.3/3	1.2
Oatmeal, ¾ cup	156	27	7	0	2.6/15	2
Skim milk, ½ cup	43	6	4	2	0.2/4	62
Brown sugar, 2 T.	68	16	0	0	0/0	7
Strawberries, 1 cup	50	12	1	0	0.6/11	1.6
Cinammon Toast* (p. 57)	65	2	14	0	0/0	91

Lunch Menu

FOODS (PER SERVING)	CAL.	CARB. (G)	PROT. (G)	CHOL. (MG)	FAT (G)/%	SOD. (MG)
Roasted Vegetable Feast*	170	37	7	0	2/9	40
French bread, 2 slices	192	36	6	0	2/9	426
Spicy Carrot Cake with Cream Cheese Frosting*	160.3	25.4	3	14.4	5.6/26	246
AFTERNOON SNACK						
Crackers, nonfat, 3	60	13	2	0	0/0	150

Roasted Vegetable Feast

218

This beautiful array of roasted, grilled and steamed vegetables is a true celebration of the garden's bounty. It's a vegetarian's dream, everyone's delight.

SERVES 4

1 pound small red potatoes
2 small eggplants, cut into eight ½-inch slices (about 1 pound)
2 small red onions, quartered
2 leeks, halved
4 plum tomatoes
2 large red bell peppers, roasted, peeled and coarsely chopped (see page 107)
¼ cup red wine vinegar
2 tablespoons finely minced garlic

½ cup coarsely chopped fresh parsley
Kosher salt and freshly ground black pepper
½ pound asparagus, trimmed
½ pound green beans, trimmed
½ pound sugar snap peas, trimmed
2 tablespoons finely minced chives
8 whole heads garlic, roasted (see page 231)

NEW POTATOES

1. Preheat the oven to 400°F. Lightly spray a roasting pan with olive oil spray.

2. Spread the potatoes in the pan and roast for about 45 minutes, until tender and crispy.

3. Preheat the broiler. Place the eggplant, onion and leek in a roasting pan, keeping the vegetables separate. Spray with olive oil spray and broil 5 to 6 inches from the heat source for 3 to 4 minutes on each side, until golden. Set aside.

4. Cut the tomatoes in half horizontally and lay them on a baking sheet, cut side up. Broil for about 5 minutes, until they begin to brown.

5. Cut the eggplant into ½-inch strips and the tomatoes into large chunks, removing the skin of both as you do so. Transfer the eggplant, tomatoes, onion, leek and potatoes to a bowl and toss with the pepper, vinegar, minced garlic and 6 tablespoons chopped parsley. Season to taste with salt and pepper and set aside.

SUGAR SNAP PEAS

These crispy, sugar-sweet peas eaten pod and all are by far my favorites. A cross between an English pea and a snow pea, they're also a "snap" to cook.

Every spring, when they're heaped high at the Farmers' Market, I try to include them in almost everything—soups, the crudite basket, steamed in salads, rice and pasta dishes, stir frys, stews and unadorned by the handful. They're loaded with protein and fiber, fat- and cholesterol-free and have only 117 calories per cup. Steam or microwave. But don't overcook or they'll lose their snap!

6. Put the asparagus and beans in a steaming basket set over 2 inches of boiling water and steam for 2 minutes. Add the peas and continue steaming for about 1 minute longer, until the vegetables are crisp-tender. Transfer to a bowl and spray with olive oil spray. Add the chives and toss well.

7. Arrange all the vegetables and the roasted garlic on a large platter or divide among 4 plates. Sprinkle lightly with the remaining chopped parsley and serve at room temperature.

CAL. 170   CARB. 37G   PROT. 7G   CHOL. 0MG   FAT 2G/9%   SOD. 40MG

Spicy Carrot Cake with Cream Cheese Frosting

This lighter version of carrot cake also has a much lighter (but equally yummy) cream cheese frosting. You can skip the frosting if you like and sprinkle the cake lightly with confectioners' sugar.

SERVES 24

1 recipe Spicy Carrot Muffins (see page 84)
¼ cup nonfat cottage cheese
6 ounces Neufchâtel cream cheese, at room temperature
8 tablespoons confectioners' sugar
1 teaspoon lemon juice
1 teaspoon vanilla extract

1. Preheat the oven to 350°F. Lightly spray a 9 × 13 × 2-inch baking pan with vegetable oil spray.

2. Spread the muffin batter in the pan and bake for 25 to 30 minutes, or until a toothpick inserted in the center comes out clean. Let the cake cool in its pan set on a wire rack for at least 1 hour, until completely cool before frosting.

3. In a blender, process the cottage cheese until smooth.

4. In a bowl, beat the cream cheese with a fork or wire whisk until light and fluffy. Using a rubber spatula, fold in the cottage cheese, sugar, lemon juice and vanilla. Frost the cake and serve.

CAL. 160.3   CARB. 25.4G   PROT. 3G   CHOL. 14.4MG   FAT 5.6G/26%   SOD. 246MG

220

GREEN BEANS WITH ROASTED RED PEPPERS

Smoky red peppers add immense sparkle atop dark green beans!

SERVES 4

1 pound green beans
2 tablespoons finely minced fresh basil
¼ cup finely chopped roasted red pepper (see page 107)
Salt and freshly ground black pepper to taste

1. Put the green beans in a steaming basket set over 2 inches of boiling water and steam for 5 to 7 minutes, until tender.

2. Transfer the beans to a bowl and toss with the basil and peppers. Lightly spray with olive oil spray and toss to coat evenly. Season with salt and pepper and serve immediately.

CAL. 38   CARB. 8.6G   PROT. 2G
CHOL. 0MG   FAT 0.2G/3%
SOD. 104MG

Herbed Scalloped Potatoes

These are pleasingly moist and loaded with flavor.

SERVES 4

1 pound Yukon Gold or russet potatoes, peeled and thinly sliced
1 tablespoon finely minced fresh thyme
4 fresh or dried bay leaves
2 tablespoons crumbled goat cheese
1 cup skim milk
2 tablespoons instant potato flakes
Freshly ground black pepper

1. Preheat the oven to 350°F.

2. Lay half the potatoes in an 8 × 8 × 2-inch casserole. Sprinkle 1½ teaspoons thyme over the potatoes and then layer with the remaining potatoes. Nestle the bay leaves into the potatoes.

3. In a blender, combine the cheese, ¼ cup milk and the potato flakes and blend until smooth. Add the remaining ¾ cup milk and blend to combine. Pour over the potatoes, sprinkle with the remaining 1½ teaspoons thyme and season to taste with the pepper. Cover tightly with foil and bake for 45 minutes. Uncover and bake for about 20 minutes longer, until the potatoes are fork-tender and lightly browned. Remove and discard the bay leaves.

CAL. 139   CARB. 25G   PROT. 6G   CHOL. 5MG   FAT 2G/13%   SOD. 67MG

Dinner Menu

FOODS (PER SERVING)	CAL.	CARB. (G)	PROT. (G)	CHOL. (MG)	FAT (G)/%	SOD. (MG)
Shrimp Dip* (p. 163), 2 T.	20.4	1.2	3.6	12	0.06/4	90
Cucumber slices, ½ cup	6.7	1	0.4	0	0/0	1
Watercress, 2 cups	8	0.9	1.6	0	0/0	28
Our House Dressing* (p. 194), 1 T.	18	2	0.1	0	1.2/58	31
Broiled beef tenderloin, 3 oz.	179	0	24	71	8.5/44	54
Herbed Scalloped Potatoes*	139	25	6	5	2/13	67
Herb bread, 1 slice	93	18	3	0	1.7/15	167
Green Beans with Roasted Red Peppers*	38	8.6	2	0	0.2/3	104
Café au Lait Frozen Yogurt* (p. 109), ½ cup	153	31	7	1	0/1	157
Today's Totals	**1703**	**283**	**93**	**106**	**32/17**	**1726**

FRESH BAY LEAVES

Since I moved to Michigan, I've nurtured six 8-foot topiary bay trees planted in big terracotta pots. In winter, they line a bright wall in my cottage office. But come spring, we set them out in the garden, where they stand in a row like Roman sentinels.

I can't tell you how much their fresh, fragrant, almost citruslike presence has added to my cooking, enhancing sauces, stews and soups as you might expect, but also rice dishes, poached fish, vegetable dishes, even savory custards.

They require a minimum of care—water and moderate sunlight. Clipping leaves for cooking takes care of the pruning. They can grow to be forty feet tall.

It's lovely how they contribute as much to cooking as they do to fragrant summer walks in the garden.

221

PORTABLE FEASTS

"**snack** (snak) *n*. 1. a small portion of food or drink or a light meal, esp. one eaten between regular meals. 2. a. a share. b. a portion. 3. to have a snack or light meal, esp. between regular meals." Today . . . choose smart!

Fruit Smoothies*

Angel food cake

Eggplant dip

Frozen grapes

Lemon-Pepper Dip*

Fruit salad

Goat cheese (chèvre)

Strawberries

Baked potato

Air-popped popcorn

Tortilla Chips* and salsa

Bagels

Low-fat cottage cheese or
    yogurt dips

Pears

Primavera Pizza*

Blue cheese and spring onions

Apples

Cereal

Apple and aged Cheddar

Summertime Bruschetta*

Café au Lait Frozen Yogurt*

Sorbet

Simple Black Bean Salsa*

Vegetable juices

Spinach Dip* and crackers

Cantaloupe Frozen Yogurt*

Raisins

Chocolate Frangelico Frozen
    Yogurt*

Fat-free muffins

Potato skins and salsa

Grapes

Graham crackers

Cinnamon-raisin bagel

Tomato juice

Rice pudding

Vanilla wafers

Flavored rice cakes

Broccoli florets and nonfat dip

Granola-sprinkled yogurt

Caper and Olive Bruschetta*

Frozen orange slices

A slice of bread and jam

Roasted Pepper Dip*

Yogurt with fruit

Cucumber

Coleslaw

Fruit yogurt

Instant oatmeal

Hard pretzels

Granny Smith apple with Brie

Lime Frozen Yogurt*

Nonfat cottage cheese

Celery and carrot sticks

Whole-grain crackers

Dried fruits

Baby carrots

A perfect peach

Nonfat vanilla yogurt

Gingersnaps and skim milk

Roasted chestnuts

Nonfat cream cheese and
  chutney

Orange sections

Sugar snap peas

Skim milk

Low-cal gelatin

Pickles

Pesto Dip* with broccoli

Raw vegetables

Blackberry Frozen Yogurt*

Creamy Guacamole* with
  Tortilla Chips*

Sun-Dried Tomato Dip*

Herbed Bruschetta*

Crab Dip* and sugar snap peas

Pico de Gallo*

Melon with white wine

Peach Frozen Yogurt*

Low-fat string cheese

Low-sodium instant soup

* = recipe in the book

Great Garden Favorites

◆

Your own small garden—a few herbs, several greens, some climbing peas, a tomato plant or two—will start a connection with the natural growing process that will nurture the soul. And to walk out of your kitchen to pick a little of this or that for dinner will make you smile. Start small and watch it grow.

Sunday
DAY 21

Ruby Red Grapefruit
Pecan Coffee Cake*
Pesto Frittata*

◆

Spring Green Soup*
Minty Tabbouleh*
Breadsticks

◆

Oven-Fried Vegetables* with
Lemon-Pepper Dip*
Arugula Salad with Feta Dressing*
Pasta with Bolognese Sauce*
Italian Bread with Roasted Garlic
Sostanza Cake*

Breakfast Menu

Foods (per serving)	Cal.	Carb. (g)	Prot. (g)	Chol. (mg)	Fat (g)/%	Sod. (mg)
Ruby Red grapefruit, ½	37	9.5	0.7	0	0.1/3	0
Pecan Coffee Cake*	155	27	0.3	8	4/24	64
Pesto Frittata*	155	1.6	14.8	78	9.5/57	332

Pecan Coffee Cake

This is a classic sour cream coffee cake that we've all loved for ages. By using Nonfat Blend, the fat and cholesterol are reduced dramatically.

SERVES 24

1½ ounces pecans, coarsely chopped (about ½ cup)
¼ cup packed light brown sugar
1½ teaspoons cinnamon
2 cups granulated sugar
¼ cup canola oil
2 tablespoons finely minced lemon zest

1 large egg, lightly beaten
2 large egg whites, lightly beaten
1 cup Nonfat Blend (see page 298)
2½ teaspoons vanilla extract
4 teaspoons lemon juice
2 cups all-purpose flour
1 tablespoon baking powder

1. Preheat the oven to 350°F. Lightly spray a 10-inch Bundt pan with vegetable oil spray and lightly dust with flour. Tap out any excess flour.

2. In a small bowl, combine the pecans, brown sugar and cinnamon and stir to mix. Set aside.

3. In the bowl of an electric mixer set on medium-high speed, beat the sugar, oil and lemon zest until evenly moistened. Add the egg and egg whites and mix for about 1 minute. Add the Nonfat Blend and mix until blended. Add the vanilla and lemon juice and mix until blended.

4. Whisk together the flour and baking powder and then slowly add to the batter, stirring until completely blended. Pour two-thirds of the batter into the prepared pan.

5. Sprinkle the nut mixture evenly over the batter and then gently pour in the remaining batter, smoothing into place

226

BREAKFAST AROUND THE WORLD

Globally, breakfast offers great variety. Egypt's morning staple is mudammas (beans). Latin Americans favor rice, beans and tortillas. The Japanese eat rice and miso soup. Israelis enjoy huge buffets of fruits, cheeses and flatbreads. In Scandinavia, lavish smorgasbords of meats, cheeses, breads and even vegetables are set out each morning. And in Italy on weekends it is often a frittata.

Eating healthfully in the morning may be a new experience to Americans used to bacon, eggs or sticky doughnuts, but with time it'll become a habit. And when you eat right all day long, you'll look forward to breakfast, for you'll be—happily— hungry!

with a spatula. Bake for 50 to 55 minutes, or until a toothpick inserted near the center of the cake comes out clean. Cool in the pan for 4 to 5 minutes and then invert on a wire rack and release by gently tapping the pan. Cool completely on the wire rack.

CAL. 155   CARB. 27G   PROT. 0.3G   CHOL. 8MG   FAT 4G/24%   SOD. 64MG

Pesto Frittata

This recipe represents a guide for making frittatas—a great way to serve eggs to more than two people. You may increase the whites even more to lower the cholesterol, and certainly use your imagination with vegetables, cheese and other flavor combinations. This frittata happens to be my favorite.

SERVES 4

3 large egg whites
3 large eggs, separated
2 teaspoons olive oil
2 tablespoons low-fat, low-sodium chicken broth
2 ounces turkey ham, thinly sliced and diced (about ⅓ cup)
2 ounces part-skim mozzarella cheese, finely diced
2 tablespoons Spinach Pesto (see page 86)

1. Preheat the oven to 425°F. Lightly spray a medium-sized oven-safe skillet with olive oil spray.

2. Put all 6 egg whites in one bowl and the 3 yolks in another. Whisk the whites for at least 2 minutes to aerate them.

3. Set the skillet over medium-high heat, add the olive oil and chicken broth and heat until warm.

4. Lightly whisk the egg yolks and add to the whites. Whisk just to combine and pour into the skillet. Add the ham, mozzarella and Spinach Pesto, stirring rapidly to incorporate them into the egg mixture. Cook for 3 to 4 minutes, just until the bottom is set; the top will still be wet.

5. Place the skillet in the oven for 5 minutes, until the frittata is firm and golden. Serve immediately or cool and serve at room temperature.

CAL. 155   CARB. 1.6G   PROT. 14.8G   CHOL. 78MG   FAT 9.5G/57%   SOD. 332MG

"Almost every person has something secret he likes to eat."
M.F.K. FISHER

227
◆

Lunch Menu

FOODS (PER SERVING)	CAL.	CARB. (G)	PROT. (G)	CHOL. (MG)	FAT (G)/%	SOD. (MG)
Spring Green Soup*	111	19	10	0	0.5/4	96
Minty Tabbouleh*	103	19	3	0	2.6/22	6
Breadsticks, 2	160	26	12	0	4/22	420

Spring Green Soup

This soup is a great way to greet spring, even though there may still be snow on the ground!

SERVES 4

5 cups low-fat, low-sodium chicken broth
10 scallions, halved lengthwise and cut into 2-inch pieces
1 large onion, halved and thinly sliced
One 10-ounce package frozen peas
2 cups fresh spinach chiffonade (see page 169)
12 asparagus spears, cut into 2-inch pieces
½ cup finely minced fresh dill
Salt and freshly ground black pepper

1. In a stockpot, bring the chicken broth to a boil over high heat, add the scallions and onion, reduce the heat and simmer, partially covered, for 20 minutes.

2. Add the peas, spinach and asparagus and cook for 5 minutes longer, until the asparagus is fork-tender. Add the dill, season to taste with salt and pepper and serve immediately.

CAL. 111 CARB. 19G PROT. 10G CHOL. 0MG
FAT 0.5G/4% SOD. 96MG

228

"To own a bit of ground, to scratch it with a hoe, to plant seeds, and watch their renewal of life, this is the most commonest delight of the race, the most satisfactory thing a man can do."
CHARLES DUDLEY WARNER

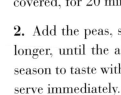

Minty Tabbouleh

With almost no oil to mask the flavor, the freshness of loads of veggies and mint makes this a cool, refreshing side salad.

SERVES 4

⅓ cup bulgur wheat

2 plum tomatoes, coarsely chopped (about ¾ cup)

Six ¼-inch slices cucumber, cubed

6 to 8 scallions, coarsely chopped, green parts only

⅓ cup finely minced loosely packed fresh mint

4 teaspoons finely minced fresh Italian parsley

2 tablespoons lemon juice

1½ teaspoons finely minced lemon zest

4 teaspoons low-fat, low-sodium chicken or vegetable broth

2 teaspoons extra-virgin olive oil

Salt and freshly ground black pepper to taste

1. In a small saucepan, combine the bulgur with ¾ cup water. Bring to a boil over high heat and cook for 1 minute. Remove from the heat, cover and set aside for 15 to 20 minutes, until the water is absorbed. Spread on a baking sheet and cool for 15 minutes.

2. In a bowl, combine the tomatoes, cucumber and scallions with the mint and parsley. In another bowl, whisk together the lemon juice, lemon zest, chicken broth and oil. Add to the vegetables, toss and season with salt and pepper. Add the bulgur, toss gently, adjust the seasonings, cover and refrigerate until serving.

CAL. 103   CARB. 19G   PROT. 3G   CHOL. 0MG   FAT 2.6G/22%   SOD. 6MG

229
♦

Pasta with Bolognese Sauce

The key to this "classic" Italian sauce is to simmer it slowly for a long time. We've made double the amount you'll need for four servings; freeze the other half. Of course, you can always invite more guests and make a larger green salad to accompany more pasta and sauce! I think the sauce is just fine without any olive oil at all.

SERVES 4
MAKES 5 CUPS SAUCE

1 cup plus 2 tablespoons beef broth

1 cup coarsely chopped onion

¼ cup finely minced garlic

1 small eggplant, coarsely chopped (about 2 cups)

Three 14½-ounce cans diced tomatoes, with juice

1 cup fruity red wine

3 fresh or dried bay leaves

1 tablespoon seeded, finely minced jalapeño

¼ cup balsamic vinegar

¼ cup Madeira

3 tablespoons tomato paste

1 pound ground turkey

1½ teaspoons dried marjoram

1½ teaspoons dried oregano

1½ teaspoons dried basil

⅛ teaspoon ground nutmeg

⅛ to ¼ teaspoon crushed red pepper flakes, or to taste

Salt and freshly ground black pepper to taste

8 ounces dried linguine

2 tablespoons finely minced fresh Italian parsley

Grated Parmesan cheese (optional)

1. In a stockpot, heat 2 tablespoons broth over medium heat and cook the onions and garlic for about 5 minutes, until translucent. Add the remaining ingredients, except the linguine, parsley and Parmesan cheese.

230
◆

MEAT AS A SIDE

Giving meat a lesser role in the main meal is one of the hardest healthy changes to make. For generations, meat has "made" the meal, in ever-increasing quantities.

Yet meat is laden with fat and cholesterol. We've learned we're eating too much protein, too few vegetables and complex carbohydrates.

Start thinking of meat as a side dish. Flip your usual ratio of meat to vegetables. Use unrefined carbohydrates such as bread, cereals, potatoes, pasta and rice instead. It's time to change the balance.

ROASTED WHOLE GARLIC

Roasted whole heads of garlic are luscious. Squeeze the pulp from the skin and spread it on thick slices of toasted peasant bread.

MAKES 4 HEADS GARLIC

4 whole heads garlic
2 tablespoons olive oil
1½ cups low-fat, low-sodium chicken broth

1. Preheat the oven to 350°F.

2. Carefully remove the outer papery skin from the garlic heads, leaving the whole heads intact.

3. Arrange the garlic heads in a small baking dish so that they fit comfortably. Sprinkle with oil and add the chicken stock. Bake, basting frequently, for 1 to 1¼ hours. Cool slightly before serving or using in a recipe.

CAL. 79   CARB. 12G   PROT. 3G
CHOL. 0MG   FAT 2.4G/25%
SOD. 216MG (ANALYZED PER HEAD)

2. Bring to a boil, reduce the heat to low and simmer, uncovered, for about 2 hours, stirring occasionally, until thick and richly colored. Taste and adjust the seasonings. Cool slightly, divide the sauce in half and transfer 2½ cups to a container with a tight-fitting lid. Freeze for future use.

3. In a saucepan of boiling water, cook the pasta over medium-high heat for 8 to 12 minutes, or until al dente. Drain and toss with the remaining 2½ cups sauce and cook over low heat for about 2 minutes, so that the pasta can absorb some of the sauce. Serve immediately, sprinkled with the parsley and Parmesan cheese, if desired.

CAL. 365   CARB. 58G   PROT. 24G   CHOL. 28MG   FAT 2.4G/8%   SOD. 2MG

Oven-Fried Vegetables

These are fantastic with Lemon-Pepper Dip (see page 162) or just a squeeze or two of lemon.

SERVES 4

1 cup plain bread crumbs or Panko (see page 205)
1 teaspoon garlic powder
½ teaspoon paprika
4 large egg whites
16 to 20 large button mushrooms, stemmed
20 broccoli florets
12 to 16 cauliflower florets

1. Preheat the oven to 450°F.

2. In a plastic bag, combine the bread crumbs, garlic powder and paprika. In a shallow bowl, lightly beat the egg whites with a fork.

3. Coat the vegetables, a few at a time, in the egg whites and then drop into the bag of crumbs and shake to coat. Shake off any excess crumbs and lay the vegetables on a baking sheet. Repeat until all the vegetables are coated. Spray lightly with olive oil spray and bake for 30 minutes, tossing every 10 minutes, until vegetables are crispy and lightly browned. Serve immediately.

CAL. 167   CARB. 29G   PROT. 11G   CHOL. 2MG   FAT 2G/10%   SOD. 310MG

231
◆

Sostanza Cake

The oldest trattoria in Florence, Italy, Sostanza on Via Porcellana always has this cake on a stand near the front door. It is a fabulous light-as-a-feather meringue dessert that is nevertheless an indulgence because of the whipping cream and toasted coconut. You can easily see how quickly a rich dessert increases the day's fat percentages from 16% to 22%.

SERVES 16

12 large egg whites, at room temperature
2 tablespoons white vinegar
¹/₄ teaspoon cream of tartar
4¹/₄ cups sugar
3 cups heavy cream
Seeds of 1 vanilla bean or 1 teaspoon vanilla extract
2 cups sweetened coconut, toasted

1. Preheat the oven to 275°F. Line 2 baking sheets with parchment paper and, using a pencil, trace two 8-inch circles on each sheet of parchment.

2. In the bowl of an electric mixer set on medium speed, beat the egg whites and vinegar until foamy. Add the cream of tartar and beat for 5 to 6 minutes, until the whites are shiny and hold stiff peaks, adding 4 cups sugar gradually as the whites stiffen. Do not overmix.

232

NUTS

Nuts are bursting with magnesium, potassium, folic acid, calcium and the anti-aging vitamin E. They have lots of protein and fiber and virtually no cholesterol.

But indulge sparingly. A mere ounce averages 180 calories and 17 grams of fat. It's monounsaturated fat, at least, the "good" kind that helps lower bad LDL cholesterol and blood pressure, and protects arteries from closing.

RED WINE AND RAISINS

The French Paradox of drinking two 6-ounce glasses of wine a day does have validity, suggests recent research by John Folts at the University of Wisconsin-Madison Medical School. The chemicals in grapes can help thin the blood, much as aspirin does, preventing bad LDL cholesterol from oxidizing and clogging arteries, a trigger for heart attacks and strokes.

Why is red wine best and not white? Because it's made from the whole grape, including skins and seeds, which is where the disease-fighting antioxidants are concentrated.

The message is clear. If you drink alcohol, consider switching to red wine in moderation. If you don't, drink purple grape juice (you'll need three times as much) or eat raisins, a concentrated source with three times the antioxidants.

3. Divide the meringue into fourths and, using a spatula or the back of a spoon, spread each one onto the parchment into a circle about 8 inches in diameter and 1 inch thick. Bake for about 45 minutes, until lightly golden. The discs will be firm on the outside and crunchy on the inside. Carefully lift the parchment from the baking sheets and set on wire racks to cool for at least 1 hour.

4. In the bowl of an electric mixer set on medium-high speed, whip the cream until it holds stiff peaks. Add the remaining ¼ cup sugar and the vanilla bean seeds or extract when the cream begins to thicken.

5. Using a wide spatula, carefully remove a meringue disc from the parchment paper and put it on a flat serving plate. Spread a quarter of the whipped cream over the disc and sprinkle with ½ cup coconut. Top with another disc and layer with more cream, coconut and the third disc. Layer with more cream and coconut and the final disc. Spread the top with the remaining whipped cream and sprinkle with the remaining ½ cup coconut.

6. Tent the cake with aluminum foil and refrigerate for at least 2 hours, until chilled. Slice with a serrated knife.

CAL. 432   CARB. 60G   PROT. 4G   CHOL. 61MG   FAT 20.6G/42%   SOD. 89MG

233

Dinner Menu

FOODS (PER SERVING)	CAL.	CARB. (G)	PROT. (G)	CHOL. (MG)	FAT (G)/%	SOD. (MG)
Oven-Fried Vegetables*	167	29	11	2	2/10	310
Lemon-Pepper Dip* (p. 162), 2 T.	18	1.2	3.6	0	0/0	108
Arugula, 2 cups	14.6	1.9	2.2	0	0.09/6	36
Feta Dressing* (p. 119), 1 T.	16	1	1	3.9	0.9/51	57
Pasta with Bolognese Sauce*	365	58	24	28	2.4/8	2
Italian bread, 2 slices	192	36	6	0	2/10	426
Roasted garlic, 1 head	79	12	3	0	2.4/25	216
Sostanza Cake*	432	60	4	61	20.6/42	89
Today's Totals	**2115**	**323**	**100**	**181**	**51/22**	**2502**

Comfort Food

◆

At times we crave foods that soothe the soul, that make us feel warm and cozy all over. Often these foods are rich, creamy and loaded with fats and calories. But they don't have to be. They can be sinfully scrumptious without being over-the-top. Best of all, you won't have to search your soul for excuses to savor them.

Monday
DAY 22

Fresh Orange Juice
Cool and Green Fruit Salad*
Fresh Bagel with Spreadable Fruit
Great Granola* with Skim Milk

◆

Pineapple Spinach Salad*
Turkey Pesto Grilled Cheese*

◆

Watercress and Cucumber Salad
with Our House Dressing*
A Cozy Chicken Potpie*
Orange Custard*

Breakfast Menu

Foods (per serving)	Cal.	Carb. (g)	Prot. (g)	Chol. (mg)	Fat (g)/%	Sod. (mg)
Orange juice, 6 oz.	83.5	19.4	1.4	0	0.3/3	1.2
Cool and Green Fruit Salad* (p. 101)	158	41	1.9	0	0.8/4	25
Bagel, 1, plain	195	38	7.5	0	1/4	379
Spreadable fruit, 1 T.	36	9	0	0	0/0	0
Great Granola* (p. 64), ½ cup	282	56	7	0	5/14	57
Skim milk, ½ cup	43	6	4	2	0.2/4	62
Morning Snack						
Grapes, 1 cup	114	29	1	0	0.9/7	3

Lunch Menu

Foods (per serving)	Cal.	Carb. (g)	Prot. (g)	Chol. (mg)	Fat (g)/%	Sod. (mg)
Pineapple Spinach Salad*	193	35	5	0	5/25	62
Turkey Pesto Grilled Cheese*	146	16.8	11	14.8	4/26	270
Afternoon Snack						
Apple, 3½ oz.	59	15	0.2	0	0.4/6	0

Turkey Pesto Grilled Cheese

This is a winner! It is filled with turkey, pesto and cheese for oozing goodness without the least feeling of deprivation.

SERVES 4

3 tablespoons plus 2 teaspoons Spinach Pesto (see page 86)
8 slices whole-wheat bread
4 ounces turkey breast slices
4 ounces part-skim mozzarella cheese
6 tablespoons skim milk
2 large egg whites

1. Spread the pesto on 4 slices of bread and top each slice with turkey and cheese. Top each with another bread slice.

2. Lightly spray a nonstick skillet with olive oil spray and heat over medium-low heat.

"It's a funny thing about life; if you refuse to accept anything but the best, you very often get it."

Somerset Maugham

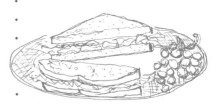

BREAKFAST TORTILLAS

Sprinkle flour tortillas with your favorite wake-up flavors.

Lightly brush olive oil on both sides. Sprinkle lightly with vanilla sugar and mint. Or brush with canola oil and shake on brown sugar and cinnamon.

Pop in the toaster oven for 6 to 8 minutes. Pop out hot, bubbly and brown.

Everybody loves 'em. No wonder—the combinations are endless . . . delicious.

JAZZ UP SALADS

Add to simple greens:

◆ Kohlrabi

◆ Fennel

◆ Roasted peppers

◆ Pineapple chunks

◆ Sprouts

◆ Mushrooms

◆ Sweet onions

◆ Capers

◆ Green peppercorns

◆ Ginger (candied or fresh)

◆ Raisins

◆ Apples

◆ Green beans

◆ Radishes

◆ Water chestnuts

◆ Broccoli

◆ Pea pods

◆ Berries

◆ Pears

◆ Daikon radish

◆ Sugar snap peas

◆ Shredded carrots

◆ Grated red cabbage

3. In a shallow bowl, beat the milk and egg white together with a fork and coat both sides of the sandwiches with the mixture by dipping them into it for 10 to 12 seconds on each side.

4. Cook the sandwiches for 3 to 4 minutes on each side, spraying the side that faces up briefly with olive oil spray before turning it. The sandwich will toast and the cheese melt as it cooks. Serve immediately.

CAL. 146   CARB. 16.8G   PROT. 11G   CHOL. 14.8MG   FAT 4G/26%   SOD. 270MG

Pineapple Spinach Salad

SERVES 4

½ teaspoon finely minced fresh ginger
¼ cup light brown sugar
Pinch of cinnamon
½ teaspoon vanilla extract
2 tablespoons water
2 cups pineapple chunks,
  diced small
¼ cup coarsely chopped toasted pecans
2 teaspoons finely minced lime zest
¼ cup finely minced fresh chervil or Italian parsley
8 cups cleaned, stemmed and slivered fresh spinach
2 small red onions, thinly sliced

1. In a small saucepan, combine the ginger, sugar, cinnamon, vanilla and water and heat over medium heat, stirring, until the sugar dissolves. Add the pineapple and cook for 15 to 20 minutes, until the sauce thickens and the pineapple is coated completely with the syrup. Remove from the heat and add the pecans and lime zest. When cool, add the chervil.

2. In a salad bowl, combine the spinach and onion. Add the pineapple-ginger mixture and toss well. Serve immediately.

CAL. 193   CARB. 35G   PROT. 5G   CHOL. 0MG   FAT 5G/25%   SOD. 62MG

A Cozy Chicken Potpie

Sometimes, especially on "Rainy days and Mondays," nothing is more perfect than a chicken potpie.

SERVES 4

1 whole chicken breast, bone-in, skinless (about 1 pound)
2 cups low-fat, low-sodium chicken broth
2 medium onions, 1 quartered and 1 cubed
½ pound carrots, cut into rounds
¼ pound sugar snap peas, trimmed (about 1¼ cups)
½ pound asparagus, cut into 2-inch lengths
¾ cup skim milk
3 tablespoons instant potato flakes
1 tablespoon potato starch
¼ cup finely minced fresh dill
Salt and freshly ground black pepper to taste
8 cloves garlic, coarsely chopped
1 cup rinsed, stemmed and coarsely chopped fresh spinach
1 recipe Buttermilk Biscuits

1. In a large, deep skillet or stockpot, combine the chicken, chicken broth and quartered onion. Bring to a boil over high heat, cover, reduce the heat and simmer for about 30 minutes, until the chicken is cooked through. Remove from the heat and allow to cool to room temperature.

2. Put the carrots in a steamer basket set over 2 inches of boiling water and steam, tightly covered, for 2 to 3 minutes. Add the peas and asparagus and steam for 1 to 2 minutes longer, until the asparagus are fork-tender. Transfer to a colander and rinse under cold running water. Reserve ¼ cup of the steaming liquid.

3. In a blender, puree the cooled broth and onion until smooth.

4. Preheat the oven to 375°F. In the skillet used for the chicken, cook the pureed broth over medium-high heat for 3 to 4 minutes, until slightly thickened. Add ¼ cup milk, the potato flakes and potato starch and cook over medium heat, stirring, until smooth. Slowly add the remaining ½ cup milk and cook, stirring, for 3 to 5 minutes, until thickened. Add the dill and season with salt and pepper. Shred the chicken into bite-sized pieces and add to the skillet.

238

5. In a saucepan, combine the reserved ¼ cup steaming liquid, garlic and cubed onion and cook over medium heat, stirring, for 1 to 2 minutes, until the onion begins to soften. Add the spinach, cover and cook for 3 to 4 minutes, until the spinach wilts. Transfer to a colander set over a plate and set aside to drain.

6. Put the steamed vegetables in a 2-quart soufflé dish and add the sauce, chicken and spinach mixture. Drop biscuit-sized pieces of dough over the top so that they cover the chicken and vegetables and barely touch each other. Set on a baking sheet and bake for 25 to 30 minutes, until a toothpick inserted in the center of the biscuit topping comes out clean. Serve immediately.

CAL. 320   CARB. 48G   PROT. 18G   CHOL. 20MG   FAT 7G/19%   SOD. 366MG

(INCLUDES BISCUITS)

Buttermilk Biscuits

If you need a great biscuit recipe for shortcake, add two tablespoons of sugar.

MAKES 6 BISCUITS

1 cup all-purpose flour
1½ teaspoons baking powder
¼ teaspoon baking soda
⅛ teaspoon salt
½ cup buttermilk
4½ teaspoons canola oil

In a bowl, combine the flour, baking powder, baking soda and salt and whisk to combine. Add the buttermilk and oil and mix with a fork until just blended and it forms a fairly sticky dough. Do not overmix. Add 1 to 2 teaspoons more buttermilk if the dough is dry and crumbly. Use as directed in the recipe for A Cozy Chicken Potpie.

NOTE: To bake the dough as biscuits, drop the dough by heaping tablespoons 1½ inches apart, onto baking sheets lightly sprayed with vegetable oil spray. Bake in a preheated 425°F. oven for 10 to 12 minutes, until golden brown.

CAL. 117   CARB. 18G   PROT. 3G   CHOL. 0MG   FAT 3.7G/29%   SOD. 620MG

(ANALYZED PER BISCUIT)

BUTTERMILK

Buttermilk contains no butter. Originally a by-product of butter-making, authentic buttermilk is almost impossible to buy today.

Commercial cultured buttermilk is artificially soured milk. Its lower fat content gives it a longer shelf life. It's great for baking, in dips and in salad dressings.

In recipes with baking powder, you can substitute buttermilk for whole sweet milk. For each cup of buttermilk, reduce the recipe's baking powder by 2 teaspoons and add ½ teaspoon baking soda. This ensures the proper proportion of acid and alkali needed for leavening.

239

Orange Custard

This delicate custard is always pleasing and as rich as you would want it.

S E R V E S   4

4 large egg whites
1 large egg
½ cup sugar
One 12-ounce can evaporated skim milk
2 tablespoons orange juice
1 tablespoon finely minced orange zest
¼ cup heavy cream
½ teaspoon vanilla extract

1. Preheat the oven to 350° F.

2. In a large bowl, combine the egg whites, egg and sugar and whisk well. Slowly whisk in the evaporated skim milk, orange juice, orange zest, cream and vanilla until smooth.

240

3. Strain into another bowl and pour the mixture into four 6-ounce custard cups or ramekins. Put the custard cups in a roasting pan and add enough hot water to come halfway up the sides of the cups. Bake for 45 to 50 minutes, until the center of the custard is set and a knife inserted in the center comes out clean. Cool in the water bath just to room temperature. Cover and refrigerate for at least 2 hours before serving.

CAL. 256   CARB. 37G   PROT. 12G   CHOL. 77MG   FAT 6.9G/24%   SOD. 174MG

YES, YOGURT

Yogurt without gelatin in it seems richer tasting and thicker and holds up better.

Always add yogurt at the very end of cooking and heat gently just until the yogurt is warm. If you overheat it, it may separate or curdle.

D i n n e r   M e n u

FOODS (PER SERVING)	CAL.	CARB. (G)	PROT. (G)	CHOL. (MG)	FAT (G)/%	SOD. (MG)
Watercress, 2 cups	8	0.9	1.6	0	0/0	28
Cucumber, ½ cup	7	1.4	0.4	0	0.07/8	1
Our House Dressing* (p. 194), 1 T.	18	2	0.1	0	1.2/58	31
A Cozy Chicken Potpie*	320	48	18	20	7/19	366
Orange Custard*	256	37	12	77	6.9/24	174
EVENING SNACK						
Popcorn (air-popped), 2 cups	61	13	2	0	0.7/10	0.6
Today's Totals	**1975**	**368**	**73**	**114**	**33/15**	**1461**

MORE FUSION COOKING

With these flavors from around the world in your pantry, you can take a culinary trip anytime you please. Many of them you already use in your cooking. It's often just a question of flavor combinations that make a dish reminiscent of a culture's cuisine.

CARIBBEAN

- Vanilla beans
- Sweet potatoes
- Pork
- Ginger
- Pineapple
- Papaya
- Allspice
- Curry
- Pepper
- Cilantro
- Mint
- Tomatoes
- Soy Sauce
- Limes
- Raisins
- Coconut
- Bananas
- Collard greens
- Oregano
- Avocados
- Rice and beans
- Rum
- Mango

SOUTH AMERICAN

- Beets
- Corn
- Avocado
- Mango

- Beef
- Chilies
- Basil
- Cilantro
- Hearts of palm
- Tomatoes
- Bananas
- Coconuts
- Limes
- Coconut milk
- Pork
- Oranges
- Papaya
- Peaches
- Black beans
- Black olives
- Rice
- Potatoes
- Sausages
- Garlic

MOROCCAN

- Lemons
- Mint
- Cloves
- Cinnamon
- Nuts
- Raisins

- Pistachios
- Eggplant
- Couscous
- Chilies
- Olives
- Phyllo
- Chickpeas
- Pine nuts
- Garlic
- Capers
- Squash
- Sweet potatoes
- Tomatoes
- Onions
- Prunes
- Oranges
- Honey

GREEK

- Feta cheese
- Sage
- Figs
- Tomatoes
- Lemons
- Raisins
- Currants
- Pistachios
- Almonds

- Yogurt
- White beans
- Honey
- Black olives
- Grape leaves
- Lamb
- Capers
- Oregano
- Bay leaves
- Grapes
- Cinnamon
- Vanilla
- Mint
- Thyme
- Rosemary
- Dill
- Garlic
- Spinach

MEXICAN

- Black beans
- Frozen corn
- Roasted red peppers
- Jalapeño peppers
- Flour tortillas
- Salsa

Getting the Most Out of
Herbs and Spices

Herbs and spices truly animate food. I'd be lost without them. To maximize their flavor:

◆ Snip fresh herbs with scissors into the dish you're cooking. Don't leave the best part on the cutting board.

◆ Fresh herbs lose their distinctive flavor when cooked a long time. Add some extra just before serving.

◆ Use herb stems for soups and stews. They're loaded with flavor, too.

◆ Mince fresh herbs with lemon zest to brighten their flavor.

◆ Crush dried herbs with the palm of your hand to release their flavor. Then freshen with minced parsley and lemon or lime zest.

◆ Toast spices in a small dry skillet over low heat—15 to 30 seconds—to release their flavor.

◆ Whenever possible, buy whole spices and grate or grind them yourself. An extra coffee grinder works wonders.

◆ In the garden herbs crave frequent cutting. Snip chives often for a lush, sturdy plant that quickly shoots out fresh, tender growth. Pick parsley and chervil from the outside in. Basil needs its tops picked continually to prevent early flowering.

◆ For fresh herbs in winter, find a local supermarket, greenhouse or herb grower (the source for restaurants), and also grow what you can in pots in your own kitchen.

◆ If fresh herbs are plentiful, use them in bouquets; their dark green or gray leaves are beautiful with flowers. Make an edible centerpiece of herbs such as basil, dill and mint; wash fresh herbs, shake dry and arrange with salad greens in a bowl of crushed ice.

◆ Dried herbs quickly lose their flavor when exposed to light, air or heat. Don't hesitate to throw out a jar that's sat on the shelf too long. When in doubt, sniff. A tired herb won't do much for your recipe anyway.

◆ Fresh herbs are a necessity to many; others spend a lifetime cooking well without them. If you want them, try growing your own to have them close at hand.

◆ Herbs are fun to grow because they're so versatile. You don't need a farm or a greenhouse. A one-room city apartment with a sunny windowsill will do.

◆ Make your herb garden a secret garden as well. Tucked behind a favorite gnarled old tree or in the vale of a distant meadow, it's a wonderful place to retreat.

243
◆

◆ In addition to the culinary value and fragrance of herbs, I love their cool colors—silver-green sage, dusty purple basil, feathery blue-green dill. They soothe in the summer's worst heat waves.

◆ At the end of the season, pick your herbs in bunches, tie them with big bows and hang them upside down to dry in the kitchen.

◆ Be prudent when substituting fresh herbs for dried and vice versa. The usual formula is to use two to three times as much fresh as dried, but your taste buds must be the final arbiter.

Tips for Cooking with Herbs

• Pick early in the day, just after the dew dries, for juicier, more aromatic and more nutritious herbs.

• Buy fresh herbs in small quantities unless you're planning to freeze or preserve them in oil.

• Gently wash herbs and pat them dry, or let them drip dry.

• Don't combine too many different herbs and spices in one dish or you will confuse the palate.

• Use fresh herbs by the handful. Forget herb flavor charts—trust your own taste.

• If while cooking you're uncertain about what or how much herbs to use, separate a bit of your dish and add the herb a little at a time. Taste, and proceed accordingly.

• Place clean herb sprigs or edible flowers in ice trays and add distilled water. Freeze and serve with sangria, iced tea, lemonade, spritzers or just your favorite mineral water.

• Make herbed vinegars when you have a good harvest. You'll be happy to have them in the fall and winter.

• Herbs are decorative in baskets, pots and pitchers. Use them as table decorations and their aromas will waft throughout the house.

• Rub herbs into meat, fish and poultry before cooking.

♦ Vary a pesto recipe with herb and nut combinations. Tarragon with pecans, shallots and hazelnuts; dill, garlic and almonds; rosemary, parsley, garlic and pecans; oregano, parsley and walnuts.

Drying Herbs

♦ To dry herbs in a microwave oven, first wash and air-dry them. Then place them on paper towels and cook at 100% for 4 minutes. If they are still moist, turn them and cook to dry a few more minutes. This is an excellent method to retain color and flavor.

♦ Buy dried herbs in small quantities and store them in small opaque or green glass jars in a dark, cool spot for 4 to 6 months.

♦ Dried and fresh herbs may be used interchangeably in most recipes, but dried are more intense than fresh. Use 3 to 5 times more fresh herbs than dried, depending on the natural strength of the herb.

♦ Let dried herbs soak in salad dressing for 15 minutes to an hour before tossing with your greens.

Bravo Italy!

◆

For centuries, the Italians have reveled in their harvest from season to season. They've taught us an age-old respect for ingredients and how to greatly encourage, not mask, optimum flavors with simple kitchen preparations.

Tuesday
DAY 23

Fresh Orange Juice

Hot Cereal with
Brown Sugar and Skim Milk

Fresh Strawberries

◆

Spinach and Red Onion Salad with
Mango Chutney Dressing*

Tuscan Lentils with Sausage*

Breadsticks

Crisp Biscotti with Dried Cherries*

◆

Turkey Scaloppine with Tomato
and Arugula Salsa*

Lemon-Dill Rice*

Baby Artichoke Sauté*

Peasant Bread

Cool Fabulous Fudge Cheesecake
Ice Cream*

Breakfast Menu

Foods (per serving)	Cal.	Carb. (g)	Prot. (g)	Chol. (mg)	Fat (g)/%	Sod. (mg)
Orange juice, 6 oz.	83.5	19.4	1.4	0	0.3/3	1.2
Cream of Wheat, ¾ cup	90	19	2	1	0/0	64
Brown sugar, 1 T.	34	8	0	0	0/0	7
Skim milk, ½ cup	43	6	4	2	0.2/4	62
Strawberries, ½ cup	25	6	0.5	0	0.3/11	0.8
MORNING SNACK						
Grapes-Grapes* (p. 70)	101	25	1.4	0	0.6/5	12

Lunch Menu

Foods (per serving)	Cal.	Carb. (g)	Prot. (g)	Chol. (mg)	Fat (g)/%	Sod. (mg)
Spinach, 1 cup, with red onion slices, 3	24	5	2	0	0.1/4	29
Mango Chutney Dressing* (p. 119), 1 T.	9	1	0.8	0.2	0.03/3	10
Tuscan Lentils with Sausage*	332	50	24	20	5.2/14	254
Breadsticks, 2	160	26	12	0	4/22	420
Crisp Biscotti with Dried Cherries* (p. 182), 2	90	20	1.2	2.8	1.2/11	110

> "No pessimist ever discovered the secrets of the stars, or sailed to an uncharted land, or opened a new heaven to the human spirit."
>
> HELEN KELLER

Beans, Beans, Beautiful Beans

They're the fresh or dried edible seeds of leguminous plants, a large group of flowering plants that produce double-seamed pods filled with a single row of seeds.

Once considered the "poor man's meat," beans have gained new respect for their nutrition—they're loaded with protein, soluble fiber, iron and calcium. Combined with whole grains or other complex carbohydrates,

they make a complete protein. A half cup has 5 grams of fiber, less than 1 gram of fat, 0 cholesterol, 9 grams of protein, 25 grams of complex carbohydrates and 5 grams of sodium. There's evidence that they:

- may lower cholesterol
- contain anticancer compounds
- slow rises in blood pressure
- diminish risk of artery clogging, strokes and heart disease

With new hybrids coming into style and heirloom beans coming back into favor, the flavor choices have never been better:

- Adzuki
- Appaloosa
- Black turtle
- Broad or fava
- Boston or navy
- Cannellini
- Kidney
- Great Northern
- Flageolet
- Pinto
- Lima
- Soybean
- Jacob's cattle
- Black soybean
- Black-eyed pea
- Chickpea
- Dried pea
- Lentil
- Peanut

The herbs that grow wild in the rocky, arid countryside in the French region of Provence have become favorites of cooks the world over. Savory, fennel seed, rosemary, thyme, oregano, basil and marjoram in varying proportions usually comprise the flavored mix.

Use them for grilled meats, tomato sauces, beans, fish, pizzas, scalloped potatoes and more.

Tuscan Lentils with Sausage

This classic Tuscan dish—richly flavored lentils topped with slices of turkey sausage—always satisfies.

SERVES 4

$^1\!/_2$ *cup dried green lentils (de Puy lentils)*
2$^1\!/_2$ cups plus 2 tablespoons beef broth
4 tablespoons finely minced garlic
4 sprigs fresh thyme
1 medium onion, finely chopped (about $^3\!/_4$ cup)
1 tablespoon finely minced fresh sage
1 tablespoon plus 1$^1\!/_2$ teaspoons tomato paste
Pinch of ground cloves
2 ounces smoked turkey sausage, sliced into
    1/8-inch-thick slices
Fresh Italian parsley, finely minced

1. In a saucepan, combine the lentils, 1½ cups beef broth, 1 tablespoon garlic and the thyme and bring to a boil over high heat. Reduce the heat, cover and simmer for 30 to 45 minutes, until the lentils are tender. Set aside.

2. In a skillet, heat 2 tablespoons broth over medium heat. Add 2 tablespoons garlic and the onion and cook for 5 to 6 minutes. Add the sage and cook for 30 seconds. Add the lentils and any cooking liquid, the tomato paste, cloves and the remaining 1 cup beef broth. Reduce the heat to medium low and simmer for 10 to 15 minutes, until thick yet still soupy. Add the sausage and heat for 2 to 3 minutes. Stir in the final 1 tablespoon garlic.

3. Ladle into bowls and sprinkle the parsley over the top. Serve immediately.

CAL. 332   CARB. 50G   PROT. 24G   CHOL. 20MG   FAT 5.2G/14%   SOD. 254MG

249

Turkey Scaloppine
with Tomato and Arugula Salsa

This delicious hot turkey scaloppine is offset with a cool arugula and tomato salsa.

SERVES 4

2 tablespoons lemon juice

2 tablespoons finely minced garlic

2 teaspoons olive oil

1 teaspoon balsamic vinegar

1 teaspoon finely minced lemon zest

Salt and freshly ground black pepper to taste

4 cups torn loosely packed arugula,
   spinach or watercress

2 large plum tomatoes, coarsely chopped

$1/2$ cup finely minced red onion

2 large egg whites, lightly beaten with a fork

$1/2$ cup fine plain bread crumbs (see page 205)

$1/4$ to $1/2$ teaspoon cayenne, or to taste

Four 3-ounce turkey breast slices (paillards)

250

1. Preheat the oven to 500°F. Lightly spray a baking sheet with olive oil spray.

2. In a bowl, combine the lemon juice, garlic, oil, vinegar, lemon zest and salt and pepper and whisk well. Toss with the greens, tomato and onion and set the salsa aside.

3. Put the egg whites in a shallow bowl. Put the bread crumbs and cayenne in a plastic bag. Dip the turkey in the egg whites and then drop in the plastic bag a slice at a time. Shake to coat evenly and then shake the excess crumbs from the turkey. Repeat with the other slices.

4. Lay the turkey on the baking sheet, spray lightly with olive oil spray and bake for 10 to 12 minutes, turning once halfway through. Serve immediately with the salsa piled on top.

CAL. 430   CARB. 38G   PROT. 54G   CHOL. 106MG   FAT 8G/17%   SOD. 356MG

NEW HABITS

When "trying" to
develop a new habit,
remember:
There's really no such
thing as "trying."
You either do it
or you don't.
Set your mind to
"just do it."
And you probably
will have a great time
in the process!

Baby Artichoke Sauté

While I love whole baby artichokes, and often carry them home to Michigan from faraway markets in New York or Italy, I can't do so often enough to satisfy my craving. And so frozen artichokes are called into action. Even these are often not in the market, so stock up when you find them.

SERVES 4

2 teaspoons olive oil
2 tablespoons lemon juice
¼ cup low-fat, low-sodium chicken broth
*18 ounces frozen artichokes, thawed and halved
    lengthwise*
2 tablespoons finely minced garlic
4 teaspoons finely minced lemon zest
2 ounces turkey ham, sliced paper-thin and minced
¼ cup finely minced fresh Italian parsley
Salt and freshly ground black pepper to taste

1. In a large skillet, heat the oil, lemon juice and chicken broth over medium heat for 1 minute. Add the artichokes, garlic and lemon zest, cover and cook for 2 to 3 minutes. Uncover, add the ham and cook, tossing, for 4 to 5 minutes, until the artichokes start to brown.

2. Toss with the parsley and season with salt and pepper. Serve immediately.

CAL. 113   CARB. 17G   PROT. 8G   CHOL. 9MG   FAT 3G/21%   SOD. 291MG

Lemon-Dill Rice

This is always a fresh-tasting complement to a meal.

SERVES 4

2½ cups low-fat, low-sodium chicken broth
1 cup rice
2 tablespoons finely minced garlic
4 teaspoons finely minced lemon zest
2 teaspoons lemon juice
Freshly gound black pepper to taste
2 tablespoons finely minced fresh dill
4 scallions, finely minced, green part only

1. In a saucepan, bring the chicken broth, rice, garlic, lemon zest and lemon juice to a boil over high heat. Cover, reduce the heat and simmer for 20 to 25 minutes, until the liquid is absorbed and the rice is tender.

2. Remove from the heat, season with pepper, stir in the dill and scallions and fluff with a fork. Serve immediately.

CAL. 203 CARB. 43G PROT. 5G CHOL. 0MG FAT 0.3/2% SOD. 2MG

252
◆

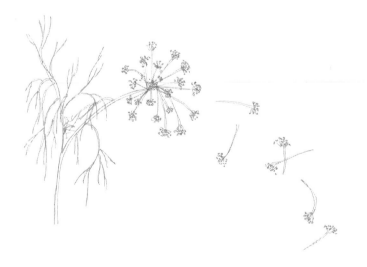

RICE

In China, the word for "rice" is the same as the word for "food."

The Burmese, the world's champion rice eaters, consume 500 pounds per person a year, about 1¼ pound a day. Americans eat twenty pounds per person per year—four pounds of which can be attributed to the brewing of beer.

Cultivated for more than 7,000 years, rice is a food staple for more than half the world. It supplies 55 percent of the daily food requirement, four times the food energy of pasta or potatoes in equal amounts. Rice is 80 percent starch, 12 percent water and contains calcium, complex carbohydrates and almost no fat. It's cholesterol-free, low in sodium, high in fiber and a fair source of protein, containing all eight essential amino acids.

Boring? Hardly. There are more than 40,000 varieties, types and sizes, including:

Arborio
Aromatic
Basmati
Black Japonica
Brown
Long-grain
Medium-grain
Texmati
Valencia
Wehani
White
Wild
Wild Pecan

COTTAGE CHEESE

Cottage cheese has come a long way from the diet plate, enjoying new life as a good-for-you ingredient, available in an array of curd sizes and textures that range from creamy to dry. Close relative pot cheese is a skim-milk form with a larger, drier curd. Farmer cheese is similar but is pressed into a block.

Read labels carefully. In $\frac{1}{2}$ cup of the creamed variety it may have 109 calories, 5 fat g and 63 mg of calcium in a cup. Nonfat has only 70 calories, no fat and 100 mg of calcium. Farmer cheese the most calories—160—and the most calcium—120 mg.

Nonfat cottage cheese whipped in the blender becomes thick and creamy—a surprising transformation. Use it in:

◆ Nonfat Blend (see page 298)

◆ Dips

◆ Toppings for pizza or pasta

◆ Baked goods

◆ Salad dressings

◆ Frozen yogurts

◆ Sweet dessert toppings

◆ Fruit salads

Cool Fabulous Fudge Cheesecake Ice Cream

If you love chocolate ice cream, here is a low-fat version. Don't think I've lost my mind when you look at the ingredients—the result is chocolaty, creamy and wonderful. It's not exactly ice cream. But it tastes fabulous!

MAKES ABOUT 1 QUART
SERVES 12

2 cups nonfat cottage cheese
1 cup semisweet chocolate chips
$\frac{1}{4}$ cup water
$\frac{1}{2}$ cup sugar
1 teaspoon vanilla extract

1. In a blender, blend the cottage cheese until smooth.

2. In a small saucepan, combine the chocolate chips and water and heat over medium heat, stirring, until the chocolate melts. Set aside to cool to room temperature.

3. In a bowl, combine the cottage cheese, sugar and vanilla and mix well. Fold in the chocolate. Chill slightly and transfer to an ice cream machine and freeze according to the manufacturer's directions. Transfer to a freezer-safe container with a lid and let mellow in the freezer for 3 or 4 hours. Eat within 48 hours.

CAL. 143   CARB. 23G   PROT. 5.3G   CHOL. 0MG   FAT 4.2G/25%   SOD. 148MG

253

Dinner Menu

FOODS (PER SERVING)	CAL.	CARB. (G)	PROT. (G)	CHOL. (MG)	FAT (G)/%	SOD. (MG)
Turkey Scaloppine with Tomato and Arugula Salsa*	430	38	54	106	8/17	356
Lemon-Dill Rice*	203	43	5	0	0.3/2	2
Baby Artichoke Sauté*	113	17	8	9	3/21	291
Peasant bread, 2 slices	118	36	6	0	3.4/15	334
Cool Fabulous Fudge Cheesecake Ice Cream*	143	23	5.3	0	4.2/25	148
Today's Totals	**1999**	**342**	**128**	**141**	**31/14**	**2101**

Pow-Pow-Ping Flavors

◆

There are simple seasonings that magnify natural ingredients: a little citrus juice or zest, garlic, balsamic vinegar, a hearty cheese, a fresh herb pureed to intensity, the sting and sweetness of onions or the heat of peppers. They all encourage nature's bounty to bring forth all of its flavors!

Wednesday
DAY 24

Raspberry Smoothie*

Orange Muffins*

◆

Arugula Salad with Our House
Dressing*

Summertime Bruschetta*

Tuscan Minestrone*

◆

Halibut with Parsley Sauce*

Zucchini and Onion Sauté*

Blue Cheese–Stuffed Potatoes*

Warm Tropical Surprise* and
Chocolate Chip Bites*

Breakfast Menu

Foods (per serving)	Cal.	Carb. (g)	Prot. (g)	Chol. (mg)	Fat (g)/%	Sod. (mg)
Raspberry Smoothie* (p. 75)	190	44	5	2	0.8/4	64
Orange Muffin*	145	25	1.5	0.4	4.8/29	222

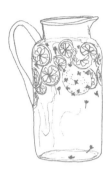

Orange Muffins

These are light-as-a-feather muffins with a light orange glaze. And there really are no eggs in these!

MAKES 12 MUFFINS

¾ cup sugar
¼ cup canola oil
Zest of 4 oranges, finely minced
½ cup buttermilk
¾ cup orange juice

1 teaspoon cinnamon
1½ cups cake flour
1½ teaspoons baking powder
1 teaspoon baking soda
¼ teaspoon salt

256

1. Preheat the oven to 400°F. Lightly spray standard-sized muffin tins with vegetable oil spray.

2. In a large bowl, combine the sugar and oil and whisk until light. Add the orange zest. In another bowl, whisk together the buttermilk, orange juice and cinnamon.

3. Sift together the flour, baking powder, baking soda and salt. Add to the sugar mixture, alternating with the buttermilk mixture. Stir until just mixed. Do not overmix.

4. Fill the muffin cups two-thirds full. Bake for 5 minutes, reduce the temperature to 350°F. and bake for 15 to 20 minutes longer, or until a toothpick inserted in the center of a muffin comes out clean. Turn the muffins out onto a wire rack. Serve warm or cooled. Store in an airtight container.

NOTE: For information on standard-sized muffin tins and using paper liners, see page 84.

CAL. 145   CARB. 25G   PROT. 1.5G   CHOL. 0.4MG   FAT 4.8G/29%   SOD. 222MG
(ANALYZED PER MUFFIN)

"Go confidently in the direction of your dreams! Live the life you've imagined. As you simplify your life the laws of the universe will be simpler."

HENRY DAVID THOREAU

Tuscan Minestrone

This soup is often thickened with loads of pureed beans, but I prefer the light, fresh taste of this version.

SERVES 2

1 onion, coarsely chopped
1 rib celery, sliced (about ¼ cup)
½ cup grated carrots
1 tablespoon finely minced garlic
2 cups plus 2 tablespoons low-fat, low-sodium chicken broth
7 cherry tomatoes, halved
½ teaspoon minced fresh thyme
1 zucchini, sliced in half lengthwise and chopped (about 1 cup)
1 small potato, coarsely chopped
½ cup cooked or canned, drained and rinsed Great Northern beans
1 tablespoon finely minced fresh Italian parsley

1. In a saucepan, combine the onion, celery, carrots, garlic and 2 tablespoons of chicken broth and cook over medium heat for 2 minutes. Add the tomatoes and thyme and cook for about 2 minutes longer, until the tomatoes soften.

2. Add the remaining 2 cups broth, the zucchini, potato and beans. Bring to a boil, reduce the heat to low and simmer, uncovered, for 30 minutes, until the vegetables are tender. Ladle into bowls, sprinkle with the parsley and serve immediately.

CAL. 228   CARB. 45G   PROT. 9G   CHOL. 0MG   FAT 1G/4%   SOD. 40MG

Lunch Menu

FOODS (PER SERVING)	CAL.	CARB. (G)	PROT. (G)	CHOL. (MG)	FAT (G)/ %	SOD. (MG)
Arugula, 2 cups	14.6	1.9	2.2	0	0.09/6	36
Our House Dressing* (p. 194), 1 T.	18	2	0.1	0	1.2/58	31
Summertime Bruschetta* (p. 95), 2 slices	282	54	10	0	2.6/8	548
Tuscan Minestrone*	228	45	9	0	1/4	40
AFTERNOON SNACK						
Apple, 1	59	15	2	0	0.4/6	0
Cheddar cheese, 1 oz.	103	0.7	6.1	22.4	8.5/74	146

257

SIMPLIFY YOUR LIFE

♦ Plan weekly menus.

♦ Shop weekly.

♦ Plant an herb garden.

♦ Watch sunsets regularly.

♦ Walk on the beach.

♦ Have coffee and talk with a friend.

♦ Sit and listen to classical music.

♦ Read a book—often.

♦ Walk the dogs.

♦ Play gin with your mate.

♦ Unplug the TV.

♦ Stop reading every magazine.

♦ Let the phone machine take messages.

Halibut with Parsley Sauce

This method of cooking halibut was inspired by a dish from l'Arpege in Paris and topped with a fabulous parsley sauce we once had in Mykonos—the best of both worlds.

SERVES 2

HALIBUT
Two 6-ounce halibut fillets or steaks
8 fresh basil leaves
8 bay leaves (see page 221)
2 tablespoons finely minced garlic
1 tablespoon finely minced lime zest
½ cup dry white wine
½ cup low-fat, low-sodium chicken broth

SAUCE
2 tablespoons chopped onion
1 tablespoon minced garlic
¼ to ⅛ teaspoon red pepper flakes, or to taste
¾ cup fresh Italian parsley leaves
1 teaspoon lemon juice
Salt and freshly ground black pepper to taste
¼ teaspoon balsamic vinegar
¼ cup chopped fresh basil
2 to 3 tablespoons fish broth, chicken broth or clam juice

258
♦

1. Preheat the oven to 375°F.

2. Prepare the halibut: In a shallow baking dish, place the halibut, skin side down. Sprinkle with the basil, bay leaves, garlic and lime zest, then add the wine and chicken broth. Bake, uncovered, for 15 to 20 minutes, depending on the thickness of the fish, until the fish is opaque and flakes when pierced with a fork.

3. Make the sauce: In a food processor fitted with the metal blade, combine the onion, garlic, red pepper flakes, parsley, lemon juice, salt and pepper, vinegar, basil and fish broth and puree. Transfer to a bowl.

FRESH FISH

When shopping for fish, nothing but the freshest will do. It's the key to cooking fish at home.

Freezing fish changes the texture of the muscle and results in a considerable loss of flavor and moisture. When frozen is the only choice, choose thick fish over thin.

WARM TROPICAL SURPRISE

In less than ten minutes you can make a dessert that will finish off a meal with a surprise visit to the tropics. Be sure the fruit is ripe but still firm—not soft and overripe.

SERVES 2

½ cup cubed cantaloupe
½ cup cubed papaya
1 cup coarsely chopped
   banana (¾-inch pieces)
1 kiwi, cut into chunks
1½ teaspoons Grand
   Marnier (optional)
1 tablespoon orange juice
½ teaspoon finely minced
   orange zest
½ teaspoon sweetened
   shredded coconut

1. Preheat the broiler. Cut two 15-inch squares of aluminum foil and place on top of each other.

2. In a bowl, combine the ingredients and toss. Spread on the foil and roll the edges of the foil over to create a tray. Broil 6 inches from the heat source for 2 to 3 minutes, until warmed and golden.

Note: You can use a shallow broiling pan to broil the fruit instead of a foil tray.

CAL. 114   CARB. 28G   PROT. 2G
CHOL. 0MG   FAT 0.8G/5%
SOD. 7MG

4. Remove and discard the bay and basil leaves from the fish and serve with the sauce on the side.

CAL. 275   CARB. 10G   PROT. 39G   CHOL. 54MG   FAT 4G/15%   SOD. 110MG

Zucchini and Onion Sauté

The deep flavors in this Italian classic are always satisfying!

SERVES 2

4 medium-sized zucchini, grated lengthwise (about 4 cups)
1 onion, sliced into thin rings (about 1 cup)
2 tablespoons finely minced garlic
2 to 4 tablespoons finely minced fresh tarragon, or to taste
½ cup low-fat, low-sodium chicken broth
Salt and freshly ground black pepper to taste

In a nonstick skillet, combine the ingredients, except the salt and pepper, and cook over medium-high heat for 10 to 15 minutes, stirring occasionally, until the zucchini wilts and begins to brown. Season with salt and pepper. Serve immediately.

CAL. 112   CARB. 24G   PROT. 7G   CHOL. 0MG   FAT 0.8G/5%   SOD. 14MG

259
◆

Blue Cheese–Stuffed Potatoes

If you love blue-veined cheeses as I do, it's amazing how far just a little bit of Roquefort goes.

SERVES 2

Two 10-ounce baking potatoes, washed, dried and pierced
several times with a fork
1 tablespoon Roquefort cheese
⅓ cup plus 2 tablespoons Nonfat Blend (see page 298)
4 tablespoons finely minced fresh chives
½ cup coarsely chopped arugula
Freshly ground black pepper to taste

1. Preheat the oven to 500° F.

2. Lay the potatoes on the oven rack and bake for 1 hour, until tender. Cool.

3. Halve the potatoes lengthwise. Carefully scoop out the insides and transfer to a bowl. Add the cheese, Nonfat Blend, chives and arugula and mash with a fork. Season with pepper.

4. Carefully stuff the potato mixture back into the skins. Set on a baking sheet lined with aluminum foil and bake for about 30 minutes longer, until heated through and lightly browned. Serve immediately.

CAL. 344   CARB. 74G   PROT. 10G   CHOL. 3MG   FAT 2G/4%   SOD. 93MG

Dinner Menu

FOODS (PER SERVING)	CAL.	CARB. (G)	PROT. (G)	CHOL. (MG)	FAT (G)/%	SOD. (MG)
Halibut with Parsley Sauce*	275	10	39	54	4/15	110
Zucchini and Onion Sauté*	112	24	7	0	0.8/5	14
Blue Cheese–Stuffed Potatoes*	344	74	10	3	2/4	93
Warm Tropical Surprise*	114	28	2	0	0.8/5	7
Chocolate Chip Bites* (p. 141), 6	156	24	1.9	7.2	6.6/37	126
Today's Totals	**2041**	**348**	**96**	**89**	**34/15**	**1437**

260

"My idea of Heaven is a great big baked potato and someone to share it with."
OPRAH WINFREY

SWEETER SWEET POTATOES

A sweet potato needs no adornment. Just pierce with a fork several times and bake at 400° F. for 1¼ to 1½ hours, until tender. When the potatoes are fork-tender, bake them for 15 minutes longer for the sugar to caramelize.

Longer baking will only make it sweeter. The portion nearest the skin nearly caramelizes, rendering butter or any added sweetness irrelevant. Just split open and enjoy. Served cold, it's a great sweet movable feast.

Baked Potatoes

A cozy comforting baked potato is one of life's true satisfactions—plus it's full of nutrients and good intentions. As it emerges hot from the oven, think carefully about what you really want to put on top.

	CAL.	FAT (G)/%
1 8-oz. medium-sized potato with skin	227	0.3/1

TOPPINGS (2 TABLESPOONS)	TOPPING ALONE		W/POTATO	
	CAL.	FAT (G)/%	CAL.	FAT (G)/%
Blue cheese	60	5/75	287	5.3/16
Butter	203	23/100	430	23.3/48
Cheddar cheese	57	5/79	284	5.3/16
Chives	2	0/0	229	0.3/1
Cottage cheese, low-fat	21	0.3/11	248	0.6/2
Cottage cheese, nonfat, blended	18	0/0	245	0.3/1
Olive oil	239	27/100	466	27.3/52
Parmesan cheese	57	4/63	284	4.3/13
Salsa	17	0/0	244	0.3/1
Sour cream	64	6/84	291	6.3/20
Sour cream, low-fat	50	0.4/72	277	4.3/14
Sour cream, nonfat	35	0/0	262	0.3/1
Yogurt, low-fat	16	0.4/23	234	0.7/3
Yogurt, nonfat	15	0/0	242	0.3/1

261
◆

Down-to-Earth Cooking

◆

Year in and year out, there are those foods that always taste fresh and new, often returning to the seasonal menus. And yet it's realistically easy to remove a great deal of the fat from traditional family favorites, while retaining all of the tastes that are most balanced and most loved.

Thursday
DAY 25

English Muffin with
Honey and Peanut Butter

Banana

◆

Oven-Fried Cottage Fries*

Red and Green Coleslaw*

Carrots Rapée*

A Quarter Pounder Your Way*

Vanilla Frozen Yogurt with
Chocolate Sauce

◆

Arugula and Red Onion Salad with
Lemon Dressing*

Summer Tomato Pasta*

Peach Cake* with Peach Sauce*

Breakfast Menu

FOODS (PER SERVING)	CAL.	CARB. (G)	PROT. (G)	CHOL. (MG)	FAT (G)/%	SOD. (MG)
English muffin with peanut butter, ½ T., and honey* (p. 124), 1 T.	231	44	7	0	5/19	240
Banana, 1	105	27	1	0	0.5/4	1
Skim milk, 1 cup	86	12	8	4	0.4/4	124

Lunch Menu

FOODS (PER SERVING)	CAL.	CARB. (G)	PROT. (G)	CHOL. (MG)	FAT (G)/%	SOD. (MG)
Oven-Fried Cottage Fries*	111	25.3	2.9	0	1.4/1	8.4
Red and Green Coleslaw*	61	15	2	0	0.13/2	23
Carrots Rapée*	35	8.8	1	0	0.1/3	20
A Quarter Pounder Your Way*	161	0.04	27	71	6/32	85
Multi-grain bun, 1	113	19	4	0	2.6/4	197
Vanilla frozen yogurt, ½ cup	167	29	7	13	3/15	25
Chocolate syrup, 2 T.	82	22	0.7	0	0.3/3	36
AFTERNOON SNACK						
Crackers, nonfat, 3	60	13	2	0	0/0	150
Cheddar cheese, 1 oz.	103	0.7	6.1	22.4	8.5/74	146

264

"The advantage of doing one's praising for oneself is that one can lay it on so thick and in exactly the right places."

SAMUEL BUTLER

Oven-Fried Cottage Fries

These are easy, easy, easy—and so satisfying!

SERVES 2

2 Yukon Gold or russet potatoes, peeled and thinly sliced

1. Soak the potato slices in ice water for 1 hour.

2. Preheat the oven to 450°F. about 15 minutes before draining the potatoes.

3. Drain and pat the potatoes dry with paper towels. Spread on a baking sheet and lightly spray with olive oil spray. Bake for 30 minutes, tossing every 5 minutes, until crispy and golden. Serve immediately.

CAL. 111 CARB. 25.3G PROT. 2.9G CHOL. 0MG FAT 1.4G/1% SOD. 8.4MG

NEW POTATOES

Red and Green Coleslaw

These days, with preshredded cabbage, making coleslaw takes about thirty seconds.

SERVES 2

3 tablespoons apple cider vinegar
1 tablespoon plus 1 teaspoon sugar
3 tablespoons nonfat sour cream
1⅓ cups shredded mixed green and red cabbage
Salt and freshly ground black pepper to taste

In a mixing bowl, combine the vinegar, sugar and sour cream and mix until smooth. Add the cabbage and toss to coat well. Season with salt and pepper. Refrigerate for at least 1 hour to allow the flavors to blend before serving.

CAL. 61   CARB. 15G   PROT. 2G   CHOL. 0MG   FAT 0.13G/2%   SOD. 23MG

CARROT POWER

Carotene gives carrots and pumpkins their cheerful orange-yellow hue. Just one carrot provides twice the RDA of antioxidant beta-carotene, thought to help delay cataracts and reduce the risk of heart disease. Available preshredded at the supermarket, carrots are easy to add to soups, tomato sauces, rice dishes, salads and stuffing.

Other deep orange vegetables and fruits and dark green leafy vegetables are rich sources of beta-carotene, too:

- ✦ Apricots
- ✦ Sweet red peppers
- ✦ Broccoli
- ✦ Brussels sprouts
- ✦ Cabbage
- ✦ Beet greens
- ✦ Mustard greens
- ✦ Kale
- ✦ Spinach
- ✦ Sweet potatoes
- ✦ Tomatoes
- ✦ Winter squash

Carrots Rapée

265
✦

This French bistro classic is usually dressed with a vinaigrette with quite a bit of oil. I think it's improved when sparked with citrus juices and mint.

SERVES 2

1 cup grated carrots
3 tablespoons dried currants
1 tablespoon orange juice
½ teaspoon finely minced orange zest
2 teaspoons lemon juice
2 teaspoons finely minced fresh mint

1. In a mixing bowl, combine the carrots and currants. Set aside.

2. In another bowl, combine the orange juice, orange zest and lemon juice. Toss with the carrot mixture. Add the mint, toss and refrigerate for at least 1 hour, or until ready to serve.

CAL. 35   CARB. 8.8G   PROT. 1G   CHOL. 0MG   FAT 0.1G/3%   SOD. 20MG

Best Burgers

Today, the Great American Hamburger as we've known it has become antiquated in healthy eating households. There are recipes for lentil burgers, rice burgers, veggie burgers, all good occasionally, but sometimes these substitutes won't do. When I crave a hamburger but can't face the fat, I mix a ratio of ground sirloin to ground turkey breast, depending on how I'm balancing my fat intake that day. And when I've exceeded my fat allowances, I'll have a turkey burger. Find one of the following combinations that meets your taste buds and dietary goals when you're craving a hamburger with all the fixings. You'll be surprised that you won't wonder: where's the beef?

	CAL.	PROT. (G)	FAT (G)/%
4 oz. ground chuck	347	27	26/67
4 oz. ground sirloin	300	33	18/54
3 oz. ground sirloin with 1 oz. ground turkey breast	255	31	14/49
2 oz. ground sirloin with 2 oz. ground turkey breast	196	30	10/46
1 oz. ground sirloin with 3 oz. ground turkey breast	155	29	6/35
4 oz. ground turkey breast	118	27	2/15

266
◆

A Quarter Pounder Your Way

Sometimes I want the taste of beef. Sometimes I just want the stuff that goes on top of the beef. So I vary my burger to match my mood and current fat allowance. The broth keeps the burger juicy. Serve plain or mixed with any of the ingredients listed below.

SERVES 2

6 ounces lean ground sirloin
2 ounces lean ground turkey breast
4 teaspoons beef broth

1. Prepare a charcoal or gas grill or preheat the broiler.

2. In a mixing bowl, combine the sirloin, turkey and chicken broth and form into 2 equal patties. Grill or broil 4 inches from the heat source for 4 to 5 minutes on each side, until cooked to desired doneness.

CAL. 161   CARB. 0.04G   PROT. 27G   CHOL. 71MG   FAT 6G/32%   SOD. 85MG
(ANALYZED PER 1 PLAIN PATTY)

267
◆

BURGER VARIATIONS: For each half pound of meat add any one of the following ingredients as you mix the meats.

½ teaspoon grated horseradish and ½ teaspoon Dijon mustard,

or 2 tablespoons beer, 3 tablespoons Worcestershire sauce and ¼ teaspoon crushed red pepper flakes,

or 2 tablespoons ketchup and ¼ cup finely diced onion,

or 2 tablespoons red wine and ½ teaspoon freshly ground black pepper,

or ½ teaspoon finely minced lemon zest and ¼ teaspoon freshly ground black pepper.

"Anybody who doesn't think that the best hamburger place in the world is in his hometown is a sissy."
CALVIN TRILLIN

Summer Tomato Pasta

The classic pasta pomodoro from Italy is best made with the summer's finest vine-ripened tomatoes. My dilemma: I love it so much I want it year-round. Window-ripened plum tomatoes and tomato paste do the trick every time—even in coldest January.

SERVES 2

¼ pound linguine, dried
½ cup pasta water
2 tablespoons tomato paste
¼ to ⅛ teaspoon crushed red pepper flakes, or to taste
2 large ripe plum tomatoes, coarsely chopped
   (about 1½ cups)
2 tablespoons finely minced fresh Italian parsley
2 tablespoons finely minced fresh basil
2 large scallions, finely minced
1 tablespoon finely minced fresh mint
2 tablespoons part-skim mozzarella, shredded
Salt and freshly ground black pepper to taste

1. In a large saucepan, cook the linguine in boiling water for 8 to 12 minutes, or until al dente. Drain, reserving ½ cup pasta water, leaving a little water clinging to the pasta, return to the pan, cover and keep warm over very low heat.

2. Meanwhile, in a large skillet, combine the pasta water and tomato paste and cook over medium heat, stirring, for 3 to 5 minutes. Crush the pepper flakes in your hand and add to the skillet.

3. Add the tomatoes to the skillet and cook for about 2 minutes, until just heated through and softened. Stir well and add to the pasta. Add the parsley, basil, scallions, mint and mozzarella and cook, tossing, over low heat for 30 seconds, until hot. Season with salt and pepper and serve immediately.

CAL. 297   CARB. 53G   PROT. 13G   CHOL. 7.5MG   FAT 4.2G/13%   SOD. 118MG

268

PASTA PERFECT— AL DENTE!

Always use a large pan and plenty of water to cook pasta. Pasta needs to "swim" while it cooks at a rapid boil.

Start testing fresh pasta for doneness after it's been cooking for 30 seconds, dry pasta after 4 minutes. Fish out a strand and bite—it should be firm yet tender, with a tiny bit of chalky white center. "Al dente" means "to the tooth"; pasta should "feel" just right when you bite it—not too soft, not too hard.

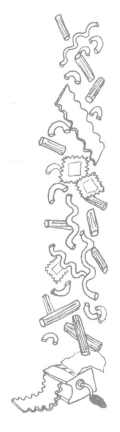

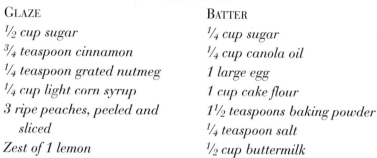

Peach Cake

This is a delightful cake, loaded with plenty of peachy flavor.

SERVES 12

GLAZE	BATTER
½ cup sugar	*¼ cup sugar*
¾ teaspoon cinnamon	*¼ cup canola oil*
¼ teaspoon grated nutmeg	*1 large egg*
¼ cup light corn syrup	*1 cup cake flour*
3 ripe peaches, peeled and sliced	*1½ teaspoons baking powder*
	¼ teaspoon salt
Zest of 1 lemon	*½ cup buttermilk*

1. Preheat the oven to 350°F. Lightly spray a 9-inch round cake pan with vegetable oil spray.

2. Make the glaze: In a bowl, mix the sugar, cinnamon, nutmeg and corn syrup. Spread in the cake pan, arrange the peaches in a circle over the glaze and sprinkle with the lemon zest.

3. Make the batter: In a bowl, combine the sugar and oil and stir together by hand. Add the egg and whisk until thick and yellow.

4. In another bowl, sift together the flour, baking powder and salt. Add to the creamed mixture, alternating with buttermilk.

5. Spread the batter over the peaches and bake for about 30 minutes, until golden and a toothpick inserted in the center comes out clean. Cool the pan on a wire rack for 5 minutes. Using a knife or spatula, loosen the cake from the pan and invert onto a plate. Serve warm or at room temperature with Peach Sauce.

CAL. 173   CARB. 30.8G   PROT. 2.2G   CHOL. 18MG   FAT 5G/26%   SOD. 139MG
(ANALYZED WITHOUT SAUCE)

269
♦

PEACH SAUCE

This provides a nice drizzle of peachy flavor to top cake, sliced fresh peaches or berries.

MAKES ABOUT 1 CUP

2 tablespoons nonfat cottage cheese
1 cup pureed fresh or canned peaches
1 tablespoon peach schnapps (optional)
1 teaspoon vanilla extract

1. In a blender, blend the cottage cheese until smooth.

2. In a bowl, combine the cottage cheese, peaches, schnapps, if desired, and vanilla and mix well. Cover and refrigerate for 1 to 2 hours before serving.

CAL. 2.1 CARB. 0.4G PROT. 0.1G
CHOL. 0MG FAT 0.03G/1%
SOD. 2.3MG (ANALYZED PER TEASPOON)

Dinner Menu

FOODS (PER SERVING)	CAL.	CARB. (G)	PROT. (G)	CHOL. (MG)	FAT (G)/%	SOD. (MG)
Arugula, 2 cups,	14.6	1.9	2.2	0	0.09/6	36
with red onion slices	15.9	3	0.5	0	0.07/4	29
Lemon Dressing* (p. 118), 1 T.	17	0.4	0.1	0	1.8/92	0.3
Summer Tomato Pasta*	297	53	13	7.5	4.2/13	118
Peach Cake* with	173	30.8	2.2	18	5/26	139
Peach Sauce*, 3 t.	6.3	1.2	0.3	0	0.03/1	6.9
Today's Totals	**1839**	**306**	**87**	**135**	**39/19**	**1385**

Fast Food

◆

Cooking at home today, especially weekday meals, needs to be accomplished with little time at the market, a swiftness and saved steps in the kitchen and a minimum of clean up. To save time you can later spend at the table, get everyone in the kitchen working together. This way you can catch up while enjoying great food.

Friday
DAY 26

Strawberry-Orange Smoothie*

Cinnamon Toast*

◆

Spiced Tomato Juice

Lime Chicken Fajitas* with Pico de
Gallo* and Creamy Guacamole*

Breadsticks

◆

Blossoming Onion* with
Spicy Dipping Sauce*

Salad Greens with
White Wine Dressing*

Oven-Fried Coconut Shrimp* with
Orange Sauce*

Red Pepper Risotto*

Peach Frozen Yogurt*

Breakfast Menu

Foods (per serving)	Cal.	Carb. (g)	Prot. (g)	Chol. (mg)	Fat (g)/%	Sod. (mg)
Strawberry-Orange Smoothie* (p. 74)	88	21	1	0	0.7/7	2
Cinnamon Toast* (p. 57)	65	2	14	0	0/0	91
Morning Snack						
Banana, 1	105	27	1	0	0.5/4	1

Lunch Menu

Foods (per serving)	Cal.	Carb. (g)	Prot. (g)	Chol. (mg)	Fat (g)/%	Sod. (mg)
Tomato juice, low-sodium, 6 oz.	29	7	1.3	0	0.1/3	17
Lime Chicken Fajitas*, 2	536	74	28	48	14/24	810
Pico de Gallo* (p. 114), 1 cup	24	6.4	0.8	0	0/0	160
Creamy Guacamole* (p. 113), ½ cup	72	9.6	2.4	0	2.4/30	14.4
Breadsticks, 2	160	26	12	0	4/22	420
Afternoon Snack						
Apple, 3½ oz.	59	15	0.2	0	0.4/6	0
Mini rice cakes, 5	50	12	1	0	0/0	2.5

YO-YO DIETING

Lots of us have slipped into the on-again off-again cycle of dieting, only to be told that we've slowed our metabolism as a result, making weight loss even harder.

While there's now controversy about whether that's true, there's a bottom-line truth about metabolism: when you don't eat enough, your body goes into "starvation mode" to conserve energy to fuel vital body processes.

Smaller, more frequent meals boost your energy and keep your metabolism humming. To kick it into high (weight-losing) gear, get moving and exercise. It's absolutely vital.

Lime Chicken Fajitas

I love to put a big platter in the center of the table, piling it with lime chicken strips, Simple Black Bean Salsa (see page 158), Lemon-Dill Rice (see page 252), Creamy Guacamole (see page 113), Pico de Gallo (see page 114), a few chopped black olives and flour tortillas so that everyone can customize their own fajitas.

SERVES 4
MAKES 8 FAJITAS

1 cup fresh lime juice
2 tablespoons finely minced lime zest
2 whole boneless, skinless chicken
    breasts (about 1¼ pounds)
2½ pounds small onions, halved
    lengthwise and cut into
    ¼-inch wedges
6 tablespoons low-fat, low-sodium
    chicken broth
2 teaspoons paprika
½ cup grated Monterey Jack cheese
8 large flour tortillas (about 10 inches), warmed

1. In a shallow glass dish, combine the lime juice and zest. Add the chicken, stir, cover and marinate in the refrigerator for at least 3 hours.

2. Prepare a gas or charcoal grill or preheat the broiler.

3. In a large skillet, combine the onions, chicken broth and paprika and cook over medium-low heat, stirring occasionally, for about 10 minutes. Uncover and cook for about 10 minutes longer, until the onions are translucent and most of the broth has been absorbed. Set aside to cool slightly.

4. Grill the chicken for about 4 minutes on each side, or until cooked through and the juices run clear when the meat is pierced with a fork. Cool slightly and slice into strips.

5. Serve by placing the chicken, onions and cheese on a platter with the tortillas. Let everyone assemble the fajitas.

CAL. 268   CARB. 37G   PROT. 14G   CHOL. 24MG   FAT 7G/24%   SOD. 405MG
(ANALYZED PER FAJITA)

---

*"Just remember,
we're all
in this alone."*
LILY TOMLIN

MINI TREATS

Eating mini versions of your favorites instantly cuts calories, fat and cholesterol. The secret is in the portion size. Bake mini muffins and bite-sized cookies. Scoop a couple of tablespoons of frozen yogurt. Have someone else "serve small," with your best interests at heart.

It sounds like a trick, but it works. It's much easier to feel satisfied after eating a whole mini muffin than to stop halfway through a big one.

273

Blossoming Onion

This deep-fried restaurant favorite really works surprisingly well with an oven-fried method. I'd rather enjoy this more frequently this way than have the onion be such an indulgence. It's great served with Spicy Dipping Sauce.

SERVES 4

2 very large red onions (about 1½ pounds)
½ cup plain bread crumbs or Panko (see page 205)
1 teaspoon garlic powder
½ teaspoon paprika
2 large egg whites

1. Preheat the oven to 375°F. Lightly spray a baking sheet with olive oil spray.

2. Peel the skin from the onions and trim the bottoms so that the onions sit flat. Starting at the center of the top of each onion and working around it, cut 20 to 30 slits, cutting only three-quarters into the onion for a "flower" effect. Transfer to the baking sheet.

3. In a small bowl, combine the bread crumbs, garlic powder and paprika. Set aside. In another bowl, whisk the egg whites lightly with a fork. Pour the whites over the onions to cover thoroughly and then sprinkle evenly with the seasoned crumbs. Spray lightly with olive oil spray and bake for 40 to 50 minutes, until the onions are lightly browned. Serve immediately.

CAL. 123.   CARB. 25G   PROT. 5G   CHOL. 0.6MG   FAT 0.9G/5%   SOD. 120MG

SPICY DIPPING SAUCE

Spicy and tantalizing, this is reminiscent of the extremely fatty sauce traditionally served with deep-fried blossoming onions—but this version is very low in fat!

MAKES ABOUT 1 CUP

¾ cup nonfat cottage cheese
¼ cup mayonnaise
1½ teaspoons prepared horseradish
1 teaspoon cayenne
Salt and freshly ground black pepper to taste

1. In a blender, blend the cottage cheese until smooth.

2. Transfer the cottage cheese to a bowl and add the mayonnaise, horseradish and cayenne. Season with salt and pepper. Mix well. Serve at room temperature or cover and refrigerate. Bring to room temperature before serving.

CAL. 11   CARB. 0.2G   PROT. 0.5G   CHOL. 0.7MG   FAT 0.9G/75%   SOD. 21MG (ANALYZED PER TEASPOON)

Oven-Fried Coconut Shrimp

This is one of my favorite splurges and now is a regular at our house for a first course or entrée.

SERVES 4

2 large egg whites
1⅓ cups fine plain bread crumbs or Panko (see page 205)
½ teaspoon ground cumin
6 tablespoons flaked sweetened coconut
2 tablespoons finely minced garlic
Freshly ground black pepper
24 large shrimp, peeled and deveined
Orange Sauce

1. Preheat the oven to 500°F. Lightly spray a baking sheet with olive oil spray.

2. In a small bowl, beat the egg whites lightly with a fork. In a small plastic bag, combine the bread crumbs, cumin, coconut, garlic and pepper.

3. One at a time, dip each shrimp into the egg whites and then into the plastic bag and shake to coat with bread crumbs. Lay the shrimp on the baking sheet and bake for 10 to 12 minutes, until the shrimp are golden and cooked through, turning once with a spatula halfway through cooking. Serve immediately with Orange Sauce.

CAL. 226   CARB. 29G   PROT. 14G   CHOL. 66MG   FAT 6G/25%   SOD. 344MG
(ANALYZED WITHOUT SAUCE)

275
◆

> *"Years may wrinkle the skin, but to give up enthusiasm wrinkles the soul."*
> SAMUEL ULLMAN

ORANGE SAUCE

This is easy to make and perfect for dipping Oven-Fried Coconut Shrimp.

MAKES ABOUT
½ CUP
SERVES 4

½ cup low-sugar orange marmalade
½ teaspoon crushed red pepper flakes
½ teaspoon molasses
4 to 6 dashes Tabasco sauce, or to taste
Pinch of cinnamon
Pinch of cumin

In a small bowl, combine the ingredients and blend well.

CAL. 112 CARB. 28.7G PROT. 0.2G
CHOL. 0MG FAT 0.1G/8% SOD. 18MG
(ANALYZED PER 2 TABLESPOONS)

Red Pepper Risotto

This is a fabulous risotto to serve as an entrée with a mixed green salad and crusty bread or as a side dish for a light meal.

SERVES 4

3 cups plus 2 tablespoons low-fat, low-sodium
  chicken broth
2 tablespoons finely minced garlic
1 cup coarsely chopped onion
1 red bell pepper, diced (about 1 cup)
1 bay leaf (see page 221)
1 cup arborio or other aromatic medium-grain rice
Freshly ground black pepper to taste
¼ cup grated Parmesan cheese
¼ cup finely minced fresh Italian parsley

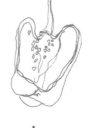

1. In a large skillet, heat 2 tablespoons chicken broth over medium heat, add the garlic and onion and cook for 1 to 2 minutes. Add the pepper and bay leaf and cook for 3 to 4 minutes.

2. In a saucepan, bring the remaining 3 cups broth to a boil, reduce the heat and keep it at a simmer.

3. Add the rice to the skillet and slowly add the broth, ½ cup at a time, stirring constantly, until all has been absorbed, about 30 to 35 minutes. When the rice is al dente, add the black pepper, cheese and parsley and stir gently. Serve slightly creamy.

CAL. 137   CARB. 23G   PROT. 7G   CHOL. 5MG   FAT 2.2G/14%   SOD. 558MG

Dinner Menu

FOODS (PER SERVING)	CAL.	CARB. (G)	PROT. (G)	CHOL. (MG)	FAT (G)/%	SOD. (MG)
Blossoming Onion*	123	25	5	0.6	0.9/5	120
Spicy Dipping Sauce*, 2 T.	66	1.2	3	4.2	5.4/75	126
Salad greens, 1 cup	9.5	1.6	0.9	0	0.1/11	14
White Wine Dressing* (p. 118), 1 T.	17	1.5	0.1	0	1.2/62	93
Oven-Fried Coconut Shrimp*	226	29	14	66	6/25	344
Orange Sauce*, 2 T.	112	28.7	0.2	0	0.1/8	18
Red Pepper Risotto*	137	23	7	5	2.2/14	558
Peach Frozen Yogurt* (p. 108), ½ cup	124	26	5.6	0.6	0.1/1	140
Today's Totals	**2002**	**336**	**98**	**124**	**38/17**	**2931**

> *"The trick is to stop and think occasionally during normal times how good things are."*
> ANDY ROONEY

SALT

I haven't cooked with it for about fifteen years. So my recipes always include "salt and pepper, to taste." I do crave salt at table on certain foods—scrambled eggs, lamb chops, sometimes fish or salad.

When you do choose salt, know your choices:

Rock salt is extracted from the earth, boiled and crystallized. **Sea salt** comes from salt water—wind and sun evaporate the water, creating salt crystals. **Table salt** is refined, with iodine added. **Kosher salt** is coarse, flaky, inexpensive and has no additives. It's my first choice for flavor.

Cool, Creamy and Ever Refreshing

When you scream for ice cream, make sure you know what you're getting. Labels can be deceiving, so scrutinize them carefully, and remember vanilla is one thing, but your favorite flavors—chocolate, praline, butter rum—all add calories, as well as loads of fat.

My advice is to make your own. Not only will you know exactly what's in it, but you can use higher-quality ingredients than any mass manufacturer can afford. These figures are all for ½-cup servings.

½ CUP SERVING	CAL.	FAT (G)/%
Vanilla ice cream, B & J	259	17/59
Vanilla ice cream, HD	230	17/67
Vanilla low-fat ice cream	100	2/18
Coffee ice cream, HD	270	18/60
Coffee Toffee Crunch ice cream, B & J	280	19/61
Mint Chocolate Cookie ice cream, B & J	260	17/59
Butter Pecan ice cream, HD	320	24/69
Frozen yogurt, Dannon	120	3/23
Chocolate Frangelico Frozen Yogurt*	137	3/20
Chocolate frozen yogurt, HD	160	3/14
Passion Fruit Papaya Frozen Yogurt*	169	0.3/2
Strawberry Frozen Yogurt*	159	0.4/2
Peach Frozen Yogurt*	124	0.1/1
Lime Frozen Yogurt*	208	0.1/0
Cool Fabulous Fudge Cheesecake Ice Cream*	215	6/25

* = *Fresh Start* recipe

B & J = Ben & Jerry's

HD = Häagen-Dazs

Country Cooking

◆

Get everyone into the act, eating and enjoying lower-fat foods. Encourage them to pitch in in the kitchen to see how easily these foods are prepared. They'll find that simple, logical changes in cooking are all that are necessary to switch gears for a lifetime of good health. That leaves plenty of time for the things that really matter most.

Saturday
DAY 27

Fresh Orange Juice

Light Lemon Pancakes* with
Very Strawberry Sauce*

Turkey Ham Slices

◆

Watercress Salad with
Roquefort Dressing*

Sausage Mushroom Pizza*

◆

Olive and Caper Bruschetta*

Crunchy Snow Peas with
Sun-Dried Tomato Dip*

Rum-Roasted Pork Tenderloin* with
Granny Smith Applesauce*

Wild Rice with Pecans*

Baked Acorn Squash

Raisin Bread Pudding* with
Vanilla Sauce*

Breakfast Menu

Foods (per serving)	Cal.	Carb. (g)	Prot. (g)	Chol. (mg)	Fat (g)/%	Sod. (mg)
Orange juice, 6 oz.	83.5	19.4	1.4	0	0.3/3	1.2
Light Lemon Pancakes*, 4	116	13.6	8	56	5.6/23	120
Very Strawberry Sauce*, 4 T.	42	10.4	0.4	0	0.2/6	16
Turkey ham, 3 oz.	90	1.5	13.5	52.5	3.8/38	990

Light Lemon Pancakes

These are light in every sense of the word—and they are also most addictive! They are great with Very Strawberry Sauce.

MAKES SIXTEEN 2-INCH CAKES

1 large egg
2 large egg whites
¼ cup plus 2 tablespoons whole-wheat flour
1 tablespoon sugar
2 tablespoons skim milk
1½ teaspoons vanilla extract
2 teaspoons grated lemon zest
¼ cup part-skim ricotta cheese
¼ cup nonfat cottage cheese

1. In a medium bowl, combine the egg, egg whites, flour, sugar, milk, vanilla and lemon zest and stir to combine.

2. In a blender, combine the ricotta and cottage cheese and blend until smooth. Add to the flour mixture and stir to blend.

3. Heat a large nonstick skillet over medium heat. Spoon the batter by tablespoonfuls into the hot skillet and when holes appear in the pancakes, flip them and cook for 1 to 2 minutes longer, until golden. Repeat until all the batter is used. Serve immediately.

Cal. 29   Carb. 3.4g   Prot. 2g   Chol. 14mg   Fat 0.7g/23%   Sod. 30mg
(ANALYZED PER PANCAKE)

WATER

At first, I felt overwhelmed. Eight glasses of water a day? I couldn't see myself standing at the kitchen sink, chug-a-lugging away.

Since then, I've learned—as have many—to sip a little water all day long. And, carrying a glass or bottle along with me has become second nature.

Exercise? You need even more water. An hour of daily exercise boosts the requirement to nine to thirteen glasses a day, depending on your weight and intensity of activity. Water regulates body temperature, carries nutrients and oxygen to cells, even cushions joints and protects organs and tissues. Extremes of cold and heat up the ante.

> *"There is the risk you cannot afford to take, and there is the risk you cannot afford not to take."*
> PETER DRUCKER

Very Strawberry Sauce

Orange and lemon juice perk up the flavor of strawberries, making them taste intensely of strawberry. This is great on pancakes, frozen yogurt, angel food cake or simply other fruits.

MAKES 1 CUP

2 cups hulled and quartered fresh strawberries
2 tablespoons orange juice
1 teaspoon finely minced orange zest
1 tablespoon honey
1½ teaspoons lemon juice

In a small saucepan, combine the ingredients and simmer gently, uncovered, for 6 to 8 minutes, stirring occasionally. Serve hot, warm or cool. To store, cover and refrigerate.

CAL. 10.5   CARB. 2.6G   PROT. 0.1G   CHOL. 0MG   FAT 0.05G/6%   SOD. 4MG
(ANALYZED PER TABLESPOON)

281
◆

Lunch Menu

Foods (per serving)	Cal.	Carb. (g)	Prot. (g)	Chol. (mg)	Fat (g)/%	Sod. (mg)
Watercress, 2 cups	8	0.9	1.6	0	0/0	28
Roquefort Dressing* (p. 120), 1 T.	9	7	7	1	0.4/36	29
"Sausage" and Mushroom Pizza* (p. 151)	245	27	23	36	5.6/20	264

Dinner

> *"The most wasted day of all is that on which we have not laughed."*
>
> Sebastien Rock Nicholas Chamfort

Olive and Caper Bruschetta

This is light, yet a real taste-bud tantalizer. It makes a great appetizer.

MAKES 8 PIECES

1½ ounces canned white tuna in water, drained and flaked

⅛ teaspoon soy sauce

1½ tablespoons finely minced fresh Italian parsley

1½ tablespoons finely minced red onions

1½ teaspoons drained capers

1½ teaspoons finely minced garlic

¾ teaspoon lemon juice

¾ teaspoon finely minced lemon zest

¼ teaspoon olive oil

1½ teaspoons finely minced pitted Kalamata olives

Eight ¼-inch-thick slices French or Italian bread

3 cloves garlic, halved

282

1. In a small mixing bowl, combine the ingredients, except the bread and garlic cloves, and mix well. Cover and refrigerate until serving.

2. Just before serving, grill or toast the bread and rub one side with the garlic cloves. Place a dollop of the olive mixture on top of each of the toasts and serve immediately.

Cal. 121   Carb. 21.4g   Prot. 5.1g   Chol. 1.6mg   Fat 1.6 g/12%   Sod. 332mg
(analyzed per bread slice)

I love to add flavor to food with wines, whiskeys and liqueurs. Use them as you would any other flavorings. The amount of alcohol left after cooking ranges from 10 to 60%, depending on the food, length of exposure, cooking method and the amount of alcohol to begin with.

Use stainless steel pans (aluminum gives a metallic taste) and simmer over low heat to preserve color and enrich flavor and character.

Rum-Roasted Pork Tenderloin

I've always loved piping-hot pork served with cool chunky apple-sauce.

SERVES 4

*1 pork tenderloin,
    approximately 1 pound
    and 12 inches long
2 large cloves garlic, slivered*

*1 cup low-fat, low-sodium
    chicken broth
2 tablespoons dark rum*

1. Preheat the oven to 400°F.

2. Make eight ½-inch vertical slits in the pork and insert the garlic slivers. Place in a shallow baking dish, pour the chicken broth and rum over the pork, cover with aluminum foil and bake for 30 minutes. Uncover and bake about 10 minutes longer, until the meat is done and reaches an internal temperature of 160°F. Serve immediately.

CAL. 158   CARB. 1G   PROT. 26G   CHOL. 83MG   FAT 4.6G/24%   SOD. 431MG

283
✦

Granny Smith Applesauce

The tartness of applesauce made with these crunchy green apples and just a little sweetness is one of my favorites.

SERVES 4

*4 cups peeled, cored and
    coarsely chopped
    Granny Smith apples*

*2 tablespoons sugar
2 tablespoons vanilla extract
    or light rum (optional)*

In a saucepan, cook the apples over medium heat for about 20 minutes, stirring occasionally. Taste and add the sugar, a tablespoon at a time, to the desired sweetness and cook for 5 minutes longer. Add the vanilla or rum, if desired, and cook for about 5 minutes longer. Taste and adjust the sweetness. Serve at room temperature or chilled.

NOTE: If you prefer, do not peel the apples. I don't.

CAL. 59   CARB. 13G   PROT. 3G   CHOL. 0MG   FAT 0G/0%   SOD. 5MG
(ANALYZED PER ¼ CUP)

Wild Rice with Pecans

I never tire of this mixture of wild rice and cracked wheat, pecans and dried fruit perked up with mint and orange zest. It tastes like . . . "more"!!!

RICE ROLES

Rice is a magical canvas on which to create wonderful flavors. Try white, brown, basmati and other rices with:

♦ Parsley, dill, tarragon, chervil, mint

♦ Scallions

♦ Parmesan cheese

♦ Toasted nuts

♦ Currants, raisins, dried cherries

♦ Garlic

♦ Lemon or orange zest

♦ Sesame seeds

♦ Peas and mint

♦ Sunflower seeds

♦ Mushroom

♦ Dry roasted peanuts

♦ Saffron

♦ Basil and chopped tomatoes

♦ Pesto

♦ Ginger

♦ Bell and chili peppers

♦ Capers

♦ Lemongrass

♦ Salsa

♦ Beans

♦ Sun-dried tomatoes

SERVES 4

¾ cup dried cherries, raisins or currants

3 tablespoons orange juice

½ cup cracked wheat

⅓ cup wild rice

3 tablespoons coarsely chopped scallions, green part only

2 tablespoons coarsely chopped toasted pecans

4 teaspoons frozen orange juice concentrate

1 teaspoon finely minced orange zest

Salt and freshly ground black pepper to taste

4 teaspoons finely minced fresh mint

4 teaspoons finely minced fresh Italian parsley

1. In a small bowl, combine the cherries and orange juice and set aside to plump for 30 minutes to 1 hour.

2. In a saucepan, bring 1½ cups water to a boil over high heat. Add the cracked wheat, cover, reduce the heat and simmer for about 15 minutes, until the liquid is absorbed. Spread on a baking sheet to dry and cool.

3. In another saucepan, bring 2 cups water to a boil over high heat. Add the wild rice, cover, reduce the heat and simmer for 35 to 40 minutes, until tender but not blooming (when the white interior shows). Drain and set aside to cool.

4. In a large bowl, combine the cooled wheat, rice, cherries and juice, if any, scallions, pecans, orange juice concentrate and orange zest. Season with salt and pepper and add the mint and parsley. Toss to coat and set aside at room temperature for about 1 hour to allow the flavors to blend.

CAL. 267   CARB. 64G   PROT. 7.3G   CHOL. 0.4MG   FAT 3.5G/10%   SOD. 4.6MG

Raisin Bread Pudding with Vanilla Sauce

This is very rich and satisfying. I love it served warm with the cool drizzle of Vanilla Sauce.

SERVES 6

8 slices raisin bread
1 large egg
1 large egg white
³/₄ cup evaporated skim milk
1 cup skim milk

¹/₂ cup sugar
¹/₂ teaspoon cinnamon
¹/₄ teaspoon ground nutmeg
1 tablespoon vanilla extract
Vanilla Sauce

1. Preheat the oven to 350°F.

2. Place the raisin bread in an 8 × 8-inch baking dish or in a 5 × 3-inch loaf pan in slightly overlapping rows.

3. In a mixing bowl, combine the rest of the ingredients except the Vanilla Sauce and lightly beat with a fork. Pour over the bread, pushing the bread down to submerge. Bake, uncovered, for 35 to 40 minutes, until golden on top. Serve warm or at room temperature, drizzled with Vanilla Sauce.

CAL. 208   CARB. 41G   PROT. 7G   CHOL. 33MG   FAT 1.9G./8%   SOD. 196MG
(ANALYZED WITHOUT SAUCE)

285
◆

VANILLA SAUCE

This is just a nice cool vanilla sauce to drizzle over warm Raisin Bread Pudding or fresh fruit.

MAKES ABOUT
1 ¹/₂ CUPS

1¹/₂ cups Vanilla Dreamy Cream (see page 87)
¹/₄ cup skim milk

In a bowl, combine the Vanilla Dreamy Cream and milk and mix well. Serve immediately.

CAL. 24   CARB. 4G   PROT. 2G
CHOL. 0.03MG   FAT 0G/0%
SOD. 56MG (ANALYZED PER
TABLESPOON)

Dinner Menu

FOODS (PER SERVING)	CAL.	CARB. (G)	PROT. (G)	CHOL. (MG)	FAT (G)/%	SOD. (MG)
Olive and Caper Bruschetta*, 2 slices	242	42.8	10.2	3.2	3.2/12	664
Snow peas, 1 cup	61	11	4	0	0.3/4	5.8
Sun-Dried Tomato Dip* (p. 163), 2 T.	24	1.8	3	2.4	8.4/30	108
Rum-Roasted Pork Tenderloin*	158	1	26	83	4.6/24	431
Granny Smith Applesauce*, ¹/₄ cup	59	13	3	0	0/0	5
Wild Rice with Pecans*	267	64	7.3	0.4	3.5/10	4.6
Acorn squash, ¹/₂	127	33	2.6	0	0.3/2	9
Raisin Bread Pudding*	208	41	7	33	1.9/8	196
Vanilla Sauce*, 3 T.	72	12	6	0.1	0/0	168
Today's Totals	**1812**	**300**	**123**	**267**	**38/19**	**3040**

A Lazy Sunday

◆

Today, easy cooking beckons us in every season but never more than in the summertime. And now that you've got a handle on how to balance your intake of various foods, it's up to you to select your choices. You know you'll love all the flavors, it's just a matter of timing your indulgences yourself.

Sunday
DAY 28

Fresh Orange Juice

Red Berries Fruit Salad*

Spicy Sausage Strata*

Spicy Carrot Muffins*

◆

Watercress Salad and
Watercress Dressing*

Roasted Garlic Pasta*

◆

Best Ever Barbecued Chicken*
or Best-Ever Barbecued Ribs*

Lemon-Dill Rice*

Ginger Green Beans*

Breadsticks

Very Creamy Cheesecake*
or Passion Fruit Papaya
Frozen Yogurt*

Breakfast Menu

Foods (per serving)	Cal.	Carb. (g)	Prot. (g)	Chol. (mg)	Fat (g)/%	Sod. (mg)
Orange juice, 6 oz.	83.5	19.4	1.4	0	0.3/3	1.2
Red Berries Fruit Salad* (p. 131)	116	28	1.4	0	0.8/6	3
Spicy Sausage Strata*	223	17.7	19.9	65	7.9/32	49.5
Spicy Carrot Muffin* (p. 84)	172	30	2.5	12	5/26	268

> *"One does not discover new lands without consenting to lose sight of the shore for a very long time."*
> André Gide

Spicy Sausage Strata

This is a dream of a way to wake up to easy Sunday-morning sausage and eggs. Everything is measured and mixed the day before. I've eliminated as much fat as possible for a dish everyone is anxious to gather for after a good night's sleep. We often serve this at our inn, and the guests love it!

SERVES 6

1 cup cleaned, stemmed and quartered mushrooms
4 slices white bread, crusts removed and reserved
1 cup nonfat cottage cheese
1 large egg
3 large egg whites
1½ teaspoons dry mustard
1 cup skim milk
2 tablespoons heavy cream
Dash of Tabasco sauce
Pinch of crushed red pepper flakes
¼ cup chopped scallions, green part only
Freshly ground black pepper to taste

288

½ cup Spicy Sausage Turkey
   (about ¼ pound) (see page 301)
1 teaspoon finely minced fresh sage
2 ounces Brie cheese, rind on
3 tablespoons Parmesan shards (see page 67)

1. In a nonstick skillet lightly sprayed with olive oil spray, sauté the mushrooms over medium heat for 4 to 5 minutes, until softened and they begin to release their liquid. Cover and refrigerate.

2. Lightly spray an 8 x 8-inch pan with olive oil spray.

3. Spread the bread crusts over the bottom of the pan and arrange the bread slices on top.

4. In a blender, blend the cottage cheese until smooth. Transfer to a bowl, add the egg, egg whites, mustard, milk and cream and blend well. Pour over the bread, cover and refrigerate overnight.

5. Preheat the oven to 350°F. Remove the strata from the refrigerator at least 30 minutes before you're ready to cook it.

6. Add the Tabasco, red pepper flakes and scallions and season to taste with pepper. Sprinkle the sausage, sage and mushrooms over the bread mixture and dot with pieces of Brie. (So that ingredients don't float to the surface, tuck some under the bread slices, if necessary.) Sprinkle with the Parmesan and bake for 45 to 50 minutes, until golden. Serve immediately.

CAL. 223   CARB. 17.7G   PROT. 19.9G   CHOL. 65MG   FAT 7.9G/32%   SOD. 49.5MG

289

EXERCISE WATCH

Be alert for chances to exercise. Walk more. Use the stairs. Bike to the store. Park farther away. Walk to work. Garden. Walk the dog. Don't depend on others or automatic devices.

Lunch Menu

Foods (per serving)	Cal.	Carb. (g)	Prot. (g)	Chol. (mg)	Fat (g)/%	Sod. (mg)
Watercress. 2 cups	8	0.9	1.6	0	0/0	28
Watercress Dressing* (p. 117), 1 T.	2.6	0.5	0.2	0	0.01/4	11
Roasted Garlic Pasta*	331	61	12.6	0	3.6/10	295

Roasted Garlic Pasta

SERVES 6

3 cups low-fat, low-sodium chicken broth
60 to 70 whole cloves garlic (6 to 7 heads)
¾ pound linguine, dried
1 tablespoon extra-virgin olive oil
¾ cup minced garlic
½ to 1 teaspoon crushed red pepper
flakes, or to taste
¾ cup fresh Italian parsley, finely minced
Salt and freshly ground black pepper to taste

1. Preheat the oven to 250° F. In a 9 × 12-inch baking dish, combine 1½ cups chicken broth and the whole garlic cloves. Roast, uncovered, tossing every 10 to 15 minutes, for 45 minutes to 1 hour, until golden brown. Set aside.

2. In a large saucepan, cook the pasta in boiling water over high heat for 8 to 12 minutes, until al dente. Drain, reserving ¾ cup of the cooking water. Return to the saucepan, cover and keep warm over very low heat.

3. In a large skillet, heat the remaining 1½ cups broth and the oil over medium heat. Add the minced garlic and pepper flakes, stir and cook for 2 to 3 minutes, until the garlic turns golden but not brown.

4. Add the pasta, roasted garlic and reserved pasta water. Toss and cook for 1 to 2 minutes to allow the pasta to absorb the sauce. Add the parsley and toss again. Season with salt and pepper and serve immediately.

CAL. 331   CARB. 61G   PROT. 12.6G   CHOL. 0MG   FAT 3.6G/10%   SOD. 295MG

290

THE GLORY OF GARLIC

With every passing year, my cooking contains more and more garlic—roasted to a subtle nutty flavor or added raw for its punch and power.

Lucky for me, it helps lower blood pressure, combat cancer and decrease blood cholesterol—the reason I've popped two garlic pills a day for a decade. But it's the flavor I crave.

There's no right or wrong way to cook with garlic. How much depends on your own taste. If a recipe seems to have too much, adjust to your liking.

Cooking and preparation determine garlic's flavor. Raw, sautéed, roasted, braised, toasted, sliced, minced, pureed or squeezed—all taste different.

Ginger Green Beans

This is a favorite Chinese-style vegetable of mine, pared down to have a minimum of fat.

SERVES 6

1 tablespoon olive oil
1 tablespoon plus 1½ teaspoons finely minced fresh ginger
1 tablespoon finely minced garlic
1½ pounds green beans, trimmed
1½ cups low-fat, low-sodium chicken broth
Freshly ground black pepper to taste

1. In a large skillet, heat the olive oil over medium heat. Add the ginger and garlic and cook for about 1 minute, until lightly browned.

2. Add the beans and cook for 2 to 3 minutes, stirring constantly. Add the chicken broth and continue cooking, tossing, for about 5 minutes, until the liquid evaporates and the beans are tender. Season with pepper and serve immediately.

CAL. 62   CARB. 9G   PROT. 3G   CHOL. 0MG   FAT 2.4G/31%   SOD. 147MG

291

♦ The more you mince garlic, the more its oils are exposed to air, increasing its power and flavor.

♦ To tame the heat a bit, sauté with onions just until tender. Too brown, garlic becomes bitter.

♦ If garlic has simmered in a dish and you want added punch, add minced fresh garlic at the end, too.

♦ Roasted garlic tastes nutty and sweet and loses its punch.

♦ Roast whole heads and squeeze the paste onto bread like butter.

♦ Place whole heads in charcoal embers until the outside is charred and the inside is soft and nutty. Spread on grilled meat, vegetables or bread.

♦ Choose large, plump, firm bulbs.

♦ Store in a cool place—but don't refrigerate.

VEGETABLES AU NATUREL

One of the smartest ways to cut fat is to stop putting it on vegetables. It's amazing how fresh steamed asparagus, broccoli, green beans and zucchini taste unadorned. They're really quite addictive, or if you want to add flavor, check below:

	CAL.	FAT (G)/%
Brown sugar, 1 T.	34	0/0
Butter, 1 T.	102	12/100
Fresh herbs, 1 T.	1	0/0
Hollandaise, 1 T.	44	4/88
Olive oil, 1 T.	119	14/100
Parmesan cheese, 1 T.	29	2/62
Rice wine vinegar, 1 T.	15	0/0
Sliced almonds, 1 T.	35	3/77

Best Ever Barbecued Chicken

The chicken is cooked in the oven but tastes like it came right from the backyard barbecue pit. But you don't have to fire up the grill for this treat—although you may, if you prefer.

SERVES 6

3 pounds chicken breasts, bone-in, skinned and halved
2¼ cups Best Ever Barbecue Sauce

1. Preheat the oven to 350°F.

2. In a shallow baking dish, bake the chicken, skin side up, uncovered, for 30 minutes. Brush generously with the sauce and continue baking for 10 minutes longer. Brush with the remaining sauce and bake for about 10 more minutes, until the juices run clear when the meat is pierced with a small, sharp knife. Serve immediately.

CAL. 475   CARB. 69G   PROT. 35G   CHOL. 90MG   FAT 7G/13%   SOD. 410MG
(ANALYSIS INCLUDES SAUCE)

Best Ever Barbecued Ribs

Country-style ribs are meaty ribs—not spareribs. If you would rather cook these on a grill, do so, using indirect heat, for about an hour.

SERVES 6

3 pounds country-style pork ribs
2¼ cups Best Ever Barbecue Sauce

1. In a large pot, cover the ribs with water by 2 to 3 inches and bring to a boil over high heat. Reduce the heat, cover and simmer for about 30 minutes. Drain and pat dry with paper towels.

2. Preheat the broiler.

3. Lay the ribs in a broiling pan or on aluminum foil and brush generously with the sauce. Broil 4 inches from the heat source for 3 minutes. Turn, brush and broil for 3 minutes. Repeat, turning

BEST EVER BARBECUE SAUCE

A spontaneous beach barbecue introduced me to the best barbecued ribs I'd ever tasted. Our friends, the Leonards, have made this recipe for barbecue sauce forever—and now we will, too. It's not too sweet, not too tomatoey, not too spicy—and it has no added fat. The secrets are in the cinnamon and blackberry jam. It's just a perfect complement to chicken or ribs cooked indoors or out.

MAKES ABOUT
4½ CUPS

1 cup packed light brown
  sugar
1½ cups Quick Tomato
  Sauce (see page 304)
1½ cups canned pineapple
  chunks, with juice
1 tablespoon cinnamon
¾ cup blackberry
  unsweetened spreadable
  fruit or seedless jam
¾ teaspoon Dijon mustard

Combine the ingredients and use immediately or cover and refrigerate until ready to use.

CAL. 17   CARB. 4.3G   PROT. 0.12G
CHOL. 0MG   FAT 0.03G/1%
SOD. 20.1MG (ANALYZED PER
1 TABLESPOON)

and brushing the ribs for about 12 minutes longer (for a total cooking time of about 18 minutes), until the ribs are cooked through and slightly crisp on the outside. Serve immediately.

CAL. 538   CARB. 69G   PROT. 28G   CHOL. 87MG   FAT 20G/37%   SOD. 396MG
(ANALYSIS INCLUDES SAUCE)

Very Creamy Cheesecake

There are numerous low-fat cheesecakes, all touted as being wonderful. Most are from a box or are made with ricotta cheese, and have never appealed to me. I like cheesecake silky smooth and creamy. This one does the trick! It satisfies on every level.

MAKES 24 SERVINGS

CRUST
2 cups crushed low-fat graham crackers (about 15 whole)
1/3 cup sugar
1 teaspoon cinnamon
1/2 teaspoon grated nutmeg
1/2 teaspoon ground ginger
1/4 cup canola oil
2 tablespoons frozen apple juice concentrate

FILLING
2 cups nonfat cottage cheese
Two 8-ounce packages Neufchâtel cream cheese
1 1/2 cups sugar
4 large egg whites
6 tablespoons cornstarch
6 tablespoons cake flour
3 tablespoons lemon juice
1 tablespoon plus 1 teaspoon vanilla extract
2 cups nonfat sour cream
*1 tablespoon finely minced
    lemon zest*

293
◆

(continued on next page)

1. Make the crust: In a mixing bowl, combine the graham crackers, sugar, cinnamon, nutmeg, ginger, canola oil and apple juice concentrate and toss with a fork until the mixture holds together. Press evenly into a 10-inch springform pan. Refrigerate.

2. Preheat the oven to 325°F.

3. Make the filling: In a food processor fitted with the metal blade, blend the cottage cheese until smooth. Add the cream cheese a little at a time and blend until smooth. Gradually add the sugar, mixing well, after each addition. Add the egg whites, one at a time, beating until mixed. Add the cornstarch, flour, lemon juice and vanilla and blend. Add the sour cream and lemon zest and blend until smooth. Wrap the bottom of the pan in foil to come halfway up the sides. Transfer to the prepared springform pan.

4. Place the pan in a larger pan. Add enough hot water to come halfway up the foil but not over its edges and bake for about 1 hour, or until firm around the edges.

5. Turn off the oven and let the cheesecake stand in the oven for 2 hours. Remove and let cool completely on a wire rack. Release the sides of the pan and chill the cheesecake until ready to serve.

N O T E : Some food processor bowls may not hold the entire mixture. If this is the case, pour half the batter into a bowl while you complete mixing the rest of the ingredients. Combine all the batter in the bowl and stir vigorously with a spatula to blend. Transfer to the springform pan.

CAL. 249   CARB. 38G   PROT. 7.6G   CHOL. 10.6MG   FAT 7.7G/27%   SOD. 280MG

294

"Slow down and enjoy life. It's not only the seeing you miss by going too fast—you also miss the sense of where you're going and why."
EDDIE CANTOR

Passion Fruit Papaya Frozen Yogurt

**FRUIT FOR
DESSERT**

Unlike Europeans, Americans seldom order fruit for dessert. But fruit is perfect at meal's end when you want something sweet. It's light and pretty, ever so special poached in wine, topped with a sweetened yogurt sauce, skewered as a kebab and grilled, served with a dash of fortified wine or liqueur, sprinkled with chocolate shavings or accompanied by a tiny wedge of cheese.

For a grand finale in Italy, fruit is brought to the table in a large bowl. Each guest receives a bowl of ice water, then selects and washes his own fruit. Thus, the host honors guest with the most perfect fruit possible, free from discoloration caused by washing in advance—a ritual that can be made very dramatic.

I adore a wonderful local lady, Marie Palazzola, who makes some of the best gelatos and sorbettos around. I'm addicted to her Passion Fruit Sorbetto, and you will be to this one!

MAKES ³/₄ QUART

6 ripe passion fruits (pulp and juice)
1 medium-sized ripe papaya, peeled, seeded and cut
   into chunks
1¹/₂ cups plain nonfat yogurt
1 tablespoon lemon juice
¹/₂ cup sugar

1. In a blender, combine the passion fruit and papaya and blend until smooth. Transfer to a mixing bowl and add the yogurt, lemon juice and sugar. Mix well.

2. Transfer the mixture to an ice-cream machine and freeze according to the manufacturer's directions. Transfer to a freezer-safe container with a lid and let mellow in the freezer for 3 to 4 hours. Eat within 48 hours.

CAL. 169 CARB. 39.1G PROT. 4.2G CHOL. 1.1MG FAT 0.3G/2% SOD. 53.6MG
(ANALYZED PER ¹/₂ CUP)

Dinner Menu

FOODS (PER SERVING)	CAL.	CARB. (G)	PROT. (G)	CHOL. (MG)	FAT (G)/%	SOD. (MG)
Best Ever Barbecued Chicken*	475	69	35	90	7/13	410
or						
Best Ever Barbecued Ribs*	538	69	28	87	20/37	396
Lemon-Dill Rice* (p. 252)	203	43	5	0	0.3/2	2
Ginger Green Beans*	62	9	3	0	2.4/31	147
Breadsticks, 2	160	26	12	0	4/22	420
Very Creamy Cheesecake*	249	38	7.6	10.6	7.7/27	280
or						
Passion Fruit Papaya Frozen Yogurt*, ¹/₂ cup	169	39.1	4.2	1.1	0.3/2	53.6
Today's Totals						
Chicken and Yogurt	**2005**	**343**	**98**	**168**	**32/14**	**1690**
Chicken and Cheesecake	**2085**	**342**	**102**	**178**	**39/17**	**1917**
Ribs and Yogurt	**2068**	**343**	**91**	**165**	**45/19**	**1676**
Ribs and Cheesecake	**2148**	**342**	**95**	**175**	**52/22**	**1903**

295
◆

"Tomorrow is the most important
thing in life. Comes in to us at midnight
very clean. It's perfect when it arrives and
puts itself in our hands and hopes we've
learned something from yesterday."

JOHN WAYNE

Basics

◆

Nonfat Blend

Roasted Garlic Puree

Rich Onion Confit

Quick and Easy Onion Confit

Pepper Croutons

Wickwood Gorp

Spicy Turkey Sausage

Basic Pizza Dough

Roasted Tomato Pizza Sauce

Quick Tomato Sauce

Faux White Sauce

Nonfat Blend

At the beginning of every week, I whip up a batch of this in the blender. (But I never use the food processor; its power breaks down the mixture and makes it watery.) I stash it in a plastic container in the fridge to use by the cup or spoonful in myriad ways as the week progresses. You'll find it used repeatedly throughout *Fresh Start* as a replacement for sour cream, mayonnaise or heavy cream.

MAKES ABOUT 2 CUPS

1 cup nonfat plain yogurt   *1 cup nonfat cottage cheese*

In a blender, combine the yogurt and cottage cheese and blend until smooth. Transfer to a container, cover and refrigerate for up to 1 week.

CAL. 9.3   CARB. 0.9G   PROT. 1.3G   CHOL. 0.14MG   FAT 0G/0%   SOD. 33.3MG
(ANALYZED PER 1 TABLESPOON)

"The key to whatever success I enjoy today is: Don't ask. Do."
VIKKI CARR

298

Roasted Garlic Puree

This intense, rich, nutty and sweet garlic puree surely will become a staple in your home. It's great on grilled meats and fish, as well as stirred into soups or stews. You'll find a million uses for it.

MAKES ²/₃ CUP

8 heads garlic, cloves separated and peeled
¾ cup low-fat, low-sodium chicken broth
2 tablespoons brandy

1. Preheat the oven to 250°F.

2. Spread the garlic cloves on a baking sheet with a rim. Sprinkle with ½ cup chicken broth and spray lightly with olive oil spray. Roast on the middle rack of the oven for 45 minutes, stirring occasionally. Increase the oven temperature to 350°F. and roast for about 15 minutes longer, or until tender and golden.

3. In a blender or a food processor fitted with the metal blade, combine the roasted garlic, the remaining ¼ cup broth and the brandy. Process until smooth. Cover and refrigerate until needed.

CAL. 12   CARB. 1.5G   PROT. 0.3G   CHOL. 0MG   FAT 0.005G/4%   SOD. 0.2MG
(ANALYZED PER 1 TABLESPOON)

Rich Onion Confit

The rich robust flavor of this onion confit intensifies as the onion and balsamic vinegar slowly cook.

MAKES 1 CUP

2 tablespoons low-fat, low-sodium chicken broth
6 cups halved and thinly sliced onions
    (6 to 8 medium-sized onions)
2 tablespoons balsamic vinegar

1. In a large saucepan, heat the chicken broth over medium heat. Add the onions, cover and cook for about 1 hour, until translucent and soft.

2. Uncover, reduce the heat to low and simmer gently for 1 hour, stirring. Add the vinegar and cook for about 30 minutes longer, until the onions are dark brown, very soft and caramelized. Use immediately or cover and refrigerate for up to 10 days.

CAL. 34   CARB. 8G   PROT. 1.0G   CHOL. 0MG   FAT 0.14G/3%   SOD. 12MG
(ANALYZED PER 1 TABLESPOON)

Quick and Easy Onion Confit

When there's no time at all, this is a very adequate stand-in for Rich Onion Confit. But because of the size limitations of the microwave, you cannot make as much at a time.

MAKES ABOUT ½ CUP

2 cups halved and thinly sliced onions
    (2 to 3 medium-sized onions)
¼ cup low-fat, low-sodium chicken broth
2 tablespoons balsamic vinegar

Put the onions and chicken broth in an 8 × 8-inch glass pan, cover and microwave on high for 10 minutes. Stir, add the vinegar, cover and cook on high for 3 minutes longer. Stir and check to see if the onions are dark brown and very soft. If not, cover and cook on high for 2 to 3 minutes longer. Use immediately or cover and refrigerate for up to 10 days.

CAL. 12   CARB. 30G   PROT. 0G   CHOL. 0MG   FAT 0G/3%   SOD. 18MG
(ANALYZED PER 1 TABLESPOON)

Pepper Croutons

Use the best-quality multi-grain bread you can buy (or bake it yourself!). I suggest buying it at a good local bakery.

MAKES ABOUT 4 CUPS

1 teaspoon freshly ground black pepper
½ teaspoon crushed red pepper flakes
4 cups cubed multi-grain bread (5 to 6 slices)

1. Preheat the oven to 425°F.

2. In a small bowl, mix the black pepper and red pepper flakes. Spread the bread on a baking sheet and lightly spray with olive oil spray. Sprinkle with the pepper mixture and toss to coat evenly. Bake for 10 to 15 minutes, tossing every 2 to 3 minutes, until browned, crisp and dry. Allow to cool completely before using. Store in an airtight container.

CAL. 231   CARB. 58G   PROT. 11.5G   CHOL. 0MG   FAT 0.009G/1%   SOD. 777MG
(ANALYZED PER ½ CUP)

300

WICKWOOD GORP

Make your own signature snack as we do at our inn— it's a healthy one, to boot. Mix dried fruits such as tart cherries, apple rings, figs or apricots with peanuts or almonds. Indulge by adding a few chocolate chips and then set the mixture out in easy reach of everyone. The following mixture, which I affectionately call "gorp," is so satisfying it tames my "snack" tooth right away.

MAKES ABOUT
2 CUPS

1 cup dry-roasted peanuts
1 cup dried tart cherries
¼ cup chocolate chips

CAL. 163   CARB. 18G   PROT. 5G
CHOL. 0.1MG   FAT 11G/61%
SOD. 2MG   (ANALYZED PER ¼ CUP)

Spicy Turkey Sausage

I often use ground turkey breast to replace ground beef and sausage but because it can easily dry out when browning, I make it as moist and tasty as possible. I devised this method for flavoring the turkey, which retains its moisture so well that it looks and tastes like sausage.

VEGETABLE JUICES

Carrot juice is by far the most popular vegetable juice. It is sweet and bright and makes a fabulous base for other highly concentrated vegetables and herbs, which can be bitter on their own.

Fresh carrots are loaded with beta-carotene, which converts to vitamin A and may help prevent some forms of cancer. Plus, it has a positive effect on vitality, appetite and digestion. Add darker green vegetables to it and you'll add cholorophyll, vitamins A, C, E, K, B$_2$ and iron and magnesium.

For maximum benefit, drink concentrated vegetable juices as quickly as possible after juicing. Every moment's delay means fewer benefits.

MAKES ABOUT $^1/_2$ POUND

$^1/_2$ pound ground turkey breast
1 teaspoon finely minced fresh sage
$^1/_4$ teaspoon crushed red pepper flakes
1 tablespoon finely minced garlic
$^1/_8$ teaspoon ground cumin
$^1/_4$ teaspoon fennel seeds
Pinch of ground cloves
1 cup beef broth

1. In a large nonstick skillet, brown the turkey over medium heat for 2 to 3 minutes. Add the sage, red pepper flakes, garlic, cumin, fennel and cloves and cook, stirring to break up the turkey, for about 8 minutes, until evenly browned.

2. Add the chicken broth and simmer for 10 to 12 minutes, or until the broth evaporates. Use immediately or cover and refrigerate until ready to use.

CAL. 140   CARB. 2.6G   PROT. 29G   CHOL. 55MG   FAT 1.78G/11%
SOD. 3MG
(ANALYZED PER $^1/_4$ POUND)

Basic Pizza Dough

When you have time to make yeast-risen pizza dough, try this classic recipe, which includes whole-wheat flour and is also my favorite. It makes a terrific thin-crusted pizza, or if you prefer, one with a thick crust—the thickness depends on how you roll out the dough. Use this with any of the pizza toppings suggested for the tortilla pizzas in the book.

MAKES TWO 12-INCH PIZZAS (4 SERVINGS)
MAKES FOUR 6-INCH PIZZAS (4 SERVINGS)
MAKES EIGHT 3-INCH PIZZAS (8 APPETIZER SERVINGS)

1 cup warm water
One $\frac{1}{4}$-ounce package active dry yeast or $\frac{1}{4}$ ounce compressed yeast

About $1\frac{1}{2}$ cups all-purpose flour
2 tablespoons olive oil
$\frac{1}{2}$ teaspoon salt
1 cup whole-wheat flour

1. In a large bowl, combine the water, yeast and $1\frac{1}{2}$ cups all-purpose flour and mix well. Add the oil, salt and whole-wheat flour. With your hands or a large wooden spoon, work the ingredients together until the dough holds its shape. Turn the dough out onto a lightly floured surface and knead for about 5 minutes, until it is smooth and elastic. If the dough becomes sticky, sprinkle with a little more all-purpose flour.

2. Transfer the dough to a lightly oiled 2-quart bowl. Cover with plastic wrap or a kitchen towel and let the dough rest for about 1 hour, until it doubles in size. Turn out onto a lightly floured surface, divide into 2 or more parts and shape each one into a ball. Cover the balls with a towel and let rest for 15 to 20 minutes. The dough is now ready to be rolled as thin (or thick) as you like, shaped, topped and cooked.

NOTE: To bake the pizza dough, transfer the dough to a sturdy pizza pan (or shape it as you desire and transfer to a sturdy baking sheet). Make sure either the pan or baking sheet has been lightly sprayed with olive oil spray and sprinkled with cornmeal. Top with the topping of your choice and bake in a preheated 500°F. oven for 15 to 20 minutes, until the crust is golden brown and the sauce in the topping is bubbling.

302

"If you wish to grow thinner, diminish your dinner, and take light claret instead of pale ale; look down with an utter contempt upon butter and never touch bread till it's toasted—or stale."

H.S. LEIGH

Keep in mind that, depending on the thinness of the crust and the ingredients in the topping, the cooking time may vary. Rely on your own good sense!

You can make this dough ahead of time, wrap it in plastic and refrigerate for up to 24 hours. Let it come to room temperature before shaping and baking.

CAL. 338   CARB. 66G   PROT. 9G   CHOL. 0MG   FAT 3G/9%   SOD. 270MG
(ANALYZED FOR 4 SERVINGS)

Roasted Tomato Pizza Sauce

Slowly roasting the tomatoes intensifies their flavor, making a rich sauce with no olive oil. This is an anytime-of-year fresh tomato sauce—and a "no-brainer." It can easily be doubled.

MAKES 1 CUP

8 plum tomatoes (about 1 pound)
1 cup low-fat, low-sodium chicken broth
1 tablespoon finely minced fresh basil
1 tablespoon finely minced garlic
1 teaspoon dried oregano
Freshly ground black pepper to taste

1. Preheat the oven to 250°F.

2. Put the whole tomatoes on a baking sheet and roast for 2 hours, turning once or twice during roasting. Cool for about 20 minutes and then slip off and discard the skins. Hold the tomatoes over a bowl while removing the skins to catch the juices. Put the tomatoes in the bowl and mash with a fork. Set aside.

3. In a nonstick skillet, heat 2 tablespoons broth over medium heat. Add the basil, garlic and oregano and cook for 2 minutes. Add the tomatoes and 7 tablespoons of the remaining broth. Simmer for about 5 minutes, stirring occasionally, until the liquid evaporates. Add the remaining 7 tablespoons broth, season with pepper and simmer for about 5 minutes longer, stirring occasionally, until the liquid evaporates. Use immediately, or cool, cover and refrigerate or freeze until using.

CAL. 8.6   CARB. 1.8G   PROT. 0.5G   CHOL. 0MG   FAT 0.1G/10%   SOD. 38MG
(ANALYZED PER 1 TABLESPOON)

303

Quick Tomato Sauce

This is a fresh-tasting, chunky tomato sauce that can be made any time of year. It freezes very well, which is lucky because this is great to have on hand.

MAKES 5 1/2 CUPS

1 tablespoon low-fat, low-sodium chicken broth
1/4 cup finely minced garlic
1 cup coarsely chopped onion
Two 28-ounce cans plum tomatoes, plus the juice from 1 can
1 teaspoon dried oregano
3 tablespoons tomato paste
Salt and freshly ground black pepper to taste
3 tablespoons finely minced fresh Italian parsley

1. In a large saucepan, heat the chicken broth over low heat. Add the garlic and onion and cook, stirring, for 4 to 5 minutes, until translucent. Add a little more broth if necessary to prevent sticking. Add the tomatoes, tomato juice, oregano and tomato paste.

2. Simmer gently over medium heat, uncovered, for about 30 minutes, stirring occasionally and, using the spoon, breaking the tomatoes into smaller pieces. Season with salt and pepper and add the parsley. Use immediately or cover and refrigerate until ready to use.

CAL. 19   CARB. 4.5G   PROT. 1.2G   CHOL. 0MG   FAT 0.05G/2%   SOD. 215MG
(ANALYZED PER 1/4 CUP)

FRUIT JUICES

Orange, lemon, cran-raspberry, apple, lime, raspberry, peach, pear, apricot. Concentrated or full strength, fruit juices are a great way to moisten food and gently transmit flavor. They can spark a salad, lift a grain to new dimensions, add juiciness to lean meat and gently sweeten baked goods. Use fresh whenever possible, or frozen concentrate, full-strength or diluted depending on the recipe. But never use juice from a jar. It's usually sugar water and doesn't supply the needed punch.

Faux White Sauce

This is the easiest and tastiest low-fat white sauce I've been able to create. It takes about fifteen minutes from start to finish—and it is white, thick and pretty terrific! Flavor the sauce with spices, herbs or chopped scallions, depending on what you are serving it with.

MAKES ABOUT 3 CUPS

2 ¼ cups skim milk

4 tablespoons instant potato flakes

2 tablespoons potato starch

½ cup low-fat, low-sodium chicken broth

Pinch of freshly ground nutmeg or paprika, or
*   2 tablespoons minced fresh herbs, such as dill, chervil or*
*   Italian parsley, or 2 tablespoons finely chopped scallions*
Salt and freshly ground black pepper to taste
1½ teaspoons unsalted butter (optional)

"If we fasten our attention on what we have, rather than on what we lack, a very little wealth is sufficient."

FRANCIS JOHNSON

1. In a nonstick saucepan, heat ¼ cup milk over medium heat. Whisk in the potato flakes until smooth. Gradually add another ¾ cup milk, whisking constantly.

305

2. In a small bowl, combine the potato starch and another ¼ cup milk and whisk to dissolve the starch. Add to the saucepan and whisk well.

3. Gradually add the chicken broth and remaining 1 cup milk, whisking constantly over medium heat so that the sauce remains thick. Season with nutmeg or paprika, herbs or scallions and salt and pepper. Add the butter, if using, cooking only until it has melted. Use immediately or cool to room temperature before using.

CAL. 28   CARB. 4.8G   PROT. 2G   CHOL. 0.8MG   FAT 0.08G/3%   SOD. 49MG
(ANALYZED PER ¼ CUP WITHOUT BUTTER)

CAL. 32   CARB. 24.8G   PROT. 2G   CHOL. 2.1MG   FAT 0.6G/16%   SOD. 49MG
(ANALYZED PER ¼ CUP WITH BUTTER)

- Acquire a taste for bread without butter.
- Have eggs poached instead of fried.
- Eat low-fat granola or Cheerios.
- Use 3 to 4 times as many vegetables as meat in soups or stews.
- Have a private tasting of regular, low-fat and nonfat mayo to see which your taste buds can tolerate.
- Try steamed asparagus, green beans and broccoli without any embellishment.
- Find a favorite evening drink that refreshes and relaxes—not wine, beer or alcohol.
- Substitute Canadian bacon or turkey ham for bacon.
- Watch your bagel fat calories.
- Reach for crunchy carrots instead of crunchy potato chips.
- Have an English muffin instead of an oversized bran muffin.
- Eat only half of your dessert at a dinner party.
- Switch from chocolate-covered raisins to plain.
- Snack on nonfat plain yogurt with honey and fresh raspberries rather than custard-style.
- Dip celery sticks in nonfat cream cheese instead of regular.
- Replace fried chicken with "oven-fried" chicken.
- Learn to drink coffee with skim milk.
- Make a white sauce from skim milk and instant potato flakes rather than a roux of butter and flour.
- Switch from regular to nonfat sour cream.
- Reduce your steak to a piece that fits in the palm of your hand.
- Make a grilled cheese sandwich with part-skim mozzarella in a nonstick pan with olive oil spray.
- Have chocolate nonfat frozen yogurt instead of chocolate ice cream.
- Choose a sandwich or multi-grain bread over a croissant.
- Split an indulgence with a friend. A couple of bites satisfies nicely.
- Snack on a hard breadstick rather than garlic bread.
- Try peaches canned in water rather than heavy syrup.
- While you're cooking, taste with a teaspoon, not a mixing spoon.
- Squeeze lemon juice on fish instead of tartar sauce.
- Flavor your favorite creamy salads with nonfat sour cream, nonfat cottage cheese, or nonfat yogurt and just a smidgen of mayo.
- Instead of fat-laden croutons, add crunch to your salad with carrots, celery or water chestnuts.
- Accompany a hamburger with baked tortilla chips instead of fries.
- Pass on seconds. Unless it's salad.
- Enjoy steamed shrimp rather than fried.
- Choose tuna packed in water, not oil.
- If you crave Roquefort dressing on your salad, lightly sprinkle oil and vinegar and crumbled Roquefort—a little goes a long way.
- Use blended nonfat cottage cheese instead of whipped cream. Flavor it with vanilla extract, vanilla bean, amaretto, frangelico, framboise.
- Have two grilled portobello mushrooms for dinner instead of meat.

FLAVORED LIQUIDS FOR STEAMING VEGETABLES

In this section I have assembled eight lightly flavored liquids, which will make steamed vegetables really come alive—without adding a single calorie or gram of fat. Combine the ingredients for the liquids in the bottom part of a vegetable steamer and use them to steam fresh vegetables. Not only will they fill the kitchen with a tantalizing aroma, they will gently infuse the vegetables with flavor you never thought possible. Then just savor them.

CITRUS

MAKES 2 CUPS

Juice of 1 lemon
Juice of 1 lime
Juice of 1 orange
Zest of 1 lemon
Zest of 1 lime
Zest of 1 orange
½ cup minced fresh mint
1½ cups water

LIME-GARLIC

MAKES 3 CUPS

10 cloves garlic, halved
2 limes, in ⅛-inch slices
2 bay leaves
2 teaspoons peppercorns
3 cups water

ITALIAN

MAKES 2 CUPS

2 tablespoons coarsely
  chopped garlic
1 cup basil
2 cups water

MEXICAN

MAKES 2¼ CUPS

1 whole jalapeño, sliced
Juice and zest of 1 lemon
2 cups water

ASIAN

MAKES 2½ CUPS

¼ cup soy sauce
3 tablespoons chopped
  fresh ginger
¼ cup coarsely chopped
  garlic
2 cups water

INDIAN

MAKES 3 CUPS

3 tablespoons Dijon
  mustard
2 tablespoons curry powder
3 cups water

GINGER

MAKES 3 CUPS

One 3-inch piece fresh
  ginger, peeled and cut
  into chunks
2 tablespoons dry mustard
3 cups water

AUTUMN

MAKES 1½ CUPS

1 teaspoon cinnamon
2 teaspoons whole cloves
1½ cups water

THE ULTIMATE
FRESH START WEEKLY
GROCERY LIST

Farmers' Market

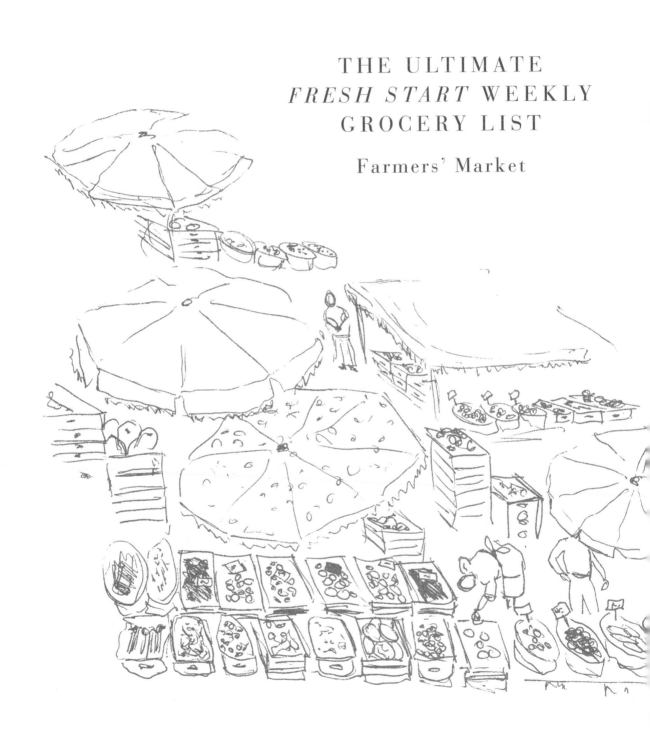

PRODUCE

___ Asparagus
___ Beets
___ Broccoli
___ Cabbage, red/green
___ Carrots
___ Cauliflower
___ Celery
___ Cucumber
___ Garlic/shallots
___ Green beans
___ Leeks
___ Lettuce
   ___ arugula
   ___ watercress
   ___ Bibb/iceberg/leaf
   ___ romaine
   ___ radicchio
___ Mushrooms, dried/
   fresh/cultivated/wild

___ Onions
   ___ red/pearl
   ___ white/yellow
   ___ scallions
___ Parsnips
___ Peas
   ___ sugar snaps
   ___ green/snow
___ Pepper
   ___ green/red
   ___ purple/yellow
   ___ hot
___ Potatoes
   ___ white/yellow
   ___ Idaho/Yukon Gold
   ___ new/russet
   ___ sweet/yam
___ Rutabaga
___ Spinach
___ Sprouts
___ Squash
___ Tomatoes
   ___ cherry/yellow
   ___ plum/beefsteak
___ Turnips
___ Zucchini, green/yellow

___ Apples
___ Bananas
___ Berries
___ Cherries
___ Grapes
___ Kiwi
___ Lemons/limes
___ Mango
___ Melons
___ Oranges
___ Papaya
___ Peaches
___ Pears
___ Pineapple

HERBS

___ Parsley/cilantro
___ Dill/chives
___ Basil/rosemary
___ Tarragon/sage
___ Oregano/chervil
___ Mint

MEAT, EGGS, POULTRY AND FISH

___ Beef
    ___ roast/steak
    ___ flank/tenderloin
    ___ London broil
    ___ ground sirloin
___ Eggs
___ Veal chop
___ Chicken
    ___ whole
    ___ boneless, skinless breasts
___ Turkey
    ___ breast
    ___ ground breast
___ Pork tenderloin
___ Game
___ Canadian bacon
___ Prosciutto
___ Sausage
    ___ hot/sweet
    ___ breakfast
___ Turkey ham
___ Lamb
___ Clams/oysters
___ Shrimp/lobster
___ Crab/scallops
___ Tuna/perch
___ Salmon
___ Sole
___ Whitefish

STARCHES

___ Dried beans
    ___ black/white
    ___ black turtle
    ___ navy/red
    ___ cannellini
    ___ giant pinto
    ___ garbanzo
    ___ split pea/lentils
    ___ heirloom
___ Rice/grains
    ___ wild/arborio
    ___ couscous
    ___ pilaf/brown
    ___ long-grain/short-grain
    ___ basmati
    ___ quinoa
    ___ wheat berries
    ___ cracked wheat
___ Pasta
    ___ long
    ___ shapes
    ___ stuffed
    ___ fresh

___ Cereals
    ___ oatmeal
    ___ steel-cut oats
    ___ granola
    ___ bran flakes/bran

BREAD

___ Rye
___ Whole-wheat/pumpernickel
___ Multi-grain
___ Sourdough
___ French/Italian
___ English muffins
___ Bagels/rolls
___ Wasa
___ Melba toast

___ Crackers
___ Baked tostadas
___ Pita bread
___ Bread crumbs
___ Croutons/stuffing
___ Phyllo dough
___ Puff pastry

DAIRY

___ Skim milk
___ Nonfat yogurt
___ Buttermilk
___ Nonfat cottage cheese
___ Nonfat cream cheese
___ Sour cream
___ Butter, salted/sweet
___ Cheese
   ___ low-fat ricotta
   ___ part-skim mozzarella
   ___ Parmesan
   ___ Swiss
   ___ American
   ___ blue
___ Horseradish
___ Tortillas
   ___ flour
   ___ corn

___ Milk
   ___ skim milk
   ___ evaporated skim
   ___ milk
   ___ buttermilk
___ Nonfat plain yogurt
___ Nonfat cottage cheese

BAKING

___ Sugar
   ___ granulated
   ___ extra-fine
   ___ light brown
   ___ confectioners'
___ Flour
   ___ all-purpose
   ___ cake
   ___ whole-wheat
   ___ cornmeal
___ Eggs
___ Honey
___ Applesauce
___ Potato starch
___ Instant potato flakes
___ Chocolate
   ___ unsweetened
   ___ chips/cocoa

___ Coconut
___ Cornstarch
___ Extracts
   ___ vanilla
   ___ almond
___ Vanilla beans
___ Spices

FROZEN FOOD

___ Sorbet/yogurt
___ Fruit juices
   ___ lemon/lime
   ___ cran-raspberry/
     apple
   ___ peach/white
     grape
   ___ orange
   ___ lemonade
___ Peas/corn
___ Artichoke hearts
___ Spinach

CANNED

___ Whole tomatoes
___ Tomato sauce
___ Tomato paste
___ Beef broth
___ Chicken broth, low-fat,
   low-sodium
___ Tuna in water

CONDIMENTS

___ Anchovies
___ Barbecue sauce
___ Capers
___ Chutney
___ Honey
___ Mayonnaise
___ Mustard
   ___ hot/sweet
   ___ Dijon/herb
___ Nuts
   ___ almonds
   ___ pecans
   ___ walnuts
   ___ pine/peanuts
   ___ macadamia
   ___ hazelnuts
___ Seeds
___ Oils
   ___ olive
   ___ cooking
   ___ salad
   ___ spray
   ___ canola
   ___ spray
   ___ butter-flavored

   ___ sesame
   ___ hot chili
   ___ nut/seed
___ Olives, green/black
___ Peanut butter, chunky
___ Pepper
   ___ ground
   ___ corns
___ Pickles
___ Salad dressing
___ Salsa
___ Salt
___ Sauce
   ___ soy
   ___ steak
   ___ Tabasco
   ___ Worcestershire
___ Syrup
   ___ corn
   ___ maple
   ___ molasses
___ Preserves, all-fruit
___ Dried fruits
   ___ apricots/prunes
   ___ currants/raisins
   ___ dates/figs

___ Vinegar
   ___ balsamic
   ___ herb
   ___ white/red
   ___ sherry
   ___ cider/rice
___ Coffee
   ___ ground
   ___ decaf
   ___ instant
___ Tea
___ Angel food cake
___ Gingersnaps
___ Low-sugar hard candy

SNACKS

___ Apples
___ Pretzels
___ Flavored rice cakes
___ Bread
___ Bagels
___ English muffins
___ Pita bread
___ Breadsticks
___ Popcorn, air-popped

Don't forget your recyclables and canvas grocery bags!

BIBLIOGRAPHY

American Heart Association. "Dietary Fat and Its Relation to Heart Attack and Strokes." *Circulation* 23 (1961).

———. *Fat and Cholesterol Counter.* New York: Times Books/Random House, 1991.

Anderson, J. W., and W. L. Chen. "Plant Fiber: Carbohydrate and Lipid Metabolism." *American Journal of Clinical Nutrition* 32 (1979).

Bailey, Covert. *Fit or Fat?* Pleasant Hills, Calif.: Covert Bailey, 1977.

———. *The Fit or Fat Woman.* Boston, Mass.: Houghton Mifflin Company, 1989.

Barnett, Robert. "Why Fat Makes You Fatter." *American Health* (May 1986).

Benditt, E. P. "The Origin of Atherosclerosis." *Scientific American* (February 1977).

Blumenfeld, Arthur. *Heart Attack: Are You a Candidate?* New York: Pyramid Books, 1971.

Brewster, L., and M. F. Jacobson. *The Changing American Diet.* Washington, D.C.: Center for Science in the Public Interest, 1978.

———. *The Changing American Diet.* Washington, D.C.: Center for Science in the Public Interest, l982.

Brody, Jane E. *Jane Brody's Nutrition Book.* New York: W. W. Norton, 1981.

———. *The New York Times Guide to Personal Health.* New York: Avon Books, 1983.

Bruce, R. A. "Primary Intervention Against Coronary Artherosclerosis by Exercise Conditioning?" *New England Journal of Medicine* 305:25 (1981).

Burkit, D. *Don't Forget Fiber in Your Diet.* New York: Arco Publishing, 1984.

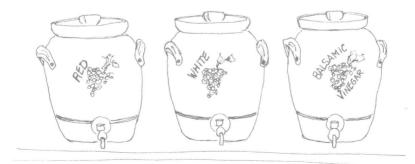

Chiang, B. N., L. V. Perlman, and F. H. Epstein. "Overweight and Hypertension." *Circulation* 39:3 (1969).

Clarke, N. E., Sr. "Artherosclerosis, Occlusive Vascular Disease and EDTA." *American Journal of Cardiology* 6 (1960).

Cohan, Carol, June B. Primm, and James R. Jude. *A Patient's Guide to Heart Surgery.* New York: HarperCollins, 1991.

Cooper, Kenneth H. *Controlling Cholesterol.* New York: Bantam Books, 1989.

Daubar. R. R., and W. B. Kannel. "Some Factors Associated with the Development of Coronary Heart Disease. Six Years Follow-up Experience in the Framingham Study." *American Journal of Public Health* 49 (1959).

Dawber, T. "Eggs, Serum Cholesterol, and Coronary Heart Disease." *American Journal of Clinical Nutrition* 36 (1982).

DeBakey, Michael E., Antonio M. Gotto, Jr., Lynne W. Scott, and John P. DeForey. *The Living Heart Brand Name Shopper's Guide.* New York: Mastermedia Limited, 1993.

"Diet, Cholesterol and Heart Disease." *New England Journal of Medicine* 304:19 (1981).

Diethrich, Edward B., and Carol Cohan. *Women and Heart Disease.* New York: Ballantine Books, 1992.

Erasmus, Udo. *Fats and Oils.* Bumby, B.C., Canada: Alive Books, 1993.

Farquhar, John W. *The American Way of Life Need Not Be Hazardous to Your Health.* New York: W. W. Norton, 1978.

Finnegan, John. *The Facts About Fats.* Berkeley, Calif.: Celestial Arts, 1993.

Fixx, James. *The Complete Book of Running.* New York: Random House, 1977.

Friedman, Meyer, and Ray H. Rosenman. *Type A Behavior and the Heart.* New York: Alfred A. Knopf, 1974.

Goulart, Francis Sheridan. "The Good and Bad of Diet Foods." *Consumers Digest* (September/October 1979).

Greenberg, Jerold S. *Managing Stress: A Personal Guide.* Dubuque, Iowa: William C. Brown Publishers, 1984.

Grundy, Scott M., M.D., Ph.D., and Mary Winston, Ed.D., R.D., eds. *The American Heart Association Low-Fat, Low-Cholesterol Cookbook.* New York: New York Times Books, 1989.

Guerard, M. *Cuisine Minceur.* New York: William Morrow and Company, 1976.

Hanssen, Maurice. *Everything You Wanted to Know About Salt.* New York: Pyramid Books, 1968.

Hausman, Patricia. *Jack Spratt's Legacy: The Science and Politics of Fat and Cholesterol.* New York: Richard Marek, 1981.

Hess, Mary Abbott, et al. *A Healthy Head Start: A Worry-Free Guide to Feeding Young Children.* New York: Henry Holt, 1990.

Horowitz, Lawrence C., M.D. *Taking Charge of Your Medical Fate.* New York: Random House, 1988.

King, C. D. *What's That You're Eating.* Newport Beach, Calif.: C. D. King Ltd, 1982.

Knowles, John. "The Responsibility of the Individual," *Doing Better and Feeling Worse: Health in the United States*, John Knowles, ed. New York: W. W. Norton, 1977.

Kraus, Barbara. *Calories and Carbohydrates.* New York: New American Library, 1981.

————. *The Dictionary of Sodium, Fats and Cholesterol.* New York: Grosset & Dunlap, 1974.

Lesser, Michael. *Fat and the Killer Disease.* Berkeley, Calif.: Parker House, 1991.

Margen, Sheldon, and the editors of the University of California at Berkeley Wellness Letter. *The Wellness Encyclopedia of Food and Nutrition.* New York: Robus, 1992.

Mayer, Jean. *A Diet for Living.* New York: Pocket Books, 1976.

McDougall, John A. *The McDougall Plan.* New York/Piscataway, N.J.: New Century Publishers, 1983.

————. *The McDougall Program.* New York: Penguin Group, 1991.

————. *The McDougall Program for Maximum Weight Loss.* New York: Penguin Group, 1994.

McGee, Harold. *On Food and Cooking: The Science Lore of the Kitchen.* New York: Charles Scribner's Sons, 1984.

Mindell, Earl R. *Food as Medicine.* New York: Simon & Schuster, 1994.

Null, Gary. *The Complete Guide to Health and Nutrition.* New York: Dell Publishing, 1984.

O'Brien, B. "Human Plasma Lipid Responses to Red Meat, Poultry, Fish, and Eggs." *American Journal of Clinical Nutrition* 33 (1980).

Ornish, Dean, M.D. *Dr. Dean Ornish's Program for Reversing Heart Disease.* New York: Random House, 1990.

Pennington, Jean A. T. *Food Values.* New York: HarperPerennial, 1989.

———— and H. N. Church. *Food Values of Portions Commonly Used.* 16th ed. Philadelphia, PA.: Lippincott, 1993.

Pollock, Michael, Jack Wilmore, and Sameul M. Fox III. *Health and Fitness Through Physical Activity.* New York: Wiley Publishing Company, 1978.

Pritikin, N., J. Leonard, and J. Hofer. *Live Longer Now.* New York: Grosset & Dunlap, 1974.

Pritikin, N., and P. M. McGrady, Jr. *The Pritikin Program for Diet and Exercise.* New York: Grosset & Dunlap, 1979.

Robbins, John. *Diet for a New America.* Walpole, NH: Stillpoint Publishing, 1987.

Sipple, H. L., and K. McNutt. *Sugars in Nutrition.* New York: Academic Press, 1974.

Starke, Rodman D., and Mary Winston. *American Heart Association Low-Salt Cookbook: A Complete Guide to Reducing Sodium and Fat in the Diet.* New York: Times Books, 1990.

Stuart, R. *Act Thin, Stay Thin.* New York: W. W. Norton, 1978.

Thompson, D. S. *Every Woman's Health: The Complete Guide to Body and Mind.* New York: Simon & Schuster, 1993.

Toufesis, Anastasia. "Dieting: The Losing Game," *Time*, January 20, 1986.

Ulh, G. S., et al. "Relationship Between High Density Lipoprotein Cholesterol and Coronary Artery Disease in Asymptomatic Men." *American Journal of Cardiology* 48:5 (1981).

Walker, A. "The Human Requirement for Calcium: Should Low Intakes Be Supplemented?" *American Journal of Clinical Nutrition* 25 (1972).

Wallis, Claudia. "Salt: A New Villain?" *Time*, March 15, 1982.

Weil, Andrew. *Natural Health, Natural Medicine.* Boston, Mass.: Houghton Mifflin Company, 1990.

Wigmore, Ann. *The Hippocrates Diet and Health Program.* Garden City, N.Y.: Avery Publishing Group, Inc., 1984.

Willan, A. *La Varenne Pratique.* New York: Crown Publishers, Inc., 1989.

Winter, Ruth. *Food Additives.* New York: Crown Publishers, Inc., 1978.

Wisser, R. W., et al. "Arteriosclerosis and the Influence of Diet: An Experimental Mode." *Journal of the American Medical Association* (1965).

Yudkin, John. "Sugar and Coronary Heart Disease." *Food and Nutrition News* 36:6 (1965).

INDEX

Conversion Chart

American cooks use standard containers, the 8-ounce cup and a tablespoon that takes exactly 16 level fillings to fill that cup level. Measuring by cup makes it very difficult to give weight equivalents, as a cup of densely packed butter will weigh considerably more than a cup of flour. The easiest way therefore to deal with cup measurements in recipes is to take the amount by volume rather than by weight. Thus the equation reads: *1 cup = 240 ml = 8 fl. oz. $\frac{1}{2}$ cup = 120 ml = 4 fl. oz.*

It is possible to buy a set of American cup measures in major stores around the world.

In the States, butter is often measured in sticks. One stick is the equivalent of 8 tablespoons. One tablespoon of butter is therefore the equivalent to $\frac{1}{2}$ ounce/15 grams.

SOLID MEASURES

U.S. and Imperial Measures		Metric Measures	
ounces	pounds	grams	kilos
1		28	
2		56	
3½		100	
4	¼	112	
5		140	
6		168	
8	½	225	
9		250	¼
12	¾	340	
16	1	450	
18		500	½
20	1¼	560	
24	1½	675	
27		750	¾
28	1¾	780	
32	2	900	
36	2¼	1000	1
40	2½	1100	
48	3	1350	
54		1500	1½
64	4	1800	
72	4½	2000	2
80	5	2250	2¼
90		2500	2½
100	6	2800	2¾

OVEN TEMPERATURE EQUIVALENTS

Fahrenheit	Celsius	Gas Mark	Description
225	110	¼	Cool
250	130	½	
275	140	1	Very Slow
300	150	2	
325	170	3	Slow
350	180	4	Moderate
375	190	5	
400	200	6	Moderately Hot
425	220	7	Fairly Hot
450	230	8	Hot
475	240	9	Very Hot
500	250	10	Extremely Hot

LIQUID MEASURES

Fluid ounces	U.S.	Imperial	Milliliters
	1 teaspoon	1 teaspoon	5
¼	2 teaspoons	1 dessertspoon	10
½	1 tablespoon	1 tablespoon	14
1	2 tablespoons	2 tablespoons	28
2	¼ cup	4 tablespoons	56
4	½ cup		110
5		¼ pint or 1 gill	140
6	¾ cup		170
8	1 cup		225
9			250
10	1¼ cups	½ pint	280
12	1½ cups		340
15		¾ pint	420
16	2 cups		450
18	2¼ cups		500
20	2½ cups	1 pint	560
24	3 cups		675
25		1¼ pints	700
27	3½ cups		750
30	3¾ cups	1½ pints	840
32	4 cups or 1 quart		900
35		1¾ pints	980
36	4½ cups		1000
40	5 cups	2 pints or 1 quart	1120
48	6 cups		1350
50		2½ pints	1400
60	7½ cups	3 pints	1680
64	8 cups or 2 quarts		1800
72	9 cups		2000